Contents

Foreword

The Martin B-26 Marauder is the story of an airplane, of the people who flew and maintained it, and of the role the B-26 played in World War II.

It is a fascinating story of the development of an aircraft from a questionable beginning to a highly successful conclusion. For the B-26 was not an instant success; it had many problems initially, not the least of which was the reputation for being "too hot, dangerous, a killer."

This story traces the evolution of the B-26 from an "ugly duckling" to a superb flying machine.

Beyond the above, this book presents the people—the combat crews and the maintenance crews that completed the loop to making the B-26 so effective.

As a former member of a B-26 group in Europe during World War II, I find this—the people part—particularly appealing. The pride, camaraderie, dedication, and resolve of people serving in a combat unit will always remain unique and wonderful, a bond. Trials and tribulations often fade, but the bond remains.

Jack Havener has rekindled the flame, identified the bond once again, and set forth a clear picture of the Marauder of World War II.

Lucius D. Clay, Jr.
General, USAF (Ret)
Colorado Springs, Colorado

General Lucius D. Clay Jr.'s distinguished career in the U.S. Air Force spanned the years 1942 to 1975. In 1971 he became the youngest four-star general to hold the position of Commander in Chief, Pacific Air Forces. And in 1973 he assumed the posts of Commander in Chief, North American Air Defense Command, and Commander, Aerospace Defense Command.

The recipient of numerous medals, General Clay now resides in Colorado Springs, Colorado, with his wife Betty Rose.

THE MARTIN
B-26 MARAUDER

J. K. Havener

AERO
A division of TAB BOOKS Inc.
Blue Ridge Summit, PA

To all the men and women who built the Marauder at
the Glenn L. Martin Co.,
those who maintained and serviced her,
those who flew her, and all those
who had faith in her—especially Col. Vincent W. Burnett.

Library of Congress Cataloging-in-Publication Data

Havener, J. K.
    The Martin B-26 Marauder / by J. K. Havener.
        p.   cm.
    Bibliography: p.
    Includes index.
    ISBN 0-8306-8287-2 (pbk.)
    1. Marauder (Bomber)   I. Title.
    UG1242.B6H38 1988   88-15690
    385.4'3—dc19   CIP

TAB BOOKS Inc. offers software for sale. For information and a catalog, please contact TAB Software Department, Blue Ridge Summit, PA 17294-0850.

Questions regarding the content of this book should be addressed to:

    Reader Inquiry Branch
    TAB BOOKS Inc.
    Blue Ridge Summit, PA 17294-0214

Cover: "Lafayette, We are Here! II.
    Aviation artist Emmett Lancaster, Tempe, Arizona, depicts the plight of his airplane (7I★D) as the 497th Squadron of the 344th Bomb Group attacked the invasion beaches on D-Day morning, 6 June 1944. Lancaster was flying copilot in R.J. "Whitey" Schwaergerl's 7I★D, and they were leading a flight in the third box of 18 aircraft in the 344th's maximum effort force of 54 aircraft. In Lancaster's words:
    "We were leading the next-to-last flight, stacked down from the cloud base to around 3000 feet. As we started our run on the beach, we came under heavy ground fire. The aircraft directly in front of us blew up, and another skidded beneath us trailing flame and smoke; pilot and copilot both slumped forward over the controls. A shell slammed into the left side of the radio compartment with an explosive force that stung my feet through the floor panels, and the ship lurched momentarily out of control, instruments gyrating wildly. We dumped our bomb load, feathered the left engine, and began to lose altitude."
    For the balance of 7I★D's story, see Chapter 6.

Acknowledgments

A debt of gratitude is owed Frances Crum, Public Relations, Martin-Marietta Corp., Bethesda, Maryland, for furnishing valuable historical material and granting permission to research the Martin archives.

Special thanks to Dotty Muller and the librarians at Martin-Marietta Aerospace Division, Baltimore, Maryland, for their help during the research in the archives of the manufacturing facility on the site of what was once the Glenn L. Martin Co. Middle River Plant, as well as to Frank R. DePietro, Martin-Marietta Corp., Bethesda, Maryland, and Buzz Bartlett, Public Relations Director at Baltimore, for editing the rough draft manuscript for authenticity regarding the Glenn L. Martin Company.

Appreciation is extended to Dr. James H. Kitchens III, archivist at the Reference Division of the USAF Historical Research Center, Maxwell AFB, and his staff for the assistance and guidance during my research there.

Aviation buffs will appreciate my elation at W. Calvin Falwell, President of Falwell Aviation, Lynchburg, Virginia, opening the door for me to the exploits of one of aviation history's greatest participants, Vincent W. Burnett.

I'll forever be indebted to Evelyn Burnett for sharing her treasured memoirs of her husband, Col. Vincent W. Burnett, with me—and to Col. Burnett, for his permission to use this material in my book.

Also, my thanks go to those Arkansans who provided valuable oral history and documentation on the aircraft disposal facility at Walnut Ridge, Arkansas: Dr. H.E. Williams, President Emeritus of Southern Baptist College; Dana Kelly of the Walnut Ridge Time Dispatch; Chalmers Clark, Walnut Ridge Chamber of Commerce Secretary; and the librarians at Arkansas State University in Jonesboro.

Enough can't be said for my wife Doris's patience and understanding during the compilation of this work. Not only did she scan the rough drafts for grammatical errors, but tolerated my "way out" reveries as I labored over it.

A hearty thanks to Mr. and Mrs. John C. Kontos, Sterling, Illinois, for bearing with me through this labor of love to diligently critique each chapter for interest and understanding from a layman's point of view.

Finally, the professional assistance of Arline Whaley and Marilynn Bollendorf, both of Middleton, Tennessee, High School, in editing and typing the submission manuscript is greatly appreciated.

Below is an alphabetical listing of those who contributed photos, personal experiences, and factual data for the project:

Baxter, A. E., Annadale, VA.
Baxter, Howard R., Marion, IN.
Bentley, D. D., Col. USAF Ret., Wilson, WY.
Borodine, P. G., Centerville, MA.
Brewer, Arthur M., Col. USAF Ret, Cape Coral, FL.
Brown, Frank, LTC USAFR Ret., Stillwater, MN.
Burnett, Evelyn (Mrs. V. W.), Lynchburg, VA.
Burnett, V.W., Col. USAFRRet., Lynchburg, VA.
Chiozza, Joe, Memphis, TN.
Clark, John E., Patrick AFB, FL.
Crumbliss, J. J., Bossier City, LA.
Damm, G. E., New York, NY.
Ehart, C. W., Eglin AFB, FL.
Falwell, W. Calvin, Lynchburg, VA.
Feldman, S. B., Albuquerque, NM.
Fitzpatrick, E. F., M/Sgt. USAF Ret., Dover, DE.
Fontana, J. V., LTC USAFR Ret., Meriden, CT.
Frank, Jim, Rock Falls, IL.
Gardella, Paul, Major USAF Ret., Colorado Springs, CO.
Gaylor, Walt, Mesa, AZ.
Gordon, Jack, Greenville, MS.
Grubb, E. B., Ft. Myers, FL.
Grubbs, J. W., Jr., LTC USAF Ret., Woodridge, IL.
Guldin, Ira S., Kutztown, PA.
Ham, C. E., LTC USAF Ret., Huntsville, TX.
Harris, R. C., Major USAF Ret., Albuquerque, NM.
Harville, Jerry, Mercedes, TX.
Henry, W. B., U.S. Air Force Museum, Wright-Patterson AFB, OH.
Hildebrand, L. F., Spokane, WA.
Holland, H. H., Capt. OK ANG, Claremore, OK.
Hughes, Paul, B/G USAF Ret., Stuart, FL.
Johnston, W. J., Croydon, PA.
Jones, Byron, Chelmsford, Essex, England.
Kingsbury, Joe, Santa Clara, CA.
Lancaster, Emmett, Tempe, AZ.
Lawrence, A. Jackson III, Ocean Springs, MS.
Lee, James, Major USAF Ret., Huntsville, AL.
Littlefield, W., Hampden, MA.
Maloney, Ed, Chino Air Museum, Chino, CA.
Mason, Ken, Ft. Worth, TX.
Maxwell, J. C., M/G USAF Ret., Memphis, TN.
McConnell, Ralph G., Springfield, PA.
Meehan, John, Ft. Lauderdale, FL.

Mickelson, David, Sunnyvale, CA.
Middlebrook, Charles K., Navy Dept. Ret., Dahlgren, VA.
Moench, John O., M/G USAF Ret., Longwood, FL.
Moran, Hugh V., Dayton, OH.
Nelson, Manly, Stanford, MT.
O'Mahony, Charles, Pittsburgh, PA.
Paden, John T., M/Sgt. USAF, Ret., Glendale, AZ.
Proffitt, David L., Louisville, KY.
Russell, Roy E., Major USAF Ret., Newark, DE.
Sharp, John F., Col. USAF Ret., Sacramento, CA.
Smiley, Howard F., LTC USAFR Ret., Sioux City, IA.
Spenser, Jay P., National Air and Space Museum,
    Smithsonian Institution, Washington, DC.
Stowe, Michael T., Millville, NJ.
Teague, George L., Glendale, AZ.
Thomas, W. A., Eugene, OR.
Vetter, M. Rudolph, Alexandria, VA.
Wagner, Ray, San Diego, CA.
Wefel, Ralph M., Oxnard, CA.
Whitehead, Leslie E., M/G USAFR Ret., Huntsville, AL.
Wilson, R. E., Carmel, IN.
Woodrum, Henry C., Redding, CA.

Introduction

This book was compiled under the frustrating circumstances I'm sure many historical aviation writers have experienced—a lack of historical data.

At its peak production period during World War II, the Glenn L. Martin Company Middle River facility in Baltimore, Maryland, employed as many as 50,000 people. During the lean postwar years and before the company became Martin-Marietta Corporation, this figure at one time dropped as low as 658! This naturally brought on severe austerity programs which resulted in decisions to lighten the workload of those few remaining employees.

As a consequence, B-26 engineering drawings, technical data, production records, test results, and related materials were scrapped. A disastrous fire had previously destroyed much of this material. Some few photographs still remain in the archives at Baltimore, but a great majority of the negatives from those days have been attrited by deterioration. Likewise, only a few issues of the company monthly news magazine, *The Martin Star,* survived the 46-year interim.

All speculations and opinions, unless specifically stated otherwise, are those of the author, and advance apology is offered for any factual or statistical errors and/or omissions in the text.

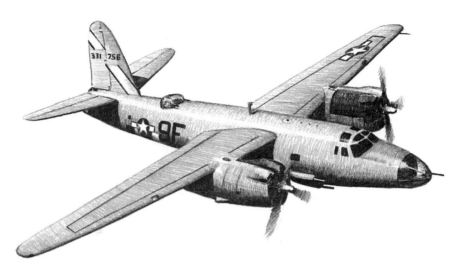

1

CONCEPTION:
An Airplane Is Born

"This ship will win the competition!" exclaimed Glenn L. Martin as he looked over a set of rough designs for a twin-engine bomber on his desk at the Martin Middle River Plant in Baltimore, Maryland, one Monday morning late in June 1939.

On 23 January of that year, the Army Air Corps had issued specifications for a new twin-engine, five-place bomber with a speed of from 250 to 350 miles per hour, a range of 3000 miles, a service ceiling of from 20,000 to 30,000 feet, to carry a maximum bomb load of 4,000 pounds and armament comprising four .30-caliber machine guns. With its eye on military developments in Europe, the Army clearly wanted a medium bomber capable of doing a specific job and with pursuit ship speed.

Since time was growing short for the 3 July opening of bids by the various aircraft companies selected to submit detailed specifications and proposals, Martin immediately sought out the designer responsible for the plans that had caught his eye. What he found was a 26-year-old aeronautical engineer named Peyton M. Magruder, who had been working on his own with a small group of designers to come up with the design. They hadn't even been officially assigned to the project, but had worked day and night through the previous weekend to finish the drawings.

Martin appointed Magruder as Project Engineer on the spot, and Martin Model Number 179 was born. It would later be designated the B-26 by the Army Air Corps.

Peyton Marshall Magruder was a tall, lanky, darkly handsome young man who not only resembled the young Howard Hughes in looks but in talent as well. He was born on an Army Post—Fort Riley, Kansas—where his father (later to become Brig. Gen. Marshall Magruder) was a lieutenant of field artillery. His early life was a kaleidoscope of army camps in the United States and abroad—Manila, Yokohama, Hawaii, and many more. He was a cocky kid—handsome, athletic, sharp-witted, and with a capacity for absorbing knowledge in the midst of outrageous behaviour, while his fellow students plodded through the courses.

He was a living paradox, so his father was resigned when Peyton snared an appointment to the Naval Academy, instead of West Point, and passed the entrance exams handily enough. The courses were a breeze for him, even if they were the most difficult in collegiate circles. That was the trouble. He still had time to get into mischief—which he did, often. In his junior year he resigned, perhaps to avoid being thrown out. Annapolis will probably never be the same.

Looking around for another spot to sate his thirst for knowledge, he spied the University of Alabama. He hooked into the end of a long line of registrants and noticed that a little way off was another line with only a few students in it.

"What line is this?" he asked the man in front of him.

"Liberal Arts," was the reply.

"And what line is that?" said Magruder, pointing to the short one.

"Lay off it, fellow," the student cautioned. "It's a tough one. That's the aeronautical engineering course."

"I haven't time to wait here all day," Peyton retorted, and headed for the short line.

So started a career. After he had finished the university, an admiral, who was a neighborhood friend of the Magruders, pulled a few strings and young Magruder found himself working on the engineering staff of the Naval Aircraft Factory in Philadelphia. He soaked up a lot of knowledge about aircraft design and construction during his short stay there.

Disenchanted with the Navy again, he was accepted for employment at the Glenn L. Martin Company in 1937. He was a very junior engineer, and for a time his light was hidden under a bushel basket of detail engineering, with the attendant routine assignments, until the day in June 1939 when the old man himself lifted the basket. From then on, Magruder's 40-watt bulb continued to increase in brightness.

Magruder was an innovator and took advantage of the Army's desire for a high top speed while having set no limit on landing speed. Using his imagination, his Model 179 incorporated a short wing, resulting in a high wing loading and fast landing speed, the latter compensated for by tricycle landing gear. A long drag profile was chosen for a circular fuselage—truly, a design far ahead of its time (Fig. 1-1).

After being selected as Project Engineer, he was given the best Martin engineering and manufacturing brains, and the team turned to the task of fulfilling

2

Fig. 1-1. *The aerodynamically perfect fuselage of this early B-26 illustrates the reason for its first nickname, "The Flying Torpedo." Note large propeller hubs, small carburetor air intakes atop engine nacelles, short rudder, old-style AAF star on wing, and flexible tail gun cone. This transition training ship is pictured on the ramp at Barksdale AAF, Shreveport, LA, on 29 March 1941. (photo courtesy Ralph G. McConnell)*

the Army's request. Working feverishly against time, they placed in the hands of the Army a Detail Specification and a Proposal during the waning days of June. The Specification outlined for the Army an airplane that Martin engineers guaranteed would do the job required by the Type Specification; the Proposal offered to build an assigned number of aircraft at a bid price.

In asking each company (seven were involved) to submit a proposed design, the Army at the same time enclosed a bulletin, called "Method of Evaluation," describing how the competing designs would be evaluated and the winner chosen. Each design was to receive a numerical rating made up of the numerical values given each of the proposed design's important characteristics. In this case it was made clear, by points assigned to maximum speed, that speed was what the Army desired above all. A possible 1000-point evaluation was the parameter.

Bids were opened on 5 July 1939, and Martin's design won the competition hands down—140 points over its nearest competitor. Only four companies had met the terms and conditions set forth by the AAF, and Martin's design was rated at 813.6 points, North American's at 673.4, Douglas's at 610.3, and Stearman's came at 442.7. Glenn L.'s prediction had come true, and his faith in Magruder was confirmed.

A contract for 201 B-26 aircraft, totaling $15,815,000, was awarded Martin on 10 August and was finally approved on 20 September. Although the first B-26 had yet to fly, much less to start in production, additional orders for 139 B-26As were placed on 16 September. Magruder was already improving on the original design, even before construction was underway.

The Army apparently had confidence in Martin's ability to come through.

Their faith was well-founded, for they realized that Glenn L. Martin, aviation pioneer, was the guiding and inspirational force behind Martin's design and production program.

Beginning in 1909, when he wheeled a frail box-kite type of airplane from his first factory (an abandoned church), Mr. Martin started his string of "firsts in aircraft industry" that would carry over to the B-26.

He had taught himself to fly, and had made the first extended over-ocean flight to Catalina Island from the coast of California, which his China Clipper was to re-enact 25 years later, when it became the first over-ocean transport, spanning the Pacific.

Although the public wasn't aware of it at the time, he threw the first bombs from an airplane in the Army's closely guarded bombing experiments in 1913. During the same year he came up with the first armed pursuit plane (crude as it may have been), called the "Aeroplane Destroyer." It was a pusher-type biplane with the pilot sitting in the rear of an extended nose. The gunner sat in front of him with a Winchester rifle mounted on a bracket on top of the front tip of the nose coaming.

Not only did Martin Aircraft pioneer many aviation firsts, but it spawned future great names in the business. One of Martin's students at his early flying school at Griffith Park in Los Angeles was William Edward Boeing, a wealthy Seattle lumberman. He promptly bought a Martin seaplane and a short time later went into the airplane manufacturing business himself, founding the Boeing Aircraft Company.

In 1913 the fledgling Martin Company was located in Los Angeles, with Lawrence Bell as general manager and superintendent of the plant. Bell later left to join Consolidated Aircraft in Buffalo, New York, and eventually formed Bell Aircraft Company, which produced the P-39 Airacobra and a host of other aircraft.

A draftsman at the Los Angeles plant during 1913 and 1914 was none other than Donald Douglas, who eventually carried the tradition of "firsts in the industry" over to his own company, Douglas Aircraft.

Yet another aviation great who worked at Martin (and later at Douglas) was James H. "Dutch" Kindleberger of North American Aviation, builder of the famous P-51 Mustang.

Prior to World War I, Martin built the Army's first two-place trainer with engine in front. During the war period it built the first American twin-engine bomber, which was standard with the Army for a decade. In the interim between World Wars I and II, Martin brought forward successful torpedo bombers and then produced a twin-engined bomber, the B-10, which was 100 miles per hour faster than the fastest bomber of the day. On the commercial side, it pioneered over-ocean commercial air transport with the famous China Clipper and her sister ships.

The production of the B-26 was in good hands. Carrying on the Martin tradition, the B-26 during its short, but illustrious lifetime, claimed many firsts:

- [ ] It was the first aircraft of World War II vintage to use four-bladed propellers. These were 13-foot 6-inch Curtis electrics that were driven by Pratt and Whitney R-2800-5 Wasp engines, which developed 1850 hp at takeoff and 1500 hp at 15,000 feet. A two-stage blower was employed for a supercharging effect at higher altitudes.
- [ ] It embodied the first horizontal tailplane with a marked dihedral—8 degrees.
- [ ] It was the first aircraft to carry a power-operated gun turret. The original armament called for four flexible .30-caliber guns, but Martin designed the 250CE dorsal-mounted, electrically operated turret with twin .50-caliber guns for increased firepower. These turrets were also later used on B-25, B-17, and B-24 American bombers as well.
- [ ] It was the first medium bomber in which the tail gunner could sit in an upright position. Original armament included a flexible .30-caliber gun in the tail position, but this was later replaced (in the B models) with twin flexible .50s, and later (in March 1943) by an electric-hydraulic Martin-Bell turret still containing twin .50s.
- [ ] It was the first WWII aircraft to use weapons pods. Two fixed .50-caliber machine guns were mounted in package pods on both sides of the forward fuselage belly, beginning with the B models.
- [ ] It incorporated the first all-plexiglass bombardier's nose—a Martin innovation.
- [ ] It was the first combat aircraft in which the designers used butted seams for the skin covering as opposed to the conventional lapped seams. This enhanced the flow of air over the streamlined torpedo-like fuselage, which increased the speed of the craft.
- [ ] It was the first combat bomber to employ an all-electrical bomb release mechanism.
- [ ] It was the first combat aircraft to have rubber self-sealing fuel tanks installed as regular equipment. These were another Martin innovation and invention, called "Mareng Cells."
- [ ] It employed the first flexible tracks for transferring ammunition from the bomb bay storage areas back to the tail gun position. Lionel, the famous toy train manufacturer, furnished these tracks (Fig. 1-2).
- [ ] It was the first combat aircraft to use plastic materials as metal substitutes on a grand scale. Martin had been pioneering the use of plastics to replace metal, and the B-26 contained over 400 such parts.
- [ ] It was the first (and last) Army bomber to use torpedoes in the WWII conflict. An external rack was installed along the keel to carry a standard 2000-pound Naval aerial torpedo.
- [ ] It was the first Allied bomber in the European Theater of Operations to complete 100 operational missions. This was accomplished by *Mild*

Fig. 1-2. *View looking down out of left waist window of the B-26 with machine gun barrel protruding. Note .50-caliber belts running to tail gun in track along top of photo. Flexible belt at right feeds shells to waist gun. (photo courtesy W. J. Johnston)*

and Bitter on an afternoon raid on a Nazi airfield at Evreux/Fauville, southwest of Rouen, France, on 9 May 1944. She was a B-26B-25, Serial Number 41-31819, of the 450th Squadron in the 322nd Bomb Group (M) of the 9th Air Force and had flown her first mission on 23 July 1943 (Fig. 1-3). She did all this on her original engines, amassing a total of 449 hours and 30 minutes on them, 310 hours and 40 minutes of that in combat! During this time she never aborted due to mechanical failure, and not one of her many crewmen was a casualty. She was taken off operations after her 100th mission and flown back to the States to conduct War Bond selling tours.

☐ Even more amazing was the fact that a B-26 was the first Allied bomber in the European Theater of War to fly 200 operational missions! In fact, *Flak Bait,* Serial Number 41-31773, actually flew 202 combat missions over a 21-month period (Figs. 1-4, 1-5). She was assigned to the 449th Squadron of the same 322nd Bomb Group and flew her first mission on 16 August 1943; when *Mild and Bitter* had completed her 100th, *Flak Bait* had 99. She never did get the press coverage that *Mild and Bitter* received, but she persevered and it paid off in the end. She flew her 202nd and last mission in early May 1945 from Airfield Y-89 at Le Culot,

Fig. 1-3. *This shot of* Mild and Bitter *was taken early in her career when she just had over 50 missions completed. Capt. Gary King, Jr., is writing up the Form 1 after just completing a flight in her. (photo courtesy Ralph G. McConnell)*

Fig. 1-4. Flak Bait *leading the 322nd Bomb Group on her 200th mission, 17 April 1945. (photo No. A-42346 courtesy Smithsonian Institution)*

Fig. 1-5. Flak Bait *on hardstand at Y-89, LeCulot, Belguim after her 200th. Note large special 200th bomb designation just right of name. (photo No. 786656 courtesy Smithsonian Institution)*

Belgium, from which she had also flown the now-famous 200th. (Sgt. W. J. Johnston, now of Philadelphia, Pennsylvania, was the engineer-gunner on the third crew assigned to *Flak Bait*, and, although he didn't realize it at the time that it was to be her last mission, he was on it. His crew flew approximately 30 mission in *Flak Bait*, including numbers 199, 201, and 202. Why not number 200 when it was ''their'' airplane? The old military truism ''Rank has its privileges'' reared its ugly head for this historic event, and Sgt. Johnston's crew had to stand down that day so the top brass of the outfit could receive the glory. At least the Sarge flew on that last one and now gloats over the fact that *Flak Bait* is probably the most famous Marauder of them all. She was appropriately named, having absorbed over 1000 enemy hits during her combat days. Her nose section—well preserved but unrestored and in original condition—now resides in a place of honor at the National Air and Space Museum of the Smithsonian Institute in Washington, D.C. After the war, Devon Francis even wrote a book about her, appropriately titled *Flak Bait.*

☐ Another B-26 may have been the first American bomber to complete *300* combat missions—and probably the only one of any type in the USAAF to do so. A photo of this unnamed ship shows her after 336 missions, during which none of her many crew members had been injured. (Unfortunately, the negative for that photo, which is the only print in the Martin Photo Library, had been destroyed by deterioration, and attempts to discover the identity of the ship or to which group she was assigned proved futile.)

☐ The army was anxious to get into production; and although the first order included a prototype, none was built, and the first production model was the first of the line to fly!

☐ It had the first aerodynamically perfect fuselage. One of its early nicknames was "The Flying Torpedo".

☐ It was the first twin-engine bomber to carry more payload of bombs than the B-17 of the time.

☐ Lastly, the B-26 was the first aircraft to test the bicycle-type landing gear that would later be adopted for use by the Air Force on the B-47 and B-52 jet bombers. The test bed was a G-25 model, Serial Number 44-68221, and was called the XB-26H. It carried the name *Middle River Stump Jumper*.

It is doubtful that any other World War II aircraft could lay claim to that many firsts.

Although *Mild and Bitter* was the first B-26 to complete 100 missions in the ETO and *Flak Bait* 200, the honor of the first B-26 to complete 100 missions anywhere has to go to *Hells Belle II* of the 17th Bomb Group in the Mediterranean Theater of Operations. She was a B-26B-10, Serial Number 41-18322, and beat *Mild and Bitter* by eight days in racking up her 100th mission on 1 May 1944, bombing the Calaviria rail viaduct in Italy. At that time she had flown a total of 724 hours, 450 to 500 of which were in combat.

The 336-mission mystery ship was undoubtedly from a Mediterranean Theater outfit also, substantiated by the fact that B-26s had been flying combat in that theater since late 1942.

The heretofore unpublicized accomplishments of *Hells Belle II* and the mystery ship only point out the fact that public relations types tend to distort or embellish the facts somewhat, or are guilty of omission. The latter is probably the reason in this case, since the air war in the ETO was the closest to Hitler's heartland, was blessed with the greatest number of USAAF combat groups, and therefore, made the juiciest news copy.

2

CONSTRUCTION:
The Breed Multiplies

Developments in Europe were making it clear every day that time was precious; the next job, one on which there could be no tarrying, was to get the B-26 out of the paper stage and into the air. Hundreds of pounds of shop blueprints for the thousands of integral parts of the airplane had to be drawn and reproduced. It was here that an ingenious Martin invention helped accelerate the program. The "Martin Photographic Reproduction System" (the "Robot Draftsman") freed precious engineering talent for more important work by redrafting original drawings photographically onto coated metal, wood, cloth, paper, and other materials.

New tools and machinery had to be designed, purchased, and set up. Thousands of tons of material had to be bought on an already tightening market. Thousands of workers new to the aircraft industry had to be hired and trained, and thousands of feet of floor space had to be added to the factory. In the Martin tradition, these problems were taken in stride. Also taken in stride was what threatened to be the most serious problem of all—there was not time to build and test a prototype.

A prototype, the first example of a new model, is usually built by hand by the best artisans available and subjected to all sorts of tests on the ground and in the air. These tests enable the engineers and manufacturing experts to detect and iron out the imperfections ("bugs") that lurk in any newly created thing, whether it be a machine, a system of government, or a pharmaceutical. Such imperfections are especially apt to be hidden away in a newly conceived, complicated mechanism such as a powerful modern airplane.

In short, Martin did not enjoy the luxury of time in which to build and test a prototype. They had to take the first airplane off the production line and let it stand or fall on its merits. In even simpler manufacturing regimes, such as tractor-drawn farm equipment, this would be unthinkable—but an airplane? Utterly impossible!

It was, therefore, a tense moment when the first B-26 came off the line (it was virtually pushed off by the airplanes inching ahead behind it), rolled out the doors of final assembly, went through its ground tests, and then took to the air for its first flight tests.

Meanwhile, anticipating they had a hot item on their hands, Martin broke ground on 4 September 1939 on a plant expansion at the Middle River facility (Fig. 2-1) without waiting for emergency plant facilities contracts, nor even for additional production contracts on the B-26. Foreseeing what was to come, they launched the program with their own money.

The expansion was necessary because Martin was already building their Model 187 Baltimore twin-engine bomber for the RAF in Plant 1, and would soon go into production on the famous PBM Mariner patrol bomber for the U.S. Navy. Later would also come the four-engined Mars patrol bomber.

Confirmation of the wisdom of the facility expansion was not long coming, and on 28 September 1940 the Army ordered 791 B-26Bs to be built in Plant 2, which brought the total aircraft on order to 1131. What was so amazing was that the B model hadn't even left the drawing boards yet, and the first "straight"

Fig. 2-1. *Aerial view of the Martin Middle River Plant in Baltimore, on 15 December 1939, before expansion for Marauder production. (photo courtesy Glenn L. Martin Co.)*

B-26 had not been flown, let alone the improved A model! The Army's faith in Martin was thus unequivocally countersunk.

Early wind tunnel test models of the aircraft had a twin tail, which designers thought would give it better control. This was dropped in favor of a single fin so that the tail gunner would have a better field of vision. The fin on the "straight" and A models was a stubby one, and maybe if they'd brought her out with twin rudders as originally intended, a veteran pilot of the South Pacific wouldn't have exclaimed: "My Gawd! When you turn onto the final approach, the needle flops to one side and the ball slides over to the other!" On the B model, the rudder was heightened for greater stability. Some sharp engineer might have even envisioned a power tail turret during the wind tunnel tests, so maybe it was an unforeseen stroke of genius that prompted the single rudder decision.

A couple of years before the Martin B-10 bomber appeared, a skinny kid, who would later be destined to play a major role in the Martin success with the B-26, was learning to fly. There was no airport in Lynchburg, Virginia, in 1929, but that didn't stop Vincent W. "Squeek" Burnett from realizing his ambition. Using cow pastures in the area, Burnett learned to fly and made his first parachute jump at age 16. By the time he was 17, he held a "Transport" license (now called "Commercial"), and flew the first glider in Lynchburg, which had been built by two local boys. His test-and check-flying expertise had therefore started at a very early age.

Burnett flew anything and everything that came along, and when Lynchburg finally did build an airport, he became a part of the first flying service there. At the time he was considered to be somewhat of a "local nut" for some of the things he did with an airplane, and the old boys around town used to shake their heads and swear that he would never live to see 21. Little did they know that Burnett was one of those rare "naturals" who became a part of every airplane he ever flew, and that his technical and engineering skills would later prove to be of the highest caliber.

It wasn't long until the flying service routine lacked the necessary challenge, and in 1935 Burnett joined a flying circus team, "The Flying Aces." For two years the team put on aerobatic shows in all the major cities and many minor ones around the country.

No one actually knows how the nickname "Squeek" came about, but the assumption is that it was because of Burnett's small stature and possibly the tone of his voice. He was only 5' 6", but was wiry and muscular. He needed the coordination and spring-steel tensility of those muscles to horse his old 1929 TravelAir biplane around in the next-to-impossible maneuvers for which he became famous. He was the first pilot to do a "Square Loop," the "Inverted Ribbon Act," and the "Beer Barrel Loop." The personal insignia on the fuselage of his TravelAir was a roundel in which a mouse ran from a doorway across a board floor, uttering a loud "SQUEEK!"

Two things happened in 1937 that had a profound effect on Squeek's life thereafter. He had made such a name for himself and had become so well-known in the aerobatic game that he decided to freelance and left the Flying Aces to accept contracts only for the bigger airshows. His skills were such that he could afford to be selective.

Also during that year, the romance of stunt flying bloomed in a different garden when he met a girl named Evelyn, who became his wife in December 1938. What could be more romantic than spending a honeymoon and the years up until the start of WWII riding the wind and barnstorming in a 1929 TravelAir? Squeek and Evelyn did just that. In fact, they had been married only a month when Squeek did his "Square Loop" publicly for the first time at the All-American Air Maneuvers at Miami, Florida, in January 1939. This maneuver was a contributing factor in his winning the coveted Freddy Lund trophy for aerobatic excellence that same month.

Between airshows, Burnett was based at College Park, Maryland, teaching students basic flying, commercial, instrument, and advanced aerobatics. During this period, he also joined in working out the training routines to be used by the Civil Aeronautics Authority.

Evelyn knew he was something special, and in spite of his reputation as a daredevil, she never categorized him as a reckless person. Every maneuver Squeek performed was a carefully thought-out plan, practiced over and over to perfection. Most daredevil pilots of that era have long since met their maker—some tragically—but Vincent W. Burnett is still with us, a testimony to his natural abilities, technical skills, and his "oneness" with every aircraft he ever flew.

As of September 1944, Burnett was qualified to fly a total of 57 different types and models of military aircraft—not to mention all the civilian and commercial types in which he was qualified!

Evelyn was in the grandstands at Miami airport in January 1940 when Squeek brought the crowd to its feet with a stunt that made all the wire services around the nation (Fig. 2-2). He flew the TravelAir across the field just three feet off the ground—inverted! Normally he'd cut a ribbon strung between two poles 10 feet off the ground in inverted flight, but this topped even the "Inverted Ribbon Act."

Squeek had been instructing for the Brinckerhoff Flying Service at College Park, and, being a freelance pilot, he had a novel arrangement with his old friend, George Brinckerhoff. During the week he instructed students in the newly formed Civilian Pilot Training Program (CPTP), and his weekends were free for him to pursue his aerobatic show work. Burnett took off with the very first student in the program, an ROTC cadet from the University of Maryland, on 10 November 1939. It was fitting that the oldest active airfield in the U.S. would be chosen by the government to start the CPT program.

With the war clouds thickening in Europe, Burnett was asked to come to Richmond, Virginia, in early 1941 to conduct the same kind of program through the University of Richmond for the Richmond Air Transport Service. Since their

Fig. 2-2. *The inverted flight that thrilled the crowd at Miami in January 1940. (photo courtesy* Miami Herald *and Evelyn Burnett)*

roots were in Virginia, he and Evelyn moved to Richmond. Then came Pearl Harbor.

What followed can best be told in Evelyn's own words: "From that day on, I could sense that Squeek was eager to move into some branch of the service. Every day recruits were coming through the airport and he would come home at night looking so restless and unhappy. One day I asked him what was troubling him. He said: 'I can do so much more for the war effort than what I'm now doing. I must get out of here!'

"I was selfish enough to feel he wouldn't have to go into the thick of things, that he would be set for the duration. So many of his old aerobatic friends were conducting these flying schools around the country. It was far more lucrative than entering the service, but Squeek never cared much about money. He would often work for nothing if it was something he really believed in. I knew he was holding back on my account; I had to do something to convince him I'd be okay. "He came home one day with a circular about ferry pilots being needed to ferry planes around the country and overseas. The pay was not too good—about half what he was receiving. I asked him, 'What do you have to do to get in the Ferry Command?' He replied, 'I'll have to report to Bolling Field, DC, for an interview and flight test.' Jokingly, I asked him what made him think he could pass those tests. He thought I was serious, and snapped back, 'Hell, girl, I've got almost 6000 flying hours!' I acknowledged, 'Yes, I know, because I keep your logbooks up to date. Go for it! I'll pack up and move back to Lynchburg so I can be close to both our families.' Deep down, I was really scared. What I really wanted to do was pack my little old ditty bag and tag along as I'd been doing all along, but I realized that this new phase in his life would call for a 'men only' situation.

"He left the next day for Bolling. In two days he was back and said, 'I have to report immediately for duty as a civilian service pilot. Do you think you can manage without me?' I said, 'Just watch me! I'm a big girl and very little scares me.' After all, I had observed him since our marriage three years before, with my heart in my throat, risk his neck every weekend in aerobatic shows around the country!'"

* * * * * * * *

Back at the Martin Middle River plant, the big day had finally arrived, and on 25 November 1940, the first B-26 off the assembly line made her maiden flight with Chief Engineer and Test Pilot William K. Ebel at the controls. It was up to Ebel to make the aircraft prove it would do all that the Army had asked it to do and the company had promised it would do (Fig. 2-3).

The original specifications had called for a 19,220-pound empty and 26,625-pound gross weight, a 323-mph top speed, 26,400-foot service ceiling, and a range of 1800 miles. When Martin No. 1226, AF Serial Number 40-1361, took off, she actually weighed 21,375 pounds empty and grossed out at 27,720 pounds. Top speed attained on the test was 315 mph at 15,000 feet, service ceiling attained was 25,000 feet, and the range had dropped to 1000 miles at 265 mph with a 3000-pound bomb load. Creeping engineering changes and altered specifications by the Army had taken their toll on performance. Unknown to anyone at the time, it would be a harbinger of what was to come.

In spite of the lower performance figures, the Army still had its coveted "300 mile per hour bomber," and the results of the test flights proved far more successful than even the bomber's most enthusiastic supporters had dared hope. Soon after, Ebel became Vice President in Charge of Engineering and a director of the company. Later on, Peyton Magruder would become Chief of New Design. Success in aircraft designing and building is not, however, a matter of enthusiasm or of gratified pride. It is a matter of cold figures and hard facts—figures and facts as attained and revealed in actual flight. That these tests were successful is a matter of record.

The test ship was then turned over to the Army for service acceptance tests. At this point, time was even more important. France had fallen and there was no telling when the victorious Nazis would stop. Just as the company had to content itself without a prototype, the Army had to content itself with a speeded-up "accelerated service test"—in other words, a quick job of testing.

Fig. 2-3. *Martin chief test pilot, William K. Ebel, togged out in winter flying gear beside some type of old twin-engine taildragging aircraft on 24 March 1941. (photo courtesy Glenn L. Martin Co.)*

Within three months of the first flight of the B-26, aircraft began moving off the assembly line in quantity at Baltimore (Fig. 2-4). On 22 February 1941, the first four aircraft were accepted by the AAF and were assigned to the 22nd Bombardment Group (Medium) at Langley Field, Virginia.

From this beginning, the flow of production B-26s to the Army— and later on, to the RAF and Free French—continued at a steady rate (in spite of what

Fig. 2-4. *One of the first B-26s off the production line on the ramp at Martin's Baltimore airport, December 1940. Note natural aluminum finish and old style AAF rudder striping. (photo courtesy Glenn L. Martin Co.)*

seemed at the time to be insurmountable obstacles) with no interruption until the day production was finally halted in early 1945 (Fig. 2-5).

When the Japanese attack on Pearl Harbor occurred, the 22nd Group was the only AAF unit operational with the B-26. On 8 December 1941, 53 of its first 56 Marauders built took off for Muroc, California. There the group remained on sea patrol duties until 31 January 1942, when it left for Australia.

Long before the original order of 201 aircraft had been completed, a fourth and subsequent orders were received (Fig. 2-6). This prompted Martin to build a duplicate of the Middle River Plant 2 facility in Omaha, Nebraska, to be used exclusively for the production of the B-26 under the so-called "Knudsen Plan" (which used subcontractors from the automotive and other related industries to supply parts and components up to and including major subassemblies and assemblies).

The Vice President and General Manager of the Omaha plant came well qualified for the job and the "Knudsen Plan" concept of manufacture. Lincoln Robert Scafe became comptroller of the Wright Airplane Company in Dayton, Ohio, while still in his twenties during World War I. After the war he was comptroller and treasurer of the Fisher Body Division of General Motors in Cleveland, Ohio, for 19 years and served on the committee for the Cleveland air races. In 1939 he went to White Motor Company and left shortly thereafter to head up the newly formed Glenn L. Martin Nebraska Company.

Meanwhile, the Army was experiencing a series of B-26 nosewheel strut failures, which caused delays in bringing the aircraft to full operational status. The strut was strengthened, but it was later found out that the accidents caused by the failure were due to improper weight distribution in the aircraft. This weight and balance factor, coupled with other circumstances (which will be discussed in the next chapter in detail), almost caused the discontinuance of B-26 production in 1942.

Fig. 2-5. *View of the Baltimore B-26 assembly line on 10 February 1941. Note provision for installation of the dorsal turret and the maze of hydraulic lines and electrical conduits in the wing's leading edge. (photo courtesy Glenn L. Martin Co.)*

Fig. 2-6. *Glenn L. Martin holding a B-26 model on 7 December 1941. Whether this publicity photo was taken before or after the news of Pearl Harbor had been received is unknown, but the Middle River Plant was already on a seven-day week. From left to right, Martin personnel: Hartson, Vollmer, McDougal, and Ebel. Painting behind Martin and photograph behind Hartson show the old Martin B-10 bomber. (photo courtesy Glenn L. Martin Co.)*

The AAF had originally intended to call the B-26 the "Martian," but the first A models delivered to the British in October 1941 were called "Marauders" by the RAF. The USAAF went along with the name. Coincidentally, this still preserved the Martin tradition of tagging their military aircraft with names beginning with M. (The British, however, changed the name of the Martin Model 187 (AAF A-30) from Maryland to Baltimore. Since the RAF had taken delivery of the lion's share of the 187 produced, Martin figured they had that right.)

The following excerpts from the Martin Company monthly news magazine, *The Martin Star,* elaborate on various items of interest related to Marauder production:

March 1942: The first R-2800 P&W engine built by the Ford Motor Company was test-flown on the B-26 on 14 February 1942—a prime example of the "Knudsen Plan" at work (Fig. 2-7). Donald Nelson, Chief of the War Production Board, and Benson Ford, Director of the Ford Motor Company, were on hand to witness the flight.

April 1942: H. G. Klemm, chief engineer of the Martin Omaha plant, and a group of his engineers have invented a tilting drafting board that enables the draftsmen to sit in swivel chairs while at work. The fatigue of bending over a flat drafting board has been reduced, and drafting efficiency has been greatly improved.

May 1942: The first B model B-26 is off the line with progressive improvements including a lengthened nosewheel strut, enlarged air intakes on the top of the engine cowling, and the installation of the R-2800-41 P&W engine, which develops 2000 hp for takeoff and 1600 hp at 13,500 feet. Top speed has been increased to 317 mph at 14,500 feet, but the weight has also increased to 22,380 pounds empty and 34,000 pounds gross, which includes a 3000-pound bomb load (Fig. 2-8).

August 1942: The Army Air Force has accepted the first C models from the Omaha plant with the longer wing installed. The span has been increased from 65 to 71 feet and the total area from 602 to 658 square feet. (*Author's note:* The longer wing was also installed on the B model at Baltimore, beginning with the 642nd production aircraft.)

Dec. 1942: The USAAF has activated nine new medium bomber groups during the course of the year, all to be equipped with the Marauder.

Jan. 1943: The British took delivery of 52 B-26As during 1941, most of which were issued to units in the Middle East.

May 1943: The Free French Air Force is being revived in North Africa and six squadrons will be equipped with Marauders.

June 1943: Defensive armament on the Marauder now consists of 12 .50-caliber guns, including two in the tail turret, two in the dorsal turret, two flexibles in the waist, and four fixed in pods mounted on the lower curve of either side of the fuselage just forward of the wing leading edge. These pod guns and a fixed .50-caliber in the lower portion of the plexiglass nose all fire forward

Fig. 2-7. *Installing the first Ford-built R-2800 P&W engine on the B-26. Ford built these engines in the midwest, which was ideal for supplying them to the Omaha plant. (photo courtesy Glenn L. Martin Co.)*

and are actuated by the pilot with a button on the control wheel. The twelfth gun of the lot is a flexible .50 in the center of the plexiglass nose, which is fired by the bombardier. The additional guns, added armor plate protection, and other modifications have now increased the weight to 24,000 pounds empty and 37,000 pounds gross, which includes a 4000-pound bomb load. As a result, the

Fig. 2-8. *B-26As on apron outside Baltimore Plant 2 awaiting delivery to the Army, 13 May 1942. Ramp for launching flying boats at upper right. Dorsal turrets have now been installed, but no machine guns are in place at any of the gun positions. Only the first few ships were delivered with the natural finish and the old red and white rudder striping; camouflage paint is now standard. Note that some ailerons are missing and all are minus propellers. A serious shortage of Curtis electric propellers, which began in the fall of 1941, was still plaguing Martin when this shot was taken. In fact, some early '26 deliveries to the 22nd Bomb Group at Langley Field, Virginia, sat on the ramps there minus propellers for some time. As soon as a ship had been ferried from Baltimore to Langley, the props were removed, mounted on a trailer dolly, and towed the 120 miles back to the Martin plant behind an automobile to be used for test-hopping new ships just off the production line. (photo courtesy Glenn L. Martin Co.)*

speed has dropped to 282 mph, and 214 mph cruise. (*Author's note:* Not too long after this, the fixed .50 in the nose was discontinued.)

Nov. 1943: Martin No. 1226, AAF S/N 40-1361, *Old Gran Pappy*, the first Marauder built, is the only first bomber of any type to still be on active service. First flown on 25 November 1940, it was later delivered to the Army in February 1941, after exhaustive flight tests by Martin which proved the mettle of the craft. The Army used it for training purposes at Patterson Field, Ohio; Jackson Army Air Base, Mississippi; Harlingen Gunnery School, Texas; and finally at Laughlin Army Air Field, Del Rio, Texas, where it was used to train new pilots to fly the B-26. While at Laughlin, it set all endurance records for training planes by hauling pilots on training flights for 2180 hours. More than 100 pilots received training in her without serious mishap or casualties of any kind. *Old Gran Pappy* has just recently been transferred to the Ford Dearborn Engine School, Michigan, to be used for instructional purposes.

Minor engineering and design changes crept into the aircraft between major alphabetical model changes and were designated numerically. As an example, many of the new ships furnished bomb groups leaving for the European Theater of Operations in late 1943 and early 1944 were B models of the -50 series (Fig. 2-9).

In early 1944, the C-45 model incorporated a thicker grip on the control wheels, improvements in the hydraulic and electrical systems, and additional emergency systems, among others.

Early models of the B-26 had two bomb bays, but the rear one was only used infrequently for light loads in the South Pacific. Eventually the rear bomb bay racks were discontinued altogether; later on, the doors and actuating mechanism were deleted as well. The space and weight factor became too critical, and the area involved was more valuable as a gunner's station after two flexible .50-caliber guns were installed in the waist window area, and ammo storage boxes were installed for the tail and waist guns. Somebody had been dreaming on this score anyway, as even later models with the 2000-hp engines would have had a difficult time staggering off the runway on a hot summer day with both bomb bays filled to capacity.

In February 1944, the model designation jumped to F. One D model had been built, which in reality was just an early B-26 that had been modified to test heated surface-type de-icing equipment (XB-26D). An E model was planned, but for some unknown reason was never built. It was a stripped version of the B, weighing 2000 pounds less and with the dorsal turret moved forward to the navigator's and radio operator's compartment just aft of the flight deck bulkhead. (Maybe someone was still trying to make use of the aft bomb bay!)

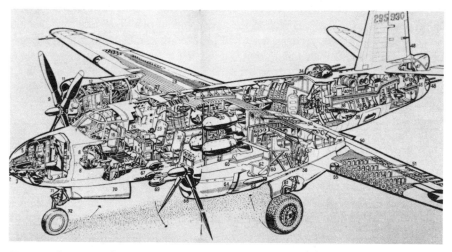

Fig. 2-9. *A cutaway view of a B-26B-50 model, showing many of the construction features and systems of the aircraft.*

The major change in the F model (in addition to the same improvements that went into the C-45) was the 3.5 degree change in the wing incidence, which Martin claimed increased the pilot's visibility, especially during takeoff and landing, and allowed the airplane to take off itself, as conventional aircraft did. They also claimed that "new fairings, fillets, exhaust nozzles, sealed doors and openings, and items of similar nature add 26 to 30 miles an hour to the top speed."

They were right about better visibility, etc., as the B-26F flew with the fuselage straight and level, due to the upward cant of the new wing, as opposed to the slight nose-high attitude of previous models. The changes that were supposed to have increased the speed either were not fully incorporated or didn't produce the desired results, as the top speed of the F actually dropped to 277 mph. With the new wing angle, though, takeoff and landing speeds were lowered.

Other significant improvements in the F were a new dural armor plate; a new fuel system, which reduced the airplane's vulnerability to gunfire; improvements in the ailerons and rudder, which made the bomber even more maneuverable; a new mechanical emergency landing gear system, reducing vulnerability and increasing safety; and further improvements to the electrical and hydraulic systems, contributing to reduced maintenance requirements.

Changes for the proposed but abandoned E model which did not carry over into the actual F production models included "new gun arrangements providing complete fire cover, better in many respects than that of the famed Flying Fortresses, new escape hatches offering added means of egress, and a reloadable 'Bazooka' twin-tube installation providing additional striking power with rocket bombs."

Martin's mention of "new gun arrangements" probably referred to the movement of the dorsal turret forward, but how the E could come out weighing 2000 pounds *less* than the B with all the added weight of a "bazooka" installation is a mystery—unless, perhaps they had planned to remove the internal bomb racks and who knows what else to turn it into a low-level ground attack version.

The last model produced was the G, which, in addition to the new wing angle, had some equipment changes and used AN fittings instead of AAF fittings for easier hydraulic system maintenance (Figs. 2-10, 2-11). One H model appeared, called the XB-26H, but this was actually the TB-26G-25MA that had been retrofitted with the bicycle-type landing gear.

Production of the B-26 finally ended at both Baltimore and Omaha on 30 March 1945 after a total of 5157 had been built (1585 of them at Omaha). Of these, 521 had gone to the British and French Air Forces (Fig. 2-12). The total included a model that was stripped of all armor and armament and used by the Navy as a target tow ship; these were painted a bright yellow, and known as the JM-1 and JM-2 (Fig. 2-13).

The Navy took delivery of 50 JM-2s all at one crack at the Naval Air Station, North Island, San Diego, California, in late 1943, according to C. Q. Middlebrook (now of Dahlgren, VA), who was a seaman stationed there at the time, having

Fig. 2-10. *Work progressing on one of the last B-26s to be built in the Martin Baltimore plant on 1 November 1944. Note butted seams in the skin and flush riveting. (photo courtesy Glenn L. Martin Co.)*

survived the sinking of the *U.S.S. West Virginia* at Pearl Harbor and subsequent duty with the Pacific Fleet.

The Army Air Force also used the target tow versions, although they retained the olive drab paint scheme. An article in the December 1943 issue of *Air Force* magazine, describing revisions in the overall Army Air Force training

Fig. 2-11. *First G model of last Army contract warming up on Baltimore flight line. Peyton Magruder, in white shirt, with other Martin officials and Army factory representative look on. Note exterior armor plating just aft of nose. (photo courtesy Glenn L. Martin Co.)*

programs, stated in part: "A significant development in gunnery training is the use of the AT-23 airplane, a B-26 stripped down for target towing. Because of its exceptional maneuverability, it is admirably suited to this purpose. Tests have shown that at 20,000 feet, the AT-23 can make 25 runs on a B-17 in 45 minutes. The calibrated airspeed of the AT-23 while towing targets at this altitude is 180 to 200 miles per hour." Later on, the AAF changed the designation from AT-23 to TB-26.

With the completion of B-26 production (Fig. 2-14), Martin could take pride in their contribution to the war effort just with the B-26 alone, not to mention the Baltimore produced for the RAF and the Mariner and Mars patrol bombers for our own Navy. The tradition went on, but competition from other aircraft companies, coupled with other circumstances, eventually forced Martin to abandon aircraft production altogether. Other major companies met the same fate in the postwar years, but in Martin's case it seemed especially tragic that such a giant in the industry, whose aircraft had been synonymous with both the Army and Navy for so many years, should topple.

However, like a phoenix, the company rose from the ashes of near-oblivion and eventually became a huge conglomerate—Martin-Marietta Corporation. True, there are no more Martin aircraft, but the company's Aerospace Division

Fig. 2-12. *Martin officials Turnbull, Furman, and Tibbs pose beside tail of 5000th B-26 at Middle River. Pat Tibbs was Martin's airport manager. Note that the only olive drab camouflage now being used is on the upper portion of the fuselage, wings, and empennage. 3 April 1945. (photo courtesy Glenn L. Martin Co.)*

now carries on the Glenn L. Martin tradition of innovation and designs and builds aerospace components, rocket launch vehicles, and systems for the aerospace industry, the military services, and NASA.

After B-26 production had ended at the Omaha plant, it was converted to the production of the Boeing B-29 Superfortress in March 1945. The special

Fig. 2-13. *The JM-1 Navy target tow version of the B-26 at Martin airport in the all-yellow paint scheme. Propeller warning stripe aft of the pilot's canopy was bright red. 13 November 1943. (photo courtesy Glenn L. Martin Co.)*

Fig. 2-14. *Martin test pilots and airport personnel pose before the last B-26 built—a G model— on the Martin Baltimore flight line, 3 April 1945. Pat Tibbs, airport manager, in center of those standing. (photo courtesy Glenn L. Martin Co.)*

bomb racks for accommodating the two atomic bombs dropped on Japan were designed and built into Superforts at the Glenn L. Martin Nebraska Company.

Even before the raids on Hiroshima and Nagasaki, Martin had an interest in the atom bomb project. Martin electric gun turrets were used as camera housings to photograph the first atomic bomb explosion in the desert wastes of New Mexico. These were the same turret housings that were built by the thousands during WWII for the B-26 and other USAAF bombers at the Martin Sinclair Division and the Omaha plant.

These camera-filled turrets were set up at various locations in the test site areas (some as close to ground zero as a fraction of a mile) and were all adapted for fully automatic operation, being connected to the robot control that actually fired the bomb.

Even after production of the B-26 had ceased at the Baltimore plant, Martin continued to work with the military on various experimental ideas. Taxi and flight tests of the bicycle landing gear-equipped B-26H were still going on in December 1945 as evidenced by Fig. 2-15.

Fig. 2-15. *The only B-26H built (actually a retrofitted G-25 model) undergoing violent 360-degree taxi turn tests of the bicycle-type landing gear at the Martin Baltimore airport on 29 December 1945. Note small outrigger wheels mounted under engine nacelles in place of the original main gear, and reversion to the old "single-stinger" tail cone. When this gear arrangement was later incorporated on the B-47 jet bomber, the outriggers were mounted outboard on the wings. The purpose of the strakes along the aft fuselage is unknown. Someone facetiously named it* Middle River Stump Jumper. *(photo courtesy Glenn L. Martin Co.)*

Fig. 2-16. *The mysterious Navy experimental model 19B-JM1, on the Martin Baltimore airport ramp. (photo courtesy Glenn L. Martin Co.)*

Another unusual experimental model appeared as late as November 1946 as can be seen in Fig. 2-16. The only clue to its purpose was the caption on the file copy, which reads: "19B-JM1 Navy version, complete assembly, ¾ front view, left."

Whether this beautiful B or C model was being used just as test bed for the small jet engine hung from its left side, the jet engine was to be used for takeoff boost instead of JATO bottles, or it was to be used for extra thrust in flight is just a matter of conjecture. At any rate, it was an aesthetically perfect installation which again drew attention to Martin's craftsmanship. Since the photo shows the "Navy" version, it is reasonable to assume that the USAAF might have been conducting similar experiments.

At the time this photo was taken, this aircraft was probably one of only a mere half-dozen B-26s still intact. All the American Marauders in the ETO and in the inventory of the USAAF and Navy stateside had already been scrapped and melted down into aluminum ingots. *C'est la guerre!*

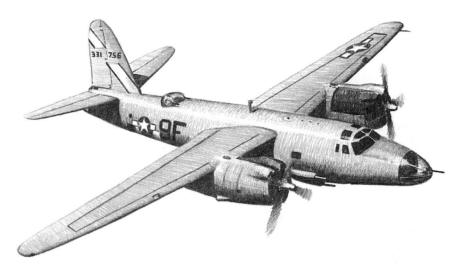

3

COMPLICATIONS:
Escaping the Executioner Thrice

The year 1942 was a critical one for the B-26, and as a result of the bad reputation it had undeservedly earned, production was nearly cancelled by Congressional action as a result of the Truman Committee Investigation.

Probably no American airplane had ever been tagged with so many derogatory nicknames. The short 65-foot wing and high wing loading of the "straight" and A models prompted wags to call her "The Flying Prostitute" or "The Baltimore Whore" (no visible means of support). Later on, in the hands of inexperienced pilots, she became known as "Widow-Maker," "Flying Coffin," "The Coffin without Handles," or "The B-Dash-Crash."

These blasphemous monikers were not without justification, however. True, the B-26 was responsible for many deaths in training accidents, and the drastic increase in the rate of such accidents and in-flight emergencies was alarming enough to draw the attention of numerous investigative bodies, one headed up by General "Tooey" Spaatz of the Air Force itself.

In actuality, this condemnation was not entirely the fault of the aircraft, but rather a combination of interrelated causes. Much of the explanatory material which follows was extracted directly from a Glenn L. Martin Company report prepared for the Committee on Military Affairs of the House of Representatives during this period.

Bearing this in mind, it is hoped that the reader will forgive the somewhat simplistic tone of the prose. Given the varied backgrounds of many Congressional Committee members, the Martin writers had to make sure that what they were trying to say would be understood. Consequently, they bent over backwards in some of their definitive explanations, and the resulting document was something even a fifth-grade student could understand (which doesn't speak too well for the intelligence level of members of Congress). The excerpts below are italicized.

The very first Marauders in the AAF inventory were flown by pilots trained with the thoroughness for which there is time in peace, and their planes, with a few exceptions for special missions, were carrying little more than the weight they were designed to carry. Even after they went into combat in the South Pacific and with the British in the Middle East, the ease with which they flew their Marauders could have been predicted from these additional facts:

After becoming a pilot, a man is given "transitional training" before he is allowed to fly solo a plane new to him. The pilots who took delivery of the B-26 at the factory—that is, came to the Martin factory and flew the planes away—required little or no transitional training to enable them to take the Marauders and fly them to the fields for which they were destined. As a matter of fact, the only such training these men received before flying the planes from the factory was three takeoffs and landings. That brief training was given by the Army Air Force representative stationed at the Martin factory. "Tactical Training" to enable such pilots to enter combat with their Marauders was correspondingly brief. New tactics had yet to be developed for a new airplane. To repeat, experienced pilots were flying the first Marauders, and the planes were being asked to carry very little more weight than they had been designed to carry.

But trouble was brewing. Most of the thoroughly trained pilots—pilots trained in the comparative leisure of peace—were being sent to the fronts. The Marauders pouring out the doors of Final Assembly were being flight-tested by Martin test pilots at the Martin airport, and with practically no accidents. [As late as mid-1942 there had never been a fatality to a Martin test pilot in a B-26 at the Martin Baltimore Airport, and these men, many of them commercially trained pilots, had test flown almost two thousand Marauders a total of almost five thousand hours.] *Then the planes took off for training fields in this country where relatively green pilots were assigned to fly them. Furthermore, most of the Army's thoroughly trained service mechanics were also being sent to the fronts; that meant that relatively green mechanics were assigned at the Army air fields to service the Marauders.*

The Army Air Force had first set up B-26 Transition Training Fields at MacDill Field, Tampa, Florida, and Barksdale Field, Shreveport, Louisiana, and many of the pilots trying to master the Marauder at these fields had *no* previous twin-engine experience—instructors and students alike!

Later on, Laughlin Army Air Field, Del Rio, Texas, and Dodge City Army Air Field, Kansas, became the transitional training bases and MacDill and Barksdale became Operational Training Unit bases, where an entire bomb group trained together for combat in combat-configured B-26s (Figs. 3-1 through 3-3). Even later, as more groups were being formed for eventual assignment to overseas duty, Barksdale changed to a Replacement Training Unit base and trained individual crews in combat flying for replacements to attrited groups overseas, as was also done at Lake Charles Army Air Field, Louisiana; Baer Field, Ft. Wayne, Indiana; and Craig Field, Selma, Alabama. Lakeland Army Air Field (Drane Field) became a sub-base of MacDill, as did Avon Park Army Air Field (both in Florida), and also conducted OTU training. The same went for Harding Field, Louisiana, a Barksdale satellite base.

Crashes at MacDill had become so commonplace in the early days of 1942 that the expression "One a day in Tampa Bay" became an albatross around the neck of the B-26 flight training program. In actuality, it was more like "one a week," but the bad reputation had spread and facts were sometimes overridden by fears. The same problems were being encountered at Barksdale, but MacDill had the dubious honor of being selected as the main culprit by virtue of the condemning rhyme.

Meanwhile fell the heaviest blow of all—and heavy is the right word. The Army, faced with tactical problems no one had foreseen when the plane was designed back in peacetime, began overloading the Marauder. This was not done whimsically; changing conditions at the warfronts required it. Be that as it may, the fact remained that relatively green men were servicing and flying a plane overloaded beyond all consideration of the laws of aerodynamics. In homey terms, it was as though a rowboat meant to hold one man and his fishing tackle had fifty pounds of rocks dumped into it with the expectation of it being able to navigate on a swift, choppy river after a third fifty pounds of rocks had

Fig. 3-1. *Postcard photo of transition training ship over Dodge City AAF. Serial number on rudder indicates this to be a C-10 model built in mid-1941. Note taller rudder, smaller propeller hubs, and larger air intakes atop engine nacelles. (photo courtesy Houston H. Holland)*

33

Fig. 3-2. *Transition training instructors at Dodge City AAF in 1943. Houston H. Holland, fourth from right in back row, and now of Claremore, Oklahoma, instructed there during 1943-44 and amassed over 900 flying hours in the B-10 and later models. Mascot,* Crew Chief, *lost his tail from a spinning prop and didn't quite make it with the leg cross like the seated officers. (photo courtesy Houston H. Holland)*

Fig. 3-3. *Dodge City transition training B-26s practicing formation flying. Instructor Holland is piloting lead ship as the flight approaches Great Bend, Kansas. Lead ship is an early short-wing, short-rudder version B model with flexible tail gun provision. The Number Three ship (upper left) is a B-40 model and the Number Two ship a B-35 model—both with no dorsal turrets but with provisions for the .50-caliber guns in the tail turrets. (photo courtesy Houston H. Holland)*

been dumped into it. The boat would stay afloat, but it wouldn't handle too well, especially with a landlubber as its crew.

That is exactly what happened to the B-26 Marauder. As the load went up and the wing loading steadily increased, which correspondingly upped the landing and stalling speeds, the aircraft became a very sensitive and demanding one to handle, especially by inexperienced pilots.

Peyton Magruder must have been horrified at how the Army had turned his streamlined beauty into a man-killer.

Of course, the weight was not added all at once; it might have been better if it had been. It was a case of half-a-ton or so here, several hundred pounds there, fifty pounds or so somewhere else. By early 1942 the plane had risen in normal gross weight from its original 26,625 pounds to a normal gross weight of 31,527 pounds, an increase of 4902 pounds or almost two and a half tons! And, out in the South Pacific, under combat conditions and usually without fighter escort, Marauder men were being asked to fly their ships at slightly less than 10,000 pounds over the designed weight!

Here are a few typical additions of weight made back at the factory before the plane even left for OTU training fields or combat duty:

Self-sealing fuel cells and lines------------------------------------*1,204 pounds*
Change from four .30-cal. to nine .50-cal. guns------------*1,903 pounds*
Armor plate--*867 pounds*
Power-operated deck turret--*350 pounds*
Additional radio equipment--*130 pounds*
Camouflage paint--*47 pounds*
Provisions for torpedo racks--*64 pounds*
Revised electrical installation------------------------------------*47 pounds*
Provisions for bomb bay ferry tanks--------------------------------*55 pounds*

While most of these additions were necessary to stay abreast of combat situations, no one had recommended that the power be increased—or if they had, no action had been taken.

Even with the tremendous increase in weight, the Marauder was still being flown successfully by properly trained pilots backed up by properly trained service mechanics. At the Martin airport, for instance, Martin test pilots, backed up by experienced service mechanics, were encountering no difficulty.

Of course, they were operating under ideal conditions. But at the training fields, the inevitable was happening. The accident rate of the Marauder began climbing, and in July the Truman Committee recommended that B-26 production be stopped. When word of this reached the South Pacific, the veteran Marauder pilots and combat leaders in that area went to bat for the airplane. Through sheer pressure via Air Force channels, they saved the B-26 from a death knell based solely on its performance out there.

This was not to last long, however, for by September the accident rate on the Marauder at training fields had risen so high that the Air Safety Board of the Army Air Forces, in conjunction with Martin personnel, and by direction of General Muir S. Fairchild, Director of Military Requirements, conducted an investigation into the causes. This was a "do or die" situation, as the Truman Committee had become adamant in again recommending the discontinuance of production in October.

About this time, a man who was destined to become a leading actor in the "Truman Committee versus the B-26" scenario had been standing in the wings. He was soon to appear on center stage. Vincent W. Burnett had been assigned to the Northeast Sector of the Ferry Command at Logan Field, Baltimore, Maryland on 12 January 1942, where his commanding officer, Col. Robert H. Baker, made him Chief Test Pilot. His duties included test-flying many types of civilian aircraft the military had absorbed, checking out pilots interested in joining the Ferry Command, and test-flying and ferrying every military aircraft type the Command had to deliver.

There were a lot of B-26s waiting to be ferried, but some of the old pilots wanted no part of flying them. In fact, many were walking away and resigning rather than ferry a '26. Having already been checked out in the B-26, Burnett had fallen in love with it and couldn't see anything dangerous about the beautiful ship. Hearing the rumors of the Truman Committee's threat to cancel B-26 production, he began flying verification tests of his own during his spare time to prove her airworthiness.

Burnett's introduction to the B-26 was somewhat of a miracle in itself and further underscored his unusual abilities as a pilot. All his thousands of hours of flying time had been single-engine, with the exception of a few hours in an old Ford Trimotor belonging to some friends in the airshow business, but checking out in the "Widow-Maker," which would have been a terrifying experience to anyone else, proved to be a "piece of cake" for Squeek.

After less than half a day familiarizing himself with the B-26 on the ground, a check pilot took him up for a spin around the field. After two turns around, the check pilot told him to land it; Burnett didn't need any more instruction! The very next day, Colonel Baker made him Chief Test Pilot of the outfit.

Subsequently the entire Logan Field unit was moved to New Castle Army Air Field, Wilmington, Delaware, as the 12th Ferrying Squadron, and where the Ferry Command eventually became a part of the Army Air Forces. On 2 May 1942 Burnett was commissioned a First Lieutenant and continued to conduct experiments with the B-26, seeking to dispel the rumors; he knew full well that she could serve well in combat and that if someone didn't find the answers, his beloved ship would end up being just a memory.

Fate was soon to take a hand in events that would eventually lead to Burnett's intense involvement with the B-26 and give him the opportunity to prove his convictions about her. In July, he ran into his old friend from civilian flying days, Major Clare Bunch, who was on Brig. Gen. James H. Doolittle's staff. Their friendship dated back to the time Bunch loaned Squeek his clipped-wing Monocoupe *Nervous Energy II* (NC511) to use in aerobatic demonstrations. As a result of these flights, Squeek probably brought more fame and recognition to the little ship than any other pilot of the time.

Bunch told Burnett that big things were brewing and that Doolittle had asked him to recruit only the best for his 4th Medium Bombardment Wing, 12th Air Force, then stationed at Bolling Field, D.C. Knowing that the 4th was flying B-26s, Burnett was ready to make the move. On 31 July, a formal request was made to Col. Baker to transfer Burnett immediately and permanently to Doolittle's 12th.

Due to an extreme shortage of ferry pilots, and not wanting to lose his Chief Test Pilot, Baker adamantly and stubbornly refused to honor the transfer request. Bunch convinced Doolittle that Burnett's aviation background and his experimental work with the B-26 would be invaluable to the 12th, so they carried the transfer request all the way to the top. On direct orders from AAF Commander, Lt. Gen. H.H. Arnold, Burnett was assigned to Doolittle as his Technical Adviser on 30 August 1942.

During September, Doolittle was informed that his personal B-26 would soon be ready for him at the Martin Omaha plant. When confirmation came through that it was off the assembly line, he sent Burnett out to pick it up. Having already dealt Japan a shocking blow with his Tokyo raid, Doolittle had a unique insignia painted on the airplane, as shown in Fig. 3-4.

On 30 September 1942 the 12th moved to England, where plans were being made for the invasion of North Africa. In November the outfit moved to Algeria, and Burnett was supposed to fly down alone but was held up for three days because Doolittle wanted him to lead a squadron of P-38s down. By that time he had been promoted to Captain.

In restrospect, the whole congressional fiasco was uncalled-for, as the AAF was keenly aware of the problem and would have rectified the situation anyway. But, as some were prone to forget, the civilian sector carried a big stick when military matters were under scrutiny.

Air Force Commanding General H. H. Arnold had already directed Doolittle to investigate the situation personally, and his preliminary report to General Fairchild in the following letter had hit the nail on the head:

TO: Director of Military Requirements   8 Sep. 1942
SUBJECT: B-26 Airplane

1. Pending the time that results of a complete analysis of the recent series of B-26 accidents is available, the following four points represent the writer's thinking on the basic reasons underlying these accidents.

   a. The airplane is more difficult to fly than other contemporary models.

   b. It has now reached a period when fatigue or "wear out" failures incline to occur.

c. At a time when the maintenance should be superior, it is poor, due largely to the rush of preparing these airplanes and units for immediate shipment overseas.

d. The operational training system is being carried on without due regard to the characteristics and inherent limitations of the airplane, again in large part, due to the requirement of getting these units overseas as rapidly as possible.

2. It is felt that a complete review of policy and practice is required in order to stop these accidents and derive the maximum utility from this airplane.

Signed,

J.H. Doolittle
Brigadier General, USA

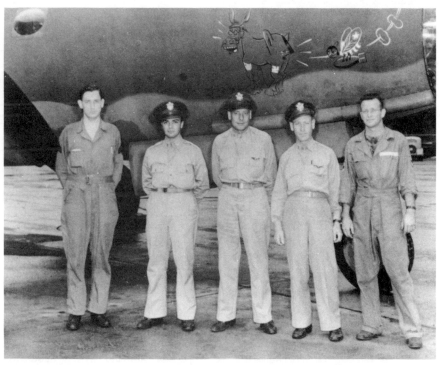

Fig. 3-4. *General Doolittle's personal B-26 at the Martin Omaha Plant, Sept. 1942. 1/Lt. Vincent W. Burnett, second from right, took delivery of the new ship and subsequently flew it to England and then to Africa. On his right is his old friend, Lt. Col. Clare Bunch. Note jackass insignia with head of Tojo, rear end of Hitler, and the USAAF be ready to sting both ends with bombs. (USAAF photo courtesy Evelyn Burnett)*

The subsequent Air Safety Board Investigation endorsed Doolittle's report and revealed the expected:

> . . . The accidents were found due to three major causes:
> 1. Inexperience of pilots.
> 2. Inexperience of maintenance mechanics.
> 3. Overloading beyond the weight when the bomber,
>   a twin-engine plane, could fly on one engine.

How did the matter of flying on one engine get into the picture? The answer is simply this: Engine failure began plaguing the airplane. The engines were supplied to Martin by the Government, but that did not lessen the Company's interest in the matter. After all, the reputation of their airplane was at stake, and word had gotten around that the B-26 would absolutely not fly on one engine.

The engine failures were investigated and found to be due to several causes. One was poor maintenance by relatively green mechanics. Another was the change from 100 octane fuel to 100 octane aromatic fuel, which damaged the diaphragm of the carburetors. And of 96 [electrical system] distributors examined, only three were found safe to fly.

Also, it was revealed that many of the instructors, themselves relatively "green" pilots, did not know how to fly the B-26 on one engine, and so could scarcely teach the technique to their student pilots. Returning to the comparison of the fellow in the rowboat into which the rocks had been dumped, one of the oars had been lost and the green man was expected to make it to shore with only one oar.

It wasn't uncommon in those days to see a lone B-26 parked off the ramp at numerous airfields around the country that had literally been abandoned due to a mechanical problem of some minor nature which caused a delay in obtaining replacement parts. Because of other commitments, the ferry crew had left the aircraft, and there it sat because no one had the courage to try to fly it out.

Part of a pilot's transitional training consists of instruction on how to fly on one engine, but what was actually happening was that the green men were being confronted with the problem of flying on one engine before they had been taught the technique. The problem just came to them with cruel suddenness and without warning or preparation. It's no wonder that so many fatalities resulted. In the mad rush to gear up for full-scale war and with both men and materials coming into the Army faster than the system could handle them, the niceties of adequate and proper training were sometimes slighted.

Even though the lives of their buddies were being wiped out in these single-engine mishaps, the American airman's ever-present ability to make light of a bad situation was evidenced by a little ditty found scrawled inside a flight line locker door at MacDill:

B-26 Single Engine Procedure

If you have altitoot,
Use your chute.
If it's on takeoff you're bent,
And an engine has gone and went,
Forget the bail-out alarm,
Brother, you've bought the farm!
Naught to do but hope and pray,
For it's certain death in Tampa Bay!

Likewise, the harried, nail-biting transition training instructors composed a parody to "I Ain't Gonna Grieve" to portray their plight:

B-26
Transition Instructor's Song

If you fly that B Dash Crash,
Oh, if you fly that B Dash Crash;
Brother, you're fixin' to bust your ass!
Gonna kill myself, Oh precious me!

If you fly that B Twenty-Six,
Oh, if you fly that B Twenty-Six;
Brother, you're in a helluva fix!
Gonna kill myself, Oh precious me!

Who built the fire on the downwind leg?
Now, who built the fire on the downwind leg?
Some dumb student went and laid an egg;
Gonna kill myself, Oh precious me!

If he hits that wrong feather switch,
Now, if he hits that wrong feather switch,
I swear I'm gonna kill the sonnuvabitch!
Gonna kill myself, Oh precious me!

There were many more verses describing in lurid detail the horrors experienced instructing students, many of whom didn't want to be there anyway, but these four verses will give an idea of the gist of the instructor's message.

After reviewing Doolittle's report to Fairchild, General Arnold, being a staunch advocate of the "put-your-money-where-your- mouth-is" approach to problem solving and having faith in both the B-26 and Doolittle's abilities, immediately wrote Jimmy a short note: "Take a B-26 and test it all ways, and then go down and take command of the B-26 outfits in Florida. Demonstrate and train the pilots thoroughly to handle the B-26."

Leaving the preparations for the move to England to his deputies, Doolittle did as directed. Of course, he didn't have to test the B-26 "all ways." Squeek Burnett had already done this, and that was good enough for Jimmy.

In the face of what seemed like unsurmountable obstacles, Doolittle insisted that the Army Air Safety Board and the Martin Company begin moving heaven and Earth to remove the causes of the accidents.

They saw to it that the physical causes of most of the engine failures were corrected. Martin sent its own maintenance mechanics to the training fields to assist and instruct Army mechanics in the maintenance of the airplanes; where possible, it sent one man for every squadron of 13 airplanes. The company also set up, in collaboration with the Army, a Service Training School right at the Baltimore factory for training Air Force mechanics in the servicing of the B-26; it had graduated over 7,000 skilled mechanics by early 1944.

With the press of the impending invasion of North Africa requiring Doolittle's presence, and seeing the wheels in motion on the B-26 "fix," Arnold let him return to his outfit after extracting a promise from him that he would still see that the demonstration and training phase was carried out. Doolittle had an ace up his sleeve in more ways than one—aerobatic "ace" and B-26 expert Vincent W. Burnett!

Retired USAF Master Sergeant Edward F. Fitzpatrick, now of Dover, Delaware, was sent to the Martin Technical School in 1942 after finishing his basic training and A&M School at Keesler Field, Mississippi. Fitzpatrick was one of the first to be sent to the special school, and at that time the students were all housed in temporary quarters—house trailers. "Fitz" didn't mind this, as he could get home every weekend; he was from Philadelphia, Pennsylvania.

He recalls seeing the famous "Doolittle demonstration" flight and remembers that the intensive course included one week each of propellers, hydraulic systems, electrical systems, and airframes.

Although he was assigned to service other aircraft subsequent to the intensive B-26 course, one of his prized possessions is a nose art shot of an ETO B-26 named *Truman's Folly,* showing the ship had completed 164 missions without an abort when the photo was taken (Fig. 3-5)—the pilot's way of expressing how wrong a Congressional Committee could be.

While Doolittle has always been given credit for saving the B-26, a little-known fact is that the pilot who flew the majority of the demonstration flights to prove to transition instructors and new pilots at OTU bases that the B-26 was a safe airplane was his Technical Adviser, Captain Vincent W. Burnett, whom Doolittle sent back to the States from Africa for this express purpose. These flights included single-engine operation, slow-flying characteristics, recoveries from unusual positions, etc. For the benefit of Army brass at Martin's Baltimore and Omaha plants, he flew a B-26 around the tower, on the deck, and with one

Fig. 3-5. Truman's Folly *with 164 mission bombs painted on her nose. She was assigned to the 453rd Squadron of the 323rd Bomb Group. (photo courtesy Edward F. Fitzpatrick)*

engine cut off and the prop feathered! The flights were made in a ship facetiously named *Epsom Salts—Just Passing Through.*

The single-engine turns around the towers shown in Figs. 3-6 and 3-7 were not done after a long dive from altitude to build up flying speed, but were executed from straight and level flight—testimonial to Burnett's expertise and the stability of the B-26 when flown by an experienced pilot.

Martin also sent its own test pilots to the fields, and they, together with Pacific veterans recalled to the States expressly for this purpose, and other experienced Army pilots from Wright Field, taught the instructors how to fly on one engine so that they in turn could teach the correct technique to their student pilots.

In some cases, recently graduated Aviation Cadets, who had only flown the single-engined AT-6 in Advanced Flying Training, were being expected to crawl into a B-26 and learn the intricacies of twin-engine flight and single-engine procedures the hard way. The Army finally began giving these men some twin-engine indoctrination in the all-metal Curtis AT-9, a twin-engined Advanced Trainer. This was a racy-looking little ship that reminded one of the British Beaufighter in that the radial engines protruded in front of the conical nose. It was a bit tricky for the novice to handle, and its miserable single-engine performance made it a logical stepping stone as a prelude to manhandling the Marauder. In fact, the AAF was already using it as a transition trainer for fighter pilots (AT-6 graduates) to give them some twin-engine experience before checking out in the P-38.

Fig. 3-6. *Burnett's epochal flight around the tower at Martin's Baltimore airport with the turn into the dead engine—this despite explicit instruction in all AAF single-engine procedures to "never turn into the dead engine"! Burnett proved it could be done, and with a B-26 to boot! Spring 1943. (Glenn L. Martin Co. photo courtesy Evelyn Burnett)*

Fig. 3-7. *Captain Burnett wheeling the B-26 around the Martin Omaha airport on the deck with one prop feathered—and again, a turn into the dead engine! Spring 1943. (Glenn L. Martin Co. photo courtesy Evelyn Burnett)*

43

As far as "manhandling" the Marauder goes, it was also dubbed a "trim tab airplane," which was a pretty fair evaluation. She could very nicely be trimmed to fly hands off, but especially during takeoff and landing maneuvers, generous use of the trim tab controls was absolutely essential. This was particularly true of the elevator trim tab. During a takeoff run, an experienced pilot would roll in trim after the nosewheel broke ground, as soon as liftoff occurred, again when the wheels came up, again when the flaps were being milked up, once again when power was reduced, again during the climbout, and finally after level out and adjustment to cruise rpm. The reverse would be true upon landing, and some hotshots were even rolling the trim tab wheel during flareout. If the B-26 wasn't properly trimmed, it was a chore of "manhandling," but when properly trimmed, she was very responsive to the controls, even though there was no hydraulic boost luxury in those days.

It got to be a joke during OTU training at how sensitive some pilots were about "having her trimmed up." A crew member changing position in the rear of the ship would throw her out of trim, and often when the "old man" had her trimmed up for straight and level on a cross-country navigational flight and had settled back in his seat and lit up a cigarette, one of the "boys in the back room" would head for the relief tube, and a blast over the intercom would pierce everyone's eardrums with: "Who in the hell is movin' around back there?!" Once in combat, and flying formation from takeoff to landing, these "trim-nit-pickers" soon learned that they'd just have to compensate for crew movement in emergency situations.

Martin also sent engineers out who showed the crews how to minimize the problems caused by overloading, by paying proper scientific attention to the plane's center of gravity.

Pilots became adept at using the weight and balance slide rule stick and the "trim fanatics" had a field day.

Even before all this was going on, the Army finally woke up to the fact that the ship was grossly overloaded, and their experts, working in full cooperation with Martin engineers, came up with design changes to make it safer for relatively inexperienced men to fly. Peyton Magruder started breathing easier, and probably slept better at night.

Besides the introduction of the R-2800-41 P&W engine in May of 1942, which developed 2000 hp for takeoff, other significant changes were the addition of three feet to each wingtip (which gave greater lift and allowed the plane to land slower), the higher vertical tail plane (which reduced the physical strength required to maintain straight and level flight with one engine out), and a new and improved aileron (which gave the pilot lighter and more positive lateral control). The increased engine power improved takeoff performance as well as during flight. In addition, the hydraulic and electrical systems were greatly improved, which simplified the problems of maintenance that all planes have. All these changes were progressively incorporated in the B and C Models.

Whereas the wing loading on the original short wing was just under 50 pounds per square foot, the Army quickly capitalized on the increased horsepower and greater lift of the longer wing to add still more weight, which boosted the wing loading to an incredible 56 pounds per square foot.

Magruder must have heaved a desperate sigh of resignation as the Army put the "Martin Murderer" almost back to square one.

Present-day jet jockeys might smirk when hearing of high wing loadings (which are commonplace today) and 130 mph landing approaches (which are SOP in today's high-performance aircraft), but back in the '40s with the designs and powerplants available at the time, these were awesome figures indeed! Remember, the Marauder had no reversible thrust propellers, no modern "high lift" flap system, no drag chute, no automatic feathering feature, no anti-skid brakes, nor any of the other performance-improving gadgets found on today's aircraft. What you saw was what you got, and you made the best of it.

Another item that plagued pilots was the Curtis Electric propeller's habit of "running away" at the most critical times. The blades would rotate into flat pitch (high drag) and sometimes would even refuse to feather, which tended to cause the ship to want to roll onto its back. Some of the emergencies and/or crashes on takeoff in the early days were due to runaway props rather than engine failures. Once the intricacies of maintaining this temperamental system were fully understood, the incidence of runaways dropped appreciably.

As late as 1944 an occasional runaway would occur on a brand-new airplane, but by then the copilots were adept at flipping the selector switch from Auto Constant Speed to the Fixed Pitch mode and then moving the toggle to the left or to the right to decrease or increase rpm as required to maintain normal operation. Once the system was properly adjusted and diligently serviced, the condition all but disappeared.

It had definitely not disappeared for Lt. Charles O'Mahony, now of Pittsburgh, Pennsylvania, and his crew, who were undergoing RTU training at Lake Charles, Louisiana in March of 1944. On the 17th, a St. Patrick's Day they'll never forget, they had a runaway prop on takeoff, and without enough altitude to correct the situation, O'Mahony had to bring her down straight ahead and ended up in a drainage ditch, as shown in Fig. 3-8.

Undaunted, O'Mahony later flew 71 combat missions with the 441st Squadron of the 320th Bomb Group over Italy, France, and Germany. He ultimately wound up being the last commanding officer of the 441st when the war in Europe ended.

While all the demonstrations, corrective measures, and design changes were having their remedial effects, the Army Pictorial Services issued a training film titled *How to Fly the B-26*. A handsome young actor played the part of a dapper lieutenant listening to the sage advice of his instructor and absorbing the techniques used during the flight demonstration. This actor was Craig Stevens, who later starred in the *Peter Gunn* television series.

The film made the whole routine seem so matter-of-fact that it was almost

Fig. 3-8. *O'Mahony's RTU B-26 in the drainage ditch off the end of the Lake Charles AAF runway, 17 March 1944. That the crew, especially the pilot and copilot, escaped serious injury in this cruncher is unbelievable—but they did. (USAAF photo courtesy Charles O'Mahony)*

ridiculous. The only real in-flight emergency actually portrayed was that caused by a lazy and indifferent flight engineer forgetting to transfer fuel. However, in retrospect, maybe it was actually the Army's intention to give the impression it was easy to fly the Marauder. With all the fear connected with the airplane, this was probably the best impression to give at the time.

Actually—as Doolittle had stated—the Marauder *was* a bit more difficult to master than contemporary twin-engine types, but that was no problem as long as proper respect for the airplane was maintained. This, of course, holds true for *all* aircraft.

While the B-26 accident rate during this period was alarming, it is a mystery as to why so much attention was focused on the problem of this particular airplane. True, for every three B-26 crashes there were only two B-25s wrecked. On the other hand, there were four A-20 Havoc and five P-38 Lightning crashes, yet they weren't dubbed ''Widow-Makers'' or some other distasteful name, and Congress didn't appoint a special committee to investigate their misfortunes. While only one airman could be lost in a fatal crash of a P-38, and three in an A-20, against the possibility of as many as six perishing in the crash of a B-26, this still did not alter the fact that the B-26 wasn't the only aircraft suffering growing pains.

There must have been some politics involved with trying to crucify the Marauder, either in the government or possibly even within the Air Force itself.

Maybe the procurement brass still carried a stone in their craw resulting from the Martin Company only agreeing to build 201 of the Army's initial requirement of 385 new medium bombers. Glenn L. Martin himself would not commit his company to more due to the fact that the firm was already committed to continue building the Maryland and Baltimore bombers for the French and British. As a consequence, the balance of the first requirement for 184 aircraft was given to the second place winner in the competition, North American, for their also-new B-25 Mitchell. Of course, as stated in Chapter 2, Martin didn't hold out for long after that, and immediately went ahead with new production facilities when they realized that hundreds more mediums would be required if Hitler was to be stopped.

Whether or not retired USAF Colonel Delwin D. Bentley, now of Wilson, Wyoming, knew of Squeek Burnett's exploits with the B-26 is a matter of conjecture, but back in early 1943 he decided to prove that not only could the Marauder fly on one engine, but that she'd fly (however momentarily) with *both* props feathered!

Bentley was then a captain and the 497th Squadron Commander in the newly formed 344th Bomb Group, which was starting OTU training at Lakeland Army Air Field, Florida. He was a "hell-for-leather" University of Wyoming graduate, wore cowboy boots constantly, and was rumored to have been the only man to have slow-rolled a B-26 deliberately and lived to tell about it. Although this rumor was widely circulated, it was completely false, but his feathering of both props was a fact.

When he boasted of doing this one day, Lt. A. J. Wood, another 497th pilot, told him he'd like to see it, so Bentley told him to take a photographer up in another ship to record the event. Wood did, and Fig. 3-9 is the photo the squadron photographer took at the exact moment when both engines were cut off and the propellers were in the full-feather position.

Nothing happened for a few days afterwards, but something like this could never have been kept a secret. Word finally got to the then Group Commander, Col. Clinton B. Hilger, about the 8½ × 11 glossy photo of the '26 with no fans turning. He called Bentley in and chewed him out royally, telling him that in light of all the recent furor over the Marauder, if word of this ever got out, there'd be Hell to pay. He demanded that all copies of the photo be destroyed or there'd be a new 497th Squadron Commander in short order!

Bentley (Fig. 3-10) swore he had the only copy (which was the truth) and tore it up before the Colonel's eyes. The old boy was too irate to realize that the negative was stashed away in Bentley's footlocker—and that's the reason the photo appears in this book.

Even before all the design changes on the B-26 could be put into production, the expected happened. Accidents at training fields began falling off, and within a month stood at a low level. The superhuman efforts of Martin and the Army had paid off, and the Truman Committee sheathed its axe. The Marauder had been spared.

Fig. 3-9. *"Look, Ma! No Hands!" Bentley's B-26 over the Lakeland, Florida, area with both props feathered. Ground details show that he had not allowed himself all that much altitude to perform the feat—but he did what he boasted he could do! (photo courtesy Col. D.D. Bentley, USAF Ret.)*

Fig. 3-10. *Newly appointed 497th Bomb Squadron Commander at his desk at Drane Field, Lakeland, Florida in early 1943. 1/Lt. Bentley was promoted to Captain soon after this photo was taken. Maybe that gleam in his eyes indicated thoughts even then of proving the B-26 could fly with no engines operating—even though she had the reputation of having "the gliding angle of a brick"! (photo courtesy Col. D.D. Bentley, USAF Ret.)*

Doolittle had investigated the situation, defined the problems, and instigated the remedial actions required, but he realized that more had to be done to remove the stigma surrounding the Marauder. Stories of the "One a day in Tampa Bay" ilk and the various derogatory nicknames still were circulating within the Air Force, and word hadn't gotten down to the grass roots level that the problems had been corrected. Pilot students in Advanced Flying Training Schools around the country still believed the Marauder was a "Flying Coffin," and very few requests for assignment to the aircraft after graduation were being made.

Wisely, it was decided that the most convincing way to get the true story across would be by actual flight demonstrations by an expert and a "straight-from-the-horse's-mouth" approach of orientation talks by this same expert. Since Vincent W. Burnett's demonstrations at the Martin factories and at Transition and OTU bases had been so successful, he was called upon again to fulfill this all-important assignment.

In addition to his love affair with the Marauder, Burnett also had developed a great fondness for the P-51 Mustang. Most every multiengine pilot in the Air Force harbored a secret desire to become a fighter pilot, to roar and zoom in aerial combat or dive bomb and strafe unencumbered by the responsibility of a crew, operating more or less as a free spirit. Burnett was no exception. In fact, Doolittle had promised him the command of his own P-51 squadron upon his return to Africa from the early 1943 demonstration flights, but the higher brass had different plans for him.

While at Miami, awaiting his return overseas, he answered a loudspeaker page to learn that instead of going back to Africa he was being assigned to Major General Robert W. Harper's Command to assist in solving the problems in the B-26 flight training program. Harper, who was then Director of all flying training in the U.S., would later remark: "If all else fails, send for Burnett!"

During the spring and early summer of 1943 Squeek made demonstration flights, gave orientation rides, and talked in symposiums to Advanced Flying School pilot students at Albany and Valdosta, Georgia; Blytheville and Stuttgart, Arkansas; George Field and Lawrenceville, Illinois; Seymour, Indiana; Columbus, Mississippi; Altus, Oklahoma; and Lubbock, Pampa, and Waco, Texas. His visits were enthusiastically received, and during the demonstration flights (on which five or six students went along and were given an opportunity to handle the controls), he demonstrated high-speed operation, steep turns, single-engine procedures, simulated bombing attack breakaways, and short field takeoffs and landings, among others. He also visited the Dodge City and Del Rio Transition Training Schools again and his report at the conclusion of the assignment was as follows:

MEMORANDUM ON B-26 TRAINING: 23 June 1943
   1. In regard to statements made to B-26 crews that arrived North African Theater, that are attached, the following facts were found after completion of lecture and flight demonstrations in a B-26 to The Twin Engine Schools in the Southeast and Gulf Coast Training Centers.

2. The attitude of these student pilots toward the B-26 was such that only 10 to 15 percent of the pilots preferred going to B-26 OTUs. This figure was increased to approximately 50 percent after the lectures and flight demonstrations on which the students rode and were given an opportunity to fly it. This indicates that if the true facts are revealed about the B-26, the problem of maintaining good morale would be very small.

3. Five days were spent at the B-26 Transition School at Del Rio, Texas, riding with students and instructors, observing methods of training and student and instructor proficiency. Although the morale was very good, the flying technique could be improved, and the training curriculum revised so that a maximum performance is derived from the airplane.

4. The ability of the instructors was found to be very good and capable of changing their technique readily and willingly with very little instruction necessary. Although the characteristics of the big-wing B-26 have been improved considerably, they are being flown like the small-wing; therefore, the full benefits of the improvements are being neglected.

5. It is felt because of the speed, maneuverability, firepower, recent modifications, that if understood and flown properly, the B-26 would be an excellent operational Medium Bombardment airplane.

Vincent W. Burnett
Major AC

For these visits, Burnett (who had been promoted to Major since the original flight demonstrations) used a combat-configured B-26 so that skeptics couldn't accuse him of subterfuge. There were still those die-hards flying armchairs in some of the Air Force ivory towers who claimed he couldn't have done what he did with the transition-configured '26 in the earlier demonstrations if it had carried the added weight of combat equipment (Fig. 3-11).

In any event, Burnett had hit the nail on the head in his report, and if it hadn't worked its way up high enough in the Air Force hierarchy, maybe this commendation from the Commanding General of the Air Force Flying Training Command helped to give it a boost upwards:

SUBJECT: Commendation
TO: Commanding General, Army Air Forces, Washington, D.C.
ATTENTION: Assistant Chief of Air Staff, Training

1. Major Vincent W. Burnett, recently assigned to this Headquarters for duty, made a tour of various twin-engine advanced schools demonstrating the B-26 type airplane and lecturing to the students on its use in combat.

2. Letters received from Commandants of stations visited by Major Burnett, copies of which are enclosed, indicate much was accomplished to stimulate confidence in the B-26 type aircraft and to increase the combat spirit among the students at the stations visited.

3. Major Burnett is highly commended for the effectiveness of his mission.

E.R. Yount
Major General
United States Army
Commanding

This initial student indoctrination program proved so successful that it was expanded and continued, with crews who had completed their tours of duty in North Africa returning to conduct the seminars. (The author recalls a combat crew from the 319th Bomb Group of the 12th Air Force visiting Ellington Field, Texas, in September 1943. As a result, the author changed his preference from the A-20 to the B-26. See Figs. 3-12 through 3-16).

Sometime after his junket to the schools, Burnett was sent to an interservice conference as the Air Force representative. Doolittle had reprieved him from the North African Theater for the express purpose of conducting the demonstration flights, but General Harper figured he might as well get as much mileage out of Squeek's expertise as possible for the benefit of the Air Force.

The purpose of the conference was to explore better methods of combat flying and to demonstrate tactics being used by all three services. It was held on the Matagorda Peninsula of southeast Texas, just south of Galveston.

Fig. 3-11. *The B-26 used by Burnett in his flying school demonstrations in 1943. That it is an earlier model is substantiated by the fixed nose gun on the underside of the bombardier's greenhouse, the torpedo rack beneath the open forward bomb bay, and the opened doors of the rear bomb bay. Burnett, in the cockpit, is probably looking askance at the misspelling of his nickname, which a Martin Omaha plant artist has inscribed on the nose. June 1943, Martin Omaha Plant. (USAAF photo courtesy Evelyn Burnett)*

Fig. 3-12. *Typical OTU training B-26 of the 497th Bomb Squadron, 344th Bomb Group, at Lakeland AAF, Florida, November 1943. Engineer-gunner John Skowski, of author's crew, on right. (This and other photos by the author to follow were taken from color slides, so the reader will appreciate that some detail and clarity has been lost through conversion to black and white.)*

Fig. 3-13. *Tight formation practice by the 497th at Lakeland. Shot of the lead ship of the flight taken from the Number One wing position. November 1943.*

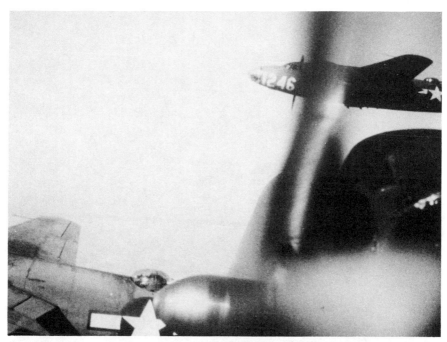

Fig. 3-14. *View of lead ship and Number Two wingman in same formation flight at Lakeland, November 1943.*

Fig. 3-15. *Easing up into the Number Four position during formation practice at Lakeland in November 1943.*

Fig. 3-16. *A study of the symmetrical beauty of the Marauder. The high flight of an 18-ship box moving into position in the skies over Lakeland, Florida, during a 344th Group simulated bombing mission in November 1943.*

Marine ace Joe Foss, with 26 Japanese planes to his credit, was there with his gull-winged Vought F4U Corsair, the hottest ship in both the Navy and Marines at the time. Foss represented his service and because of many other aces present, a *Time* magazine article referred to the conference as a "Killer's Convention."

Whether it was a part of the intended demonstrations or whether Squeek was feeling his oats after showing flying students what the B-26 could do has been blurred by time, but in any event, the gauntlet was thrown down by Burnett for an aerial duel between his B-26 and Foss and his F4U.

What transpired was the most unorthodox and engine-roaring dogfight imaginable. Foss, with all his kills in the Pacific (made with a Grumman F4F Wildcat, by the way), could not bring the '26 down, and the aerial duel was declared a draw.

Normally the B-26 would have been no match against the more maneuverable and faster F4U, but with a world-class aerobatic pilot at the controls, it was a different story—and one that Foss hadn't experienced with the caliber of the opposition he had faced in the Pacific. Never one to boast, Burnett did allow himself one bit of indulgence and steadfastly maintained he'd pit his '26 against any comparable plane any day of the week and that nobody would take him.

Final proof of the Marauders' capabilities were realized with the B and C models, and it became the dominant medium bomber in the European Theater of Operations. Cries that the B-26 was unsafe died away; its accident record came down to a minimum comparable rate with other types in training situations, and its combat loss record was lower than any other bomber. Squeek Burnett's on-the-scene skills in selling the Marauder had played a major part in her salvation, and Peyton Magruder finally stopped biting his nails.

He would have but a short respite, however, as in early 1944 a cancellation of production was again threatened by the Army's proposal to bring out a new twin-engined bomber and discontinue the B-26.

The Martin Company quickly prepared a paper in defense of the Marauder for the Committee on Military Affairs of the House of Representatives. The more significant portions of that treatise are quoted herewith:

Marauders made history in the Mediterranean with General Jimmy Doolittle. Though designed to operate at medium altitude, they were called on for ground strafing and attack bombing from zero altitudes. They helped drive the stubborn Germans mile by mile along the coast of North Africa; they pushed the Germans up through Sicily and helped roll them mile by mile up the shank of the Italian boot. In two days Marauders shot down 52 enemy fighters over southern Italy and lost five—a record for the Mediterranean Theater. But losses in North Africa had been high. Built as a medium bomber and used for strafing and low-altitude bombing, they took more antiaircraft fire than they were designed to take. The lesson of the South Pacific had still not been learned. The Marauder was being used effectively but not efficiently; and meanwhile, B-26s were being accumulated in England.

Here again, at first the old error was made. The plane was built as a medium bomber and it was not used as a medium bomber. Then all at once something happened; the Marauder began to be used as a medium bomber, bombing from an altitude of 10,000 to 12,000 feet. The plane came into its own. Press reports reveal that in the first 11 raids at these altitudes, only two planes were lost. In 47 days, Marauders made 59 raids with a total loss of only five planes. The next 892 sorties cost only two planes. As the third month of their proper employment drew to a close, over 4000 sorties had cost a total of only 13 Marauders.

Percent losses per raid run less than one half of one percent; losses of heavy bombers run more than five percent, or over ten times as high. This is not meant as a criticism of the heavy bombers, whose crews are as brave and whose designers and manufacturers are as able as the men who fly and build the Martin B 26 Marauders. Light bombers have their place, medium bombers have their place, heavy bombers have their place; together they will reduce the fancied fortress of Europe. The point is simply this: B-26 Marauders have finally been called upon to do in the European Theater the job they were built to do, and they are doing it well. We have many reports from England that heavy bomber crews are now requesting reassignment to Marauders. These requests are, in our opinion, the result of low casualties now being experienced by the Marauders.

The B-26 Marauder has had trouble—maybe it was difficult to fly in the beginning, maybe it had excessive maintenance items at first—but in spite of these difficulties it has always done a job! Due to the many design changes and improvements already made we do not hesitate to say—along with the pilots who fly them—that there is no better flying airplane in this country or abroad.

Let us now sum up the history of the present B-26 Marauder as it comes from the factory. Aircraft manufacturers, like everyone else, live in the face of certain irreducible minimums. One of these is that under the best of conditions it takes three years to design and perfect a new type of plane. It took the justly famed Flying Fortress between eight and nine years—half of them peace years—to become what it is today. The B-26 Marauder had to crowd its development to its present state of excellence into three years. They were not three years of peace, with the luxury of time in which to incorporate all the desirable refinements the Company wanted to incorporate. They were years in which a suddenly awakened Army was saying: "Give us Marauders fast. Put in a couple more tons of stuff, but don't let production slip while you're doing it! Give us Marauders fast!"

It was under these conditions—together with shortages of materials and of trained personnel, and with relatively green Army mechanics and Army pilots cracking up some of the heavily overloaded planes—that the B-26 Marauder developed into the powerful and reliable weapon it is today. At the same time, something else had been developed. The brains, expertise, personnel, tools, and military background of one of America's longest-established producers of military aircraft have been forged into one of the most efficient production machines in the country. From that highly efficient production machine, built up under all the difficulties of wartime, now flows a steady line of powerful and reliable weapons—the B-26 Marauders.

It is these Marauders which did or are doing the job of saving Australia, blasting Japs all over the Pacific, and giving the Axis flaming hell in Africa, in Sicily, in Italy, and in the so-called Fortress Europe. The plane was doing this job even during its three years of development—the three years minimum which every plane requires for development.

But that is only part of the Glenn L. Martin Company's achievement. Last summer the Company, for the first time since 1939, had the opportunity to make radical and far-reaching design changes. The changes up to that point had been mostly changes to fulfill the tactical requirements. For the most part they consisted of adding weight to the plane, with little opportunity to make design changes to refine imperfections out of the plane and make it better able to carry the weight loaded on it. Time did not permit.

But, as mentioned above, last summer Martin engineers took the opportunity to make design changes. These changes are now complete and ready to go into the line, thus giving the Army Air Forces a B-26 Marauder—to be known as the B-26E—that the Glenn L. Martin Company believes to be the most powerful and reliable air weapon available today.

The new B-26 isn't just on paper; one of these has already been turned over to the Army for study. The new plane has been going to various B-26 Marauder airfields in this country, where Army pilots have been flying it. Their enthusiasm has been highly gratifying. A few weeks ago, for instance, a general officer stepped somewhat gingerly into the new plane to ride as a passenger. After the first few minutes he expressed a desire to fly the plane himself. "Why," he said, "I'd been told the Marauder was hard to fly. I'd say she handles like a P-38!" And the Marauder, remember, is not a pursuit ship, but a medium bomber!

Author's note: Following this paragraph of the report was a detailed listing of the design changes for the E model as described in Chapter 2. As explained there, when production changed over, it was to the F Model.

That is the plane the builders of the Marauder are ready to turn off the production line without any delay in the flow of present Marauders! The tools are ready, the people are ready, the production lines are ready—above all, the plane is ready.

In other words, during the three years ordinarily required to build and iron the imperfections or "bugs" out of a new type plane, the Glenn L. Martin Company has accomplished these things for the country and for the Army Air Forces:

1. *Developed a bomber that is one of the most powerful and reliable weapons in the hands of the Army today.*
2. *Kept up a steady production flow of these bombers while incorporating mandatory design changes.*
3. *Built a highly efficient production machine made up of some of the best-trained skilled workers and some of the best production tools and techniques in the world.*
4. *Developed—while all this was going on and within the three year period that has always been necessary to the development of a plane— the new Martin B-26E Marauder, probably the most effective, best flying, and most reliable air weapon of its type.*

If a bomber of the type of the Marauder is still needed, the Glenn L. Martin Company has that bomber in its perfected form. It has something even more valuable than the perfected plane itself; it has the production potential to produce that plane. That production potential, like the Marauder itself, is something which has taken three years to create. Around the Marauder has been built a gigantic and perfected team of engineering and manufacturing skills, of highly trained artisans, of specific techniques and tools—all directed to the single job of producing the Marauder. The carefully built skill and teamwork of that organization is something that all the money, all the wishful thinking, all the patriotic enthusiasm in the world cannot replace—in less than three years. The plane which that organization of thousands of specifically trained personnel and specifically designed techniques and tools produces cannot be replaced in less than three years. Replace the Marauder by some new plane and what happens? Out the window go the three years spent in perfecting what is probably the most effective and reliable plane of its type available today; in its place comes a plane with the inevitable three years of problems and difficulties and heartbreaks to face before it gets where the Marauder is today. And out the window goes something even more valuable—the organization and skills and tools specifically created to build the Marauder; in their place comes the necessity to start all over again and take three years to build and perfect a similar organization around the new plane.

The Glenn L. Martin Company has a long and proud record as producers of reliable military aircraft. It has devoted three years to the perfecting of the Marauder and to the perfecting of an organization to build the Marauder. Because of its long and proud military record, the Glenn L. Martin Company feels privileged to say that, in its considered opinion, to jettison that perfected plane and that perfected production potential would be little short of tragic!

This impassioned plea, while somewhat repetitive and superfluously worded, was 100 percent right, and about as correct in fact and assumption as you could get.

Could you imagine the builders of the Russian Stormovik attack plane raking the Red Army over the coals, through the Politburo, as Martin did the U.S. Army Air Force in this document? *Nyet!* It could only happen in America!

Martin's publishing the photo shown in Fig. 3-17 was timely, indeed.

As it all turned out, nobody was a loser on the deal. Martin, the Army Air Force, and Douglas aircraft all came out winners. Admittedly, this could probably have only happened in wartime, and especially since the Marauders were accomplishing so much in the ETO (Fig. 3-18).

The Army still got its new medium bomber, the Douglas A-26 Invader, but no reduction was made in Marauder production. Douglas has long been working on a larger replacement for the A-20 Havoc, so it didn't take the normal three years from the date of the Martin report to bring it out. In fact, the A-26 first went operational with the 416th Light Bomb Group in the ETO in December 1944. Following that, A-26s replaced the A-20s of the 409th Light Bomb Group in the ETO in January 1945, those of the 47th Light Bomb Group in the MTO in February, and the Marauders of the ETO's 386th Medium Bomb Group in March and those of the 391st Medium Bomb Group in April. The last to convert was the ETO's 410th Light Bomb Group, in May 1945.

Unbeknown to most at the time was a plan afoot to eventually replace all medium and light bomb groups with the A-26, and eventually move most of them

Fig. 3-17. *Mechanics at an AAF training base in the summer of 1944, weeping over the retirement from service of* Old Bettsy, *second B-26 manufactured at Martin. Fine print under her name reads: "Too Rich or Too Lean." What this meant was only known to those who flew and serviced her. Deciphering the "Rich—Lean" and "Raise—Lower" under the "Mixture" and "Speed" inscriptions just beneath the pilot's window is easier, because they show the relative positions the levers had to be moved to in order to achieve those results. (photo courtesy Glenn L. Martin Co.)*

from Europe to the Pacific for the final assault on Japan when sufficient island bases had been secured within range of the Japanese homeland.

The atom bomb precluded this, however, and as a follow-on, postwar light and medium bombardment outfits were all equipped with the A-26. Both the A-20 and the B-26 were phased out, and the B-25 was used as a twin-engine Advanced Flying School Trainer. There's no doubt that the A-26 was a fine airplane, and it proved itself as a night intruder during the Korean War. Its designation was changed at that time to B-26, which was confusing to many and an especially bitter pill for the Marauder veterans to swallow. There was only one B-26 in their eyes, and that was the Martin B-26 Marauder (Fig. 3-19).

While mention has been made of the Marauder escaping cancellation at three different times, a fourth near-miss occurred in North Africa during its early operations there. An analysis was made by the Air Force itself just after the Allied campaign had ended in May 1943, but kept secret because it was feared that its figures would dangerously lower morale if they became widely known.

A comparison was made between the B-25 and B-26 operational statistics and the B-26 came off a poor second. In view of the fact that it cost half again as much to build as the B-25, it was almost cancelled at that time.

Fig. 3-18. *The USAAF Chief of Staff, General H. H. Arnold, and Glenn L. Martin at a "Poor Richard" dinner in Philadelphia sometime in 1944. Without a doubt, Martin's close friendship with Arnold had a great bearing on the Military Affairs Committee and the Army's decision to continue with B-26 production in 1944. (photo courtesy Glenn L. Martin Co.)*

Even though there had been more B-26s in the theater than B-25s for the greater share of the campaign, the figures showed this:

	B-25	B-26
Total Sorties Flown	2689	1587
Aircraft Lost	65	80
Percentage Lost per Sortie	2.4	5.00
Percentage Abortive Sorties	3.00	12.00

The wheels started turning on the discontinuance machine again, but only the Marauder's improved performance during the Italian campaign and in the ETO brought them to a halt. It's a good thing this study was kept secret (maybe through Doolittle's farsightedness), for the magnificent Marauder might not have survived if the Truman Committee had gotten into the act again—and maybe even Squeek Burnett's expertise couldn't have saved her that time!

Not only had Burnett proved the Marauder's airworthiness, but he was instrumental in perfecting the target tow version of the B-26. While touring bases in the States with Major General Robert W. Harper, they found that gunnery schools were getting feedback from combat theaters that gunners were not

Fig. 3-19. *B-26B instrument panel and control console. Button for firing package guns is on right of pilot's control wheel and propeller feathering switches are just below the mixture control knobs at the lower right of the console. Propeller governor control levers are pushed forward in the center, while the throttles are pulled back at the left. (photo courtesy LTC James V. Fontana, USAFR, Ret.)*

shooting accurately at high altitudes. At the time, the Air Force had no target tow ship that could operate above 10,000 feet, and since ballistics are quite different at high altitudes, they knew that a target tow ship had to be developed that would operate at altitudes of 20,000 feet and above.

The B-26 was selected for the experiment and General Harper asked Burnett to develop it. Squeek had Martin in Baltimore install a target tow reel system in a B-26 to determine if it would operate successfully at 200 mph indicated airspeed, and at and above 20,000 feet.

After many exhaustive flight tests, he found that it operated perfectly. Subsequently, six more B-26 aircraft were modified and sent to gunnery schools around the country. From then on, the B-26 became the standard Air Force high-altitude target tow ship.

The Air Force finally recognized Burnett's valuable contribution to the war effort when a long-belated event took place on 26 June 1945. Major General Elwood P. Quesada, then Assistant Chief of Air Staff, Intelligence, awarded the Air Medal to Burnett in the office of the War Department, Washington, D.C. (Fig. 3-20). The citation read: ''For meritorious achievement while participating

Fig. 3-20. *Major Vincent W. Burnett being awarded the Air Medal by General Quesada. "Pete"*
Quesada was very familiar with ETO B-26 operations, as he commanded the 9th Air Force Fighter
Command during the war, his fighters flying escort for the Marauders many times. (USAAF
photo courtesy Evelyn Burnett)

in aerial flights during the period May 1942 to September 1944. During this
period, Major Burnett made an outstanding contribution to the performance of
combat operations of the Army Air Forces through his experimentation with
the flying characteristics of the P-39N, P-51, and B-26 type airplanes which
proved invaluable to aeronautical engineers in designing future models. Through
his thorough understanding of these airplanes, this officer was instrumental in
instilling confidence in the young flyers being trained to fly them in combat. The
outstanding flying skill, technical ability, and leadership displayed by Major
Burnett reflect highest credit upon himself and the military service of the United
States.''

Just thereafter, Burnett was promoted to Lieutenant Colonel and assigned
to Headquarters, U.S. Group Control Council in Europe. Since the Air Medal
had been automatically awarded to ETO air crew members after completing five
combat missions, it seems that the USAAF tragically slighted Burnett. Doolittle
realized early on that this man was too valuable to risk in combat flying, and
the job he did on the B-26 alone surely called for a more prestigious award,
to say nothing of what he did for Lawrence Bell's P-39 and ''Dutch''

Kindleberger's P-51! (The story of his exploits with those two fighters will of necessity have to wait for another telling.)

At the time of the award, Burnett was still serving on General Harper's staff, and on 27 May 1947 was promoted to temporary Colonel. In January 1948 he was assigned to Mitchel Field, Long Island, New York, as Deputy CO of the 52nd Fighter Group, Strategic Air Command. On 10 April 1950 he left the service as a permanent Lt. Colonel to pursue other interests but remained active in the Air Force Reserve. He retired from the Reserve 1 June 1969 as a full Colonel, and he and Evelyn are living the retired "good" life in Lynchburg, Virginia.

Hopefully, this story will serve to give Squeek the belated recognition that he so richly deserved!

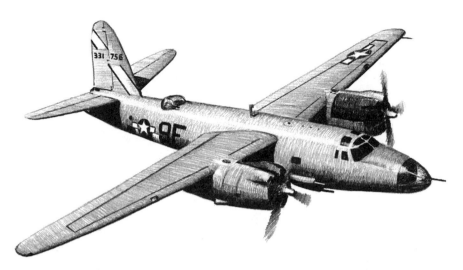

4

COMBAT, PHASE ONE:
First Blood Drawn . . . and Let

It would take volumes to relate in detail the combat record of the B-26, so these chapters on combat will of necessity only cover the highlights of her combat experience. For the sake of order, separate chapters will be devoted to each theater of operations in which the Marauder flew combat—South Pacific and Alaskan, Mediterranean, and European. Most of the chronological battle record intermingled throughout the narrative has been excerpted from the old press dispatches and communiques that were compiled by the Glenn L. Martin Company to bolster their defense of the B-26 during the Congressional Inquisitions. As a consequence, the dates are often those of the actual dispatch, which was sometimes delayed by the censors for military security reasons. However, even though the dates may not be those of the actual happenings, it is interesting to note that the progress of the Allied advances can pretty well be followed—especially in the Pacific and MTO—by reading these accounts.

The South Pacific

The Marauder saga in the South Pacific is one fraught with the frustrations of an Air Force far from being prepared for the war that faced it. Changes in command, urgent move orders, changes in organizational structure, rapid deployment, changes in plans, "hurry up and wait" situations, inadequate facilities or no facilities at all, many "do it yourself" conditions—all these plagued these Pacific pioneers.

There were two groups equipped with B-26s in this theater, the 22nd and the 38th, but only two squadrons of the 38th (69th and 70th) flew the '26. The 71st and 405th Squadrons were equipped with B-25s. In fact, the 69th and 70th were practically orphans for a time. On 29 May 1942 they were divorced from the 38th Group, and when they eventually arrived in the Pacific, they operated remotely under the direction of COMAIRPAC until they were finally assigned to the 42nd Bomb Group in March 1943.

Squadrons of the 22nd Group also operated on a remote basis much of the time. Originally the group was composed of the 2nd, 19th, and 33rd Bombardment and the 18th Reconnaissance Squadrons. Later on, the 18th became the 408th Bombardment Squadron.

With no intention of slighting the 38th Group and its 69th and 70th B-26 Squadrons, this account provides more detail on the 22nd Group merely because its records in the Air Force Historical archives offered the most pure B-26 data.

The 22nd Bombardment Groups' Marauders (by now attrited to 44) left San Francisco by ship on 6 February 1942 bound for Hickam Field, Hawaii. There they were reassembled and flew sea patrol duty until they were fitted with bomb bay ferry tanks and flown to Brisbane, Australia, where they were based at Amberley Field.

By 22 March the first flight had arrived in Australia, and subsequently the outfit moved to bases in the Townsville, North Queensland area, flying their first mission out to Garbutt Field on 5 April.

Not only was the 22nd the first Air Force bombardment group to move to a war theater from the States after Pearl Harbor, but it was the first completely armed Air Force group to fly the Pacific (from Hawaii to Australia) en masse. A B-17 group (the 7th) was already enroute to Hawaii at the time of the Pearl Harbor attack so was considered in the same category as those fighter outfits already enroute by ship and other Air Force units already in place in Hawaii, the Phillipines, and Australia.

Early missions were leapfrog affairs, with the 22nd taking off from the mainland loaded with bombs, landing at Moresby to be refueled and the pilots briefed scantily, and then taking off again for the target. Each mission was a 2600-mile round trip, 1300 of it carrying bombs, and with 2400 miles of it over open and shark-infested waters. Moresby was a malaria-infested hole, and since no adequate living quarters were available, the crews slept under the wings of their aircraft using bedding and mosquito netting hauled from Australia.

There was no fighter escort available; four B-26s holding off as many as 20 Zeroes was common odds. During the first 10 months of combat, the 22nd was credited with destroying 94 enemy aircraft in the air. The base on Moresby came under enemy bombing and strafing attacks many times, and the group's aircraft took off numerous times just to avoid being caught and destroyed or damaged on the ground. All missions were flown at low altitudes, using the primitive D-8 bombsight, and targets were usually attacked with small formations of from two to six aircraft in single flights or elements. Medium bombardment tactics were still to be developed for this new bomber, so it was a trial-and-error situation all the way around—and with target ranges certainly more suited to heavy bomber capabilities than to those of a medium. But there just weren't enough heavy bombers available to accomplish the urgent task of striking the advanced Japanese installations, so the Marauders were called upon to fill the gap.

Seaman C. Q. Middlebrook, now of Dahlgren, Virginia, was a survivor of the USS *West Virginia* sinking at Pearl Harbor, and afterwards was stationed at Luke Field Naval Air Station at Pearl Harbor. He remembers three B-26s of the 69th Squadron of the 38th Bomb Group landing there just prior to the Battle of Midway. They had come over from Hickam Field to be fitted with torpedoes after their flight from Hamilton Army Air Base, California, using bomb bay fuel tanks. This was the flight led by Captain James F. Collins, for which he was awarded the DFC. Both the 69th and 70th Squadrons flew their Marauders from Hamilton to Hawaii between 22 May and 10 June 1942. Twenty-six ships in all made the 2200-mile trip without a mishap, the first time this flight had been negotiated by a medium bomber.

The NAS Torpedo Shop boss, Chief Peterson, and a half dozen sailors (including Middlebrook) removed the bomb bay tanks and installed naval torpedoes on the '26s. The three ships then spent some time carrying the "fish" on practice flights around the islands to familiarize the crews with the torpedo configuration.

Returning from one of these practice flights, one Marauder landed right at the approach end of the runway. In fact, it was about a foot or so short of the runway when it touched down and when the main gear hit the concrete lip of the runway, it severely wrinkled the fuselage skin around the aft window hatches, necessitating the aircraft being laid up for repairs.

A few days later, Middlebrook and his buddies removed the torpedoes, reinstalled the bomb bay tanks, and the two serviceable Marauders left for Midway and the big battle, along with two Marauders from the 18th Recon Squadron of the 22nd Bomb Group that had been delayed at Hickam Field from the earlier flights to Australia.

1942

23 April: American fighting planes turning tide in Pacific—B-26s arrive and enter active combat duty in Australia under Lt. Gen. George H. Brett, USA. Lt. Ralph E. Hankey, Charlotte, N.C., awarded DFC and Oak Leaf Cluster for riding out attack by eight Zeros when his B-26 and one other were set upon.

23 May: Lone Marauder bombed Lae at 800 feet despite blinding rain squalls, terrific antiaircraft fire, and combatting 15 Zeros, downing one and getting back to base safely.

5 June: With one dead engine after bombing Lae, Marauder pilot John C. O'Donnell, Oakland, Md., flew four hours and five minutes back to Port Moresby. Enroute his B-26 was attacked by a flight of Zeros and he downed four.

13 June: Inscribing another revolutionary step in aerial warfare, Martin Marauders with torpedoes (Army bombers helping the Navy) sank a Jap cruiser with two torpedoes.

19 June: Marauders were again used as torpedo planes in the all-important U.S. victory at Midway.

An interesting but revealing firsthand report on the Battle of Midway is contained in the following letter by the 69th Squadron's Capt. James F. Collins, Jr., and illustrates the impossible conditions under which the Marauders were operating:

TO: Commanding General, VII Bomber Command,
Hickam Field, TH   6 June 1942
SUBJECT: B-26 in Battle of Midway

1. Crews were up at 0315 for the alert. At 0600 the order came to warm up engines, shut them off, and to stand by the planes. At 0615 the order was given to attack carriers 180 miles on a bearing of 320 degrees. We departed at 0625 and sighted enemy at 0705. The formation of four (4) B-26s turned slightly to the left and then sharply to the right in order to best pass through the ack-ack of the surface vessels. It was at this time that we sighted six Navy single-engined torpedo planes which had left Midway about 15 minutes before we did. They were just going in for their attack and were approaching from our right and across our path. We did not see them again. At this time we went through heavy fire from all ships and met six Zeros head on at an altitude of approximately 700 feet. We dove to 200 feet, causing most of their fire to pass overhead. It is my opinion that it was at this point I lost my Number Two and Three wingmen. By again turning right we made our attack from about 20 degrees off the carrier's bow. He was turning sharply to his right and consequently toward my left, but we were on the middle of his circle and he would have slim chance to miss the torpedo if it made a true run. Just after release, I could see the Number Four ship slightly under us and to our left making his attack. His navigator said our torpedo hit the water cleanly and when last seen was making a true run toward the carrier. We released from about 220 feet and 210 statute miles per hour. Zeroes were still with us and after shooting down two and possible three we still had one to contend with for the next 15 or 20 minutes. We went through ack-ack by abruptly changing altitude when they appeared to be getting the range. We were making 255 mph by then and just getting into cloud formations that were pretty spotty from 1000 to 2000 feet. Here the last Zero left us.

2. Both turret guns hung up repeatedly. One tail gun would not fire after the first burst. The motors would not pull ammo through the tracks to either tail gun. It had to be jerked by hand. I consider all guns to have been unsatisfactory during the entire flight. I believe that .50-caliber guns should be out the side windows instead of the .30 guns provided and that

100-round ammo cans should be provided for them instead of 30-round cans. I believe that at least four .50-cal. guns should be provided fixed in the wings and that a single or twin .50 should be mounted movable in the nose. I believe that these guns are virtually necessary because no one bomber is a match for a bunch of fighters and particularly so when the few guns it has won't shoot and the gunners have not had sufficient training to shoot them. Although none of the crew was shot, the ship was considerably shot up and a crash landing had to be made on the field upon our return.

3. Only two of the four B-26s returned to the field. Both of these ships will require considerable repair before they will be fit for duty again. Only two of the six Navy torpedo planes returned to the field. Neither of these are fit for duty. I believe that if a coordinated attack of dive bombers and level bombers had been there to help us, we would have sustained fewer loses.

James F. Collins, Jr.
Captain, Air Corps

This dramatically points out how news communiques can be so misleading. Sure, "only" two B-26s were lost, but only four were involved in the mission. The Navy fared even worse, losing four out of six of their torpedo bombers, and they were only half the size of a B-26! On the other side of the coin, Captain Collins had a genuine understanding of what was needed in defensive armament, and some of his suggestions were later incorporated in the production B-26.

He had done admirably well considering that the only experience they'd had was those few practice flights in Hawaii, during which no actual drops had been made. The Marauder carried an 18-inch 2000-pound Naval serial torpedo slung on an external rack along the keel of the ship. Takeoff with a fish on board was a bit hairy, to say the least, as the torpedo hung on the B-26 "straights" only cleared the ground by about four inches when taxiing.

Although early deck-level torpedo runs were promising, it soon became evident that the B-26 was entirely too large for this type of attack when losses mounted on subsequent missions. Torpedo operations were finally discontinued, but even as late as November 1943, groups in OTU training were still practicing skip-bombing on the deck at Tampa Bay. If the Marauder was too large for torpedo runs, it certainly followed that it would be too large for skip-bombing runs also. The Army was slow to learn that the Marauder was a medium bomber and *not* a low-level attack aircraft.

Collins had understated the damage to his and the other surviving Marauder, flown by Lt. James Muri. Three of Muri's crew members were wounded, and the ship had over 500 holes in it! Collins' ship had acquired 186 flak and bullet holes, some of which had knocked out his hydraulic system. In actuality, both ships were so shot up that they were beyond repair and were junked.

The 69th and 70th Bomb Squadrons had been stationed at Jackson Army Air Base, Mississippi, with the 38th Bomb Group, flying B-18s, until they started receiving B-26s in September of 1941. On 8 December the 70th's aircraft and crews were detached to Savannah, Georgia, from where they flew Atlantic patrol missions for six days, returning to Jackson after the Army finally decided there was no danger of attack from that quarter—just another case of war jitters. It was bad enough that such confusion had reigned over the famous false alarm enemy plane attack on Los Angeles, but to suppose that Japanese aircraft carriers or submarines would be attacking the East Coast was a bit far-fetched.

The entire 38th Group moved to California in mid-January 1942, and by the end of the month all ground echelons and the air echelons of the 71st and 405th B-25 squadrons were aboard ship and bound for Australia. The 69th and 70th air echelons remained at Fort McDowell until 8 March, when they were sent to Patterson Field, Ohio, for further B-26 instruction and training.

In May they were equipped with B-26Bs, and between 19 and 21 May had flown to California on the first leg of the movement to New Guinea and the Fiji Islands. At Sacramento Air Depot the bombers were stripped of armor plate, machine guns, and unnecessary equipment and fitted with bomb bay fuel tanks for the flight to Hawaii.

The continuing flight from Hawaii was made via Christmas Island, Canton Island, and the Fijis. The 69th's aircraft had all arrived at Tontoutu, New Guinea, by 23 June, and then were moved to Plains De Gaiac where, after a period of training, they flew patrol and antisubmarine searches until 2 December, when they moved to Efate, New Hebrides. More practice, patrol, and search missions were flown from there, interrupted only by a 12-day TDY operating out of Guadalcanal, until 27 February 1943, when all their B-26s were transferred to the 70th and were replaced by B-25s.

By 9 July 1942, all 12 aircraft of the 70th Squadron had arrived at Nandi air base in the Fijis. Training began, and the next three months were devoted to search missions, practice torpedo and skip-bombing runs, and copilot transition. Some of the copilots had come directly to the outfit from cadet school!

Combat operations began for the 70th on 14 November 1942, when the aircraft took off for Espiritu Santo loaded with torpedoes. There they were exchanged for two 1000-pound bombs each and takeoff for Guadalcanal followed. They arrived at dusk, and the crews spent the night in foxholes as a naval battle raged off the coast. Next morning they took off to bomb the Japanese transports that were trying to land reinforcements on the island. After landing to refuel after the mission, they then headed back to their home base in the Fijis. Such was the hassle they went through trying to fight a war.

The 70th was progressively based at Henderson Field, Guadalcanal, back to the Fijis, and then again to Guadalcanal in August 1943, when all their B-26s were replaced by B-25s (which had been filtering into their inventory since June).

May-Oct. 1942: Marauder bombardment groups down 90 Jap Zeros while losing only six in Southwest Pacific and New Guinea Theaters.

70

The reader may wonder how the Marauders were able to down as many Zeros as reported when the airplanes of the two bomb groups out there carried only from four to six machine guns. First of all, not enough can be said for the bravery and determination of the gunners and the skill of the pilots in taking violent evasive action. Secondly, the troops in this "Hell on Earth" war theater did what American soldiers have done down through the ages: They improvised and used their ingenuity.

They realized early on that their firepower was not sufficient for the opposition they were encountering, so they first added flexible .30s in the nose and then changed all the original .30 to .50s. Some even cut openings in the sides of the ship aft of the bomb bay and mounted flexible guns there; others enlarged the astrodome opening and mounted a flexible up there. Specifications, safety inspectors, and weight and balance limitations be damned! They had a war to fight and were determined to even up the odds, whatever it took.

These modifications were left up to the discretion of individual crews, and some are graphically illustrated by the accompanying photographs of those made on 70th Squadron's Captain John F. Sharp's *Cookie Lee,* named after his two-year-old daughter, Sandra Lee. The aircraft, an early B model, Serial Number 41-17562, is shown in Fig. 4-1 on a metal landing mat in the Fiji Islands with John and his crew standing before it. Note that it still had the small air intakes atop the engine cowlings, the large propeller spinners, no package guns, and only a single .30-caliber flexible gun mounted in the nose just above center.

Fig. 4-1. Miss Cookie Lee *and crew (Sharp at extreme left) before extensive modifications. It was one of the first 81 B models. Fiji, 1942. (photo courtesy Col. John F. Sharp, USAF Ret.)*

Figure 4-2 shows the view looking aft through the rear bomb bay to the tail gun position and shows the repositioning of the ammunition cans forward of the rear bulkhead. The ship as received from the factory had the ammunition cans installed aft of the bulkhead, and, after bouncing the tail a few times during landings, the crew decided to move the cans forward for better balance. The rear bomb bay racks have already been removed and the doors wired shut.

After numerous frontal attacks by enemy fighters, the Maraudermen decided to give the bombardier some more firepower. Figure 4-3 shows the installation of a .50-caliber gun replacing the former .30-caliber flexible just above the nose center. Note the three metal strap supports added outside the plexiglass nose to support the added weight of the gun. As extra insurance, they also installed two flexible .30s on each side of the bubble. These eventually caused the bombardier to knock his head for lack of space and were finally removed. The bomb bay doors are shown open to illustrate the removal of a flat-plated frontal area that caused excess drag with the doors open. They simply cut the plate away, allowing the airstream to pass through the ends of the open doors, thereby reducing the drag on the bomb run. They were not only ingenious, but also practical.

Fig. 4-2. *Interior of Sharp's* Miss Cookie Lee *looking aft to the tail gunner's position. (photo courtesy Col. John F. Sharp, USAF Ret.)*

Fig. 4-3. *The nose of* Miss Cookie Lee *showing the added guns and reinforcement straps as well as the reduced-drag bomb bay doors. (photo courtesy Col. John F. Sharp, USAF Ret.)*

Figure 4-4 shows Captain Sharp (now of Sacramento, California) standing proudly at the nosewheel well of his ship with the freshly painted symbol of a Japanese Kawanishi 97 Mavis four-engine flying boat at the top center above the plane's name. John's Marauder participated in a running dogfight with the Mavis on 3 February 1943, and despite cannon fire from the flying boat severing the main spar of the Marauder's right wing and blowing away three feet of the leading edge, they shot the Jap down and returned safely to their Gaudalcanal base after a 2½ hour flight at just above stalling speed to prevent the wing from tearing off! This was just one of the many combat-related examples of the Marauder's rugged construction.

John says the latest modification, shown in Fig. 4-5, greatly increased the defensive armament and played a major role in downing the Mavis. Although Captain Collins had suggested wing guns be added to the B-26 after the battle of Midway, this could not be done because of the complex pattern of hydraulic and electrical lines in the leading edge. Likewise, to have hung guns suspended under the wings either just inboard or just outboard of the engines would have entailed timing them to fire through the propellers, and this would have been too costly. If guns were hung far outboard on the wings, it would have been too much of a problem to position them so as to zero in on a target—and then

Fig. 4-4. *Sharp by the nose of his ship after the wing had been repaired and the Mavis symbol painted above Lee.* (photo courtesy Col. John F. Sharp, USAF Ret.)

Fig. 4-5. *The .50-caliber package gun installation done by the outfit's innovative armament and maintenance personnel.* (photo courtesy Col. John F. Sharp, USAF Ret.)

there was the problem of containers for the ammunition. So they went the route of least expense and fewest engineering problems and installed package guns on either side of the fuselage just aft of the nosewheel well to be fired by the pilot. There was no streamlined pod, as would eventually come out of the factory, just the bare gun hanging out there. Admittedly, the riveting job was somewhat rough, done under Spartan field conditions, but it did the job and that was all that counted. These South Pacific heroes were, therefore, responsible for many of the improvements and design changes that would be incorporated in future production Marauders (Fig. 4-6).

"Necessity is the mother of invention" became the slogan these brave crews and imaginative maintenance men and armorers lived by, and their creativeness proved to be sound since the greater share of their modifications were later incorporated into the production aircraft in some form or another. If anyone proved that the Marauder was a superb combat aircraft, these men surely did—and *without* the benefits of the added defensive armament, more armor plating, increased power, engineering refinements, and excellent maintenance facilities that the ship finally enjoyed in the ETO when it belatedly assumed the role of a true medium bomber!

Maintenance conditions were rough at best in this remote part of the world, and, since by dictate the Army's first priority on men and material was the MTO

Fig. 4-6. *Captain John F. Sharp astride an aerial torpedo of the type carried in the Battle of Midway. Note thatched roof on an otherwise modern-type building behind his head. Fiji, 1942. (photo courtesy Col. John F. Sharp, USAF Ret.)*

and ETO, spares and replacement parts were scarce indeed. Improvisation was sometimes the only thing that kept the ships in the air—that and cannibalization. Holes in the wings and fuselage from enemy fire were sometimes even patched with Prince Albert tobacco tins!

5 Nov.: B-26s pound twice on successive days the town of Dilli on Timor in the East Indies, shooting down two Zeros, a third probable. Marauders hit ammunition dump while smashing Lae.

10 Nov.: B-26s sink 5,000-ton Jap troopship in Oiva area of New Guinea and raid airdrome installations at Buna.

21 Nov.: Marauders, teamed with Flying Fortresses and a Navy Task Force, aid in sinking 28 Jap ships, damaging 10 others, and downing 14 Jap planes at Solomon Islands.

24 Nov.: B-26s aid American troops attacking Buna in New Guinea by spraying Jap positions with bombs and bullets.

As the year drew to a close, attacks on naval vessels slackened off somewhat and targets such as airfields, barges, dumps, rail and road junctions, buildings, personnel, and bivouac areas became the main objectives.

1943

1 Jan.: Marauders attack Munda on New Georgia Islands, 100 miles northwest of Guadalcanal.

5 Jan.: Capt. Jerry Crossen, ex-pilot for New York's Mayor La Guardia, escapes death by belly-landing his B-26 in narrow jungle strip at Buna. Plane damaged when hit by three-inch AA shell. One bomb rack still full. He has been on 46 bombing missions and flown 570 combat hours in the B-26 *So Sorry*.

6 Jan.: Capt. Hoyt Jolly, of Auburn, Ga., leads B-26s in raid on Sanananda Point, first Jap holding on Buna-Gona front in New Guinea. Used 300 pound bombs.

10 Jan.: B-26s participate in shuttle strafing of Jap convoy off Lae, New Guinea. In running battle, Marauders and other American planes inflict losses totaling 133 planes on Nipponese, heaviest of any engagement in the war.

14 Jan.: Escorted Marauders bomb Rekata Bay installations for service and repair of warplanes and light surface vessels.

24 Jan.: After silencing antiaircraft batteries, B-26s blast Munda in four raids in one day.

2 Feb.: On successive days Marauders strike Kolombangara Islands, hitting airdrome, runways and supply dumps, and Munda. Lt. Max Wilenski, East Lynne, Conn., destroys from his B-26 a Jap flying boat in Solomon Islands. Enemy cannon destroyed much of his right wing, but he returned safely after a two-hour flight.(*Author's note:* Here is a prime illustration of how these dispatches were sometimes incomplete or in error. Wilenski was actually the bombardier on Capt. John F. Sharp's crew. The entire crew fired at the Mavis, the top turret firing forward, along with the pilot's fixed package guns and the bombardier's nose flexible, when they made passes at the flying boat from behind and below, and the tail gunner and top turret gunner firing at the Jap's nose gun position as they passed under and out in front of him.)

13 Feb.: B-26s pound Munda and Kolombangara Islands, bringing the attacks to a total of 63 since 23 November 1942.

As our armed forces pushed northward in the South Pacific, the temporary airfields used were sometimes hacked out of the undergrowth and runways were short. The model of the B-25 Mitchell available to the Air Force at that time proved to have a shorter takeoff requirement than the B-26, so it began phasing in to take over the medium bombardment island-hopping chores in that theater. Although production of the B-25 hadn't started until February 1941, a full six months after the B-26, it was considerably easier to manufacture and did not encounter the growing pain problems the Marauder suffered. Consequently, there were more B-25s available for South Pacific duty because it had been decided to send them to the Mediterranean but not to the European Theater. Eventually, all medium bomb groups in the South Pacific were equipped with the B-25.

Three of the 22nd's squadrons were changed over to the B-25 between January and October, leaving only the 19th Squadron with the Marauder. By this time the many hours of continuous combat had taken their toll on the remaining Marauders, and they were all sent back to the Garbutt Depot, near Townsville on the Australian mainland, for rebuilding and reconditioning. Since the decision to go with the B-25 had been made long before, no replacement B-26s had been sent to the Pacific, and combat attrition had reduced their numbers to just enough to equip one squadron and have a few spares in reserve. Cannibalization of battle casualties, which had gone on all along, reached major proportions at the Australian Depot.

Those that came back into the 19th's inventory at Dobodura, New Guinea, in July had all their camouflage paint removed and a coat of wax applied to the skin. They were known from then on as the "Silver Fleet." This did increase the speed of the ship by a few miles per hour and eliminated one 47-pound "rock in the rowboat," and, since most of the missions still involved long stretches over water, it was felt that camouflage was no longer necessary. Amazingly, among these was the third ship to come off the Martin assembly line in Baltimore—No. 40-1363! While *Old Gran Pappy* (#1) and *Bettsy* (#2) had endured the rigors of transition training, #3 had taken a different kind of beating— combat of the worst kind—and had survived.

Although the 19th received notoriety as the Silver Fleet (they even had a special insignia painted at the top of the rudder with "The Silver Fleet" lettered on it), it is interesting to note that they weren't the first of the 22nd Bomb Group to fly silver Marauders in the Pacific.

Lt. Col. James W. Grubbs, Jr., USAF Ret., now of Woodridge, Illinois, was the radio operator on Lt. George E. Sutton's B-26 *Wild Willie* of the 2nd Bomb Squadron. A photo taken of the ship and crew at Reid River, near

Townsville, Australia, in March 1942 shows the ship in its natural finish (Fig. 4-7). Grubbs explains that their squadron originally picked up their new airplanes at Wright-Patterson Air Base during June and July 1941 where they had been undergoing service acceptance testing by the Air Force. Since these ships were among the first built by Martin, they were in the natural finish and stayed that way until replaced by B-25s early in 1944.

Another amazing fact about *Wild Willie* is that Lt. Sutton had only three or four hours of B-26 flying time when he received his new airplane—and the copilot had even less! Due to the demands of war, these early birds really learned to fly the Marauder the hard way.

Some of the B-26 crewmembers stayed on with the B-25s when the changeovers were taking place; some were sent back to the States to aid in the instruction of new B-26 crews, some went over to North Africa for another tour in 26s, and even later on some were also assigned to B-26 groups in OTU or already in England.

4 June: Posthumous award of the DFC made to Lt. Arthur W. Hughes, Ridgewood, N.J., for a raid on Lae, New Guinea. His flight of three Marauders successfully bombed the runway and other installations. Then Lt. Hughes protected another B-26 under attack, shot down two Zeros, and returned safely to his base, although his plane was damaged. Lt. Hughes was later killed in action.

Fig. 4-7. *Lt. Sutton's silver Marauder at Reid River, Australia, March 1942. Radio operator James W. Grubbs, Jr. is third from right. Serial Number 40-1396 indicates she was the 35th Marauder built. Note teardrop housing for the radio compass loop antenna just behind the pilot's canopy. This unit was moved to a spot on the underside of the fuselage on later models. (photo courtesy LTC James W. Grubbs, Jr., USAF Ret.)*

9 June: Capt. Franklin A. Allen, Los Angeles, Cal., relates the experiences of his B-26 *The Sea Wolf* in the Southwest Pacific. It had flown 378 hours of combat time, was never unfit for duty; once it was flown for a week with a patched bed sheet in place of a hole in the elevator. It was on 18 combat missions. Capt. Allen, a veteran Marauder pilot, holds the Air Medal and the Soldier's Medal.

12 June: Col. Brian (Shanty) O'Neill, 32, former Daily News Golden Gloves boxing champion from Yonkers, N.Y., led an unescorted formation of three Marauders over Lae. They were attacked by 15 Zeros. They shot down eight and returned safely to base.

4 July: *Miss Cookie Lee,* a B-26 piloted by Capt. John R. Sharp, Salt Lake City, Utah, survived cannon fire from a four-engine Jap flying boat, which the Marauder later shot down. The plane, a veteran of 21 missions, returned safely to its base at Guadalcanal, despite a severely damaged wing. (*Author's note:* The news scribes finally got the complete story on Sharp's encounter with the Mavis, but look how long it took to get the facts straight! Unavoidable as these slips or delays may have been, they certainly compounded the anxieties of the families back home.

29 July: S/Sgt. W. M. Hamilton, Fabius, N.Y., radio operator on a B-26, awarded DFC and Silver Star for courage in South Pacific. He was cited for extraordinary achievement while participating in combat over Salmaua, New Guinea, where he shot down 2 Jap planes.

21 Aug.: Lt. Russell Glassner, Chicago, Ill., returns from the Southwest Pacific area, where as a Marauder pilot he participated in 54 missions, including 21 bombing raids.

Press dispatches and communiques are very sketchy, so to give a more complete analysis of the significant role played by the 22nd Bombardment Group, these statistics on its combat performance from 6 April 1942 to 10 January 1943 will give a consolidated picture:

Total Missions		167
Total Sorties		841
Aircraft to Reach Objective		594
Percentage of Aircraft to Reach Objective		70.63
Aircraft That Took Off to Avoid Air Raids		57
Aircraft That Did Not Reach Objective		247
Shipping Target Not Found	(83)	(34%)
Mechanical Failure	(77)	(31%)
Weather	(67)	(27%)
Lost Formation	(7)	(3%)
Enemy Interception	(3)	(1%)
All Other Causes	(10)	(4%)
Enemy Shipping Sunk		6
Enemy Shipping Probably Sunk or Damaged		29
Enemy Aircraft Destroyed on Ground		80

Enemy Aircraft Damaged on Ground	13
Enemy Aircraft Encountered in Air Combat	229
Enemy Aircraft Destroyed in Air Combat	94
Enemy Aircraft Probably Destroyed in Air Combat	3
Aircraft Losses	72
Enemy AA	14
Enemy Aircraft	14
Enemy Bombing	5
Enemy Strafing	2
Mechanical Failure	14
Weather	9
Personnel Failure	3
Fuel Shortage	3
All Other Causes	8

What is so amazing in this set of figures is that in spite of the overwhelming fighter opposition encountered and the withering anitaircraft fire from most of the low-level targets, only .033 percent of the aircraft were lost to enemy combat action!

What is equally amazing is the number of enemy fighter aircraft destroyed in aerial combat—especially if conditions reported in Captain Collins' Battle of Midway letter plagued the group throughout this period.

From 1 July to 31 September 1943, the 19th Squadron was the only one of the 22nd Bomb Group flying B-26s in combat, since the other three were being retrained in the B-25. Here's the 19th's record for that period, under a much more condensed system of reporting that had gone into effect:

Percentage of Aircraft in Commission	65.8
Number of Missions	22
Number of Sorties	185
Number of Aircraft to Reach Objective	173
Percentage of Aircraft to Reach Objective	93.1
Aircraft Failed to Reach Objective	12
Mechanical Failure	12
Enemy Aircraft Encountered	9
Aircraft Losses	3
Enemy Aircraft	1
Mechanical Failure	2

Losses due to enemy action during this period dropped to .0054 percent, and there was a decided improvement in the percentage of aircraft reaching the target, and those that didn't were all due to mechanical failure. The battle veterans in the flight crews were more proficient, but maintenance continued to be a serious problem—not from lack of proficiency, but from a lack of the means and material to get the job done properly.

During the remaining months of 1943, the 19th's statistics show the following:

	Oct.	Nov.	Dec.
Percentage of Aircraft in Commission	69.8	50.5	64.7
Number of Missions	4	12	20
Number of Sorties	35	86	181
Number of Aircraft to Reach Objective	25	78	168
Percentage of Aircraft to Reach Objective	71.4	90.7	92.8
Aircraft Failed to Reach Objective	10	8	13
Mechanical Failure	3	7	12
Weather	7	-	-
Other Causes	-	1	1
Enemy Aircraft Encountered	-	-	-
Aircraft Losses	-	-	-

Although losses to enemy action were nil during this final period of operations, due to the absence of enemy aircraft, the maintenance problem still haunted the crews, and weather again became a deterrent to reaching the objective as well as reducing the number of missions during October and November.

The last mission flown by B-26s in the South Pacific was on 9 January 1944. Later that month the 22nd Bombardment Group was designated a heavy bombardment group and equipped with B-24s. The B-25s were transferred to other medium bombardment outfits. On 11 January 1944, the remaining few B-26s were flown to Eagle Farm Depot near Brisbane to be scrapped out.

At least one ship, Freddie Nichols' *The Flying Parson,* did eventually find its way to the ETO, ending up in France, and after the war was used for training purposes by the French Air Force.

One of the few airmen to pull a B-26 combat tour in both the South Pacific (with the 22nd BG) and the ETO (344th BG) was S/Sgt. George L. Teague, now of Glendale, Arizona. At the risk of stealing some thunder from the coming chapter on the ETO, it is pertinent to look at Teague's personal assessment of the difference between his dual tours of combat at this point:

"It's difficult to compare flying combat with B-26s in the Pacific Theater and that of the European Theater for a number of reasons. I'm speaking now only of my personal experiences, my personal comparison. First, when the B-26s were used in the Pacific, the Japanese had control of the air; we were heavily outnumbered and formations were small by European standards. An escort was a rarity. By the time I got to Europe, we weren't attacked by fighters very often again, for a number of reasons.

"German fighters didn't like to fly at the altitude we flew, which was between 10 and 12 thousand feet; their fighters weren't as efficient at that altitude. They didn't like our speed, which was quite a bit faster than the Fortress or

Liberator. Also, we were hitting targets mostly in the occupied countries and they saved their fighter strength for the heavies, which were hitting their homeland. Because of these reasons, flying B-26s in the Pacific was tougher and our casualties were heavier than the groups in Europe.

"There was also the difference in terrain; though the B-26 did a good job in the Pacific, I think the distances were too great for a medium bomber. Our first missions to Rabaul in the Pacific were seven to eight hour missions—just twice that of the missions in Europe and comparable to the time spent by the heavies in Europe. The heavies also hit Rabaul, and it took them 10 to 12 hours depending upon their approach. A navigator was a necessity in the Pacific because shortly after takeoff on most missions we were out of sight of land and over water. Because of this, we had a seven-man crew in the Pacific compared to six in Europe.

"A piece of shrapnel through a fuel tank in the Pacific was a serious matter, for, in many cases, we were at our extreme range and the loss of any fuel meant the plane couldn't get home. I understand from talking to gunners of B-26s in Africa that they didn't encounter any shortage of enemy fighters, but we flying from England to the continent didn't run into them very often.

"I flew in B-26s in the Pacific early in 1942, while it wasn't until 1944 I started flying my European missions. The Germans were past their peak strength by then, as the Japanese were also going downhill by the time I came home from the Pacific in June 1943.

"One thing the Germans had that the Japanese didn't was their antiaircraft guns. The 88 was much better than anything the Japanese had. The flak in Europe was rougher than anything I encountered in the Pacific except for the times I had to fly over Japanese warships. Japanese naval antiaircraft fire was good, but they had the motivation of having nowhere to hide. Even so, I think the German antiaircraft fire was more accurate and more effective; there were no Pas de Calais areas in the Pacific! I might add too that the altitude we flew in Europe was the perfect altitude for the 88; its accuracy was starting to fall off at heavy bomber altitude, so it was of greater danger to us and very effective—too often to suit us!

"Things seemed to be more efficient in Europe. Of course, by the time I got there, the United States had become an old hand at aerial warfare. Everything seemed to be planned better, and in most cases operated as planned. The airplanes were there, the equipment was there, and the personnel was there. In the Pacific, that wasn't true. We operated with what we had, from airplane to equipment to personnel. We had to play it by ear. Cannibalization of wrecked airplanes was a way of life. If we needed more combat personnel, we got them from our ground crews. We didn't see any replacements from the States for the first year of operation.

"In Europe, we went on our mission, bombed, then came back to the base. In the Pacific, it didn't work that way. One mission could take two or three days to complete, with a total flying time of 14 to 20 hours. First we took off from the satellite bases and joined up at Garbutt outside of Townsville, Australia. There we fueled up and bombed up. We then flew to Port Moresby, New Guinea. We fueled up there; then we went out and bombed, came back to fuel up again, and got out in a hurry, for Port Moresby was being bombed by the Japs several times a day. To stay there was to invite a loss of airplanes, and this happened several times when we didn't get away in time.

"One of the greatest differences was in the formations of airplanes. In Europe, it was standard to fly in a 36-plane formation, rarely without escort. This was unheard-of in the Pacific during the early days. The largest formation I flew with in the Pacific was 12 aircraft, and this with no escort. We were almost always attacked by Japanese fighters on these missions. Most missions were undertaken with from three to six airplanes. I flew on one to Rabaul in which we were the only airplane to attack though we had started out with three planes. The other two were lost before we got there. We were escorted only twice in the 46 missions I flew in the Pacific, once by P-38s, which left us to dogfight Zeros, and another time by P-39s. The only problem was we were never met by the P-39s at the rendezvous; we didn't see them until we were almost home—which is probably just as well, for a P-39 was a pushover for a Zero.

"Another difference was in the attitudes of the personnel of the 22nd Group, compared to that of the 344th. We in the 22nd had been together for two years. We had operated together in peacetime and everyone in the Group knew everyone else. As a result, when a crew was lost, it was felt more keenly than when I was in the 344th. By that, I mean in the 344th we knew the crews in our own squadron but didn't know those in other squadrons very well. Of course, I understand some of the original members of the 344th had been flying together in the States since early 1943, but that still wasn't like the 22nd.

"Another difference was that in the 344th we flew our missions at a much faster pace; it wasn't uncommon for a week to go by between missions in the 22nd. A man was busier in the 344th and he didn't have time to make fast friends. I pulled 65 missions in the 344th within six months. It took me a year and a half to pull 46 with the 22nd. Perhaps it was planned that way, but it isn't the shock to lose comparative strangers as it is someone you've known very well for two years or more.

"The living conditions in Europe were better than in the Pacific, but neither were anything to brag about. We lived in tents in the Pacific, though I can't honestly say that the Quonset huts in England were any improvement. For a while in the Pacific we were stationed just outside of Townsville, Queensland, Australia, which gave us somewhere to go during our off time. It was 20 miles by truck, but the trucks made the run daily. I think the Australians were more like the Americans than the English; they seemed to have the same easygoing manner. It's certain that they ate better than the English, though this was no fault of the British. We could get a steak the size of a dinner plate for the equivalent of 30 cents; in fact, this was the standard Australian breakfast—a steak with eggs. In England, I remember we used to get a so-called 'hamburger steak' when it was available, which consisted of mostly sawdust—at least it tasted that way. So we did eat much better in the Pacific than we did in Europe until we got to Iron Range. Up in the northern part of Australia the engineers had hacked a strip there in the middle of the jungle about 200 miles from the nearest town. Needless to say, Bishops Stortford in England was a paradise compared to this.

"In the Pacific, we went on our two rest and recreation leaves, one to Sydney and the other to Melbourne, and in Europe we went on our one same type leave to Aberdeen, Scotland. I can't compare those. It's like trying to compare a hundred dollar bill with two fifties. If I live to be a hundred, I'll never forget those leaves! They almost made getting shot at worthwhile just to be able to go.

"There was also a difference in the B-26s we flew. In the Pacific, the 22nd had the first B-26s in existence. They had a 12-volt electrical system, which proved too light almost immediately. They also had an automatic pilot which, according to the pilots, was extremely untrustworthy. There were none in the European '26s. The tail gun consisted of one .50-caliber flexible gun. At the beginning we had two .30s out the waist; these were finally thrown out in favor of .50s. There was a camera hatch just back of the waist guns in which a .30-caliber gun was mounted. The wingspan of those '26s was 65 feet instead of 71. There were several homemade package gun modifications which consisted usually of a single gun mounted through the bombardier's glasshouse, much to the disgust of the bombardier. The European B-26 package guns would have come in very handy in the Pacific on several missions, notably Rabaul and Milne Bay.

"There is at least one instance in which there was no difference between the 22nd and the 344th Group and that was in their regards for the B-26 Marauder. Both groups thought there was only one plane in which to fly combat and that was the B-26!''

One fact is certain: Teague touched practically all bases in his capsulized comparison, and it is one of the finest factual accounts seen in many a day. An enlisted man who went through the hell of both worlds can really tell it like it was!

Alaska and the Aleutians

The 28th Composite Group in the Alaskan Air Command of the 11th Air Force was formed in California during 1941. It consisted of one heavy bombardment squadron, two medium bombardment squadrons, and one fighter squadron.

The 77th Bombardment Squadron air echelon left Sacramento for Elmendorf Air Force Base, Alaska, with 14 B-26s during January 1942, but five were lost in crack-ups in the vicinity of Watson Lake and Whitehorse, Canada.

Lt. Howard F. Smiley, now of Sioux City, Iowa, was with the 77th at Gowen Field, Boise, Idaho. On 16 January 1942, six of their B-26s left Edmonton, Alberta, Canada, to fly the thousand-mile stretch up to Whitehorse, Yukon Territory, on the second leg of their move to Elmendorf.

Smiley was flying copilot on one ship only because he was outranked by a Lt. Dancer for the left seat slot by five weeks; Dancer was Class 41-F and Smiley Class 41-G in pilot training school. Other members of the crew included a bombardier-navigator, a radio operator, a turret gunner, and a tunnel gunner plus a crew chief. Their ships had no guns installed in the tail position at the time, so no tail gunner was carried.

There were no aeronautical charts of that part of the world available to them at that time, so the only maps they carried were 8½- × -11″-pencil sketches drawn up for them the night before by Canadian bush pilots. Radio silence was mandatory and radar was unheard of at that time, so the six ships had two strikes against them, navigation-wise, before they even took off.

In a snowstorm during the latter part of the short daylight hours, three of the ships (Smiley's included) became lost and, being low on fuel, all elected to make forced landings on the frozen wastes of a shallow valley that was at around the 5000-foot altitude level. Two of the ships landed with minimal damage to aircraft and crew, but Smiley's ship ended up in the condition shown in Fig. 4-8, a photograph he took a few days later after he'd recovered somewhat from injuries sustained in the landing.

The rest of the crew had come through the ordeal okay, but both Dancer and Smiley had been knocked unconscious by the impact which, as can be seen

Fig. 4-8. *Smiley's wrecked ship in "Million Dollar Valley," 18 June 1942. Note tarpaulins draped over left wing as a shelter while crew awaited rescue. What appear to be tufts of grass around the airplane are actually bushes four to five feet in height, which indicate the depth of the snow at the site. (photo courtesy LTC Howard F. Smiley, USAFR Ret.)*

85

in Fig. 4-8, had pretty well demolished the nose section. From the looks of it, it's a wonder they weren't mangled to death. When Smiley came to about an hour later, he found himself in his sleeping bag under the wing, with the back of his head bandaged up. With customary B-26 crew efficiency, the crew had used the wing covers (carried for protecting the wings from snow and ice when the aircraft was parked on the ground) to construct a shelter under the left wing by draping them over and piling snow around the base to hold them in place. Emergency rations and equipment had been broken out, and the crew settled in to await rescue. They had no idea of where they were, but found out later they were only about 90 miles from Watson Lake!

The story continues in Smiley's own words:

"At the same time we were enroute to Alaska, a flight of P-40s was also enroute to the same place; however, they were one day behind us, having stopped at Fort Nelson, B.C. When we didn't arrive at Whitehorse on schedule, word was sent to Fort Nelson for the P-40s to conduct a search in the area.

"After searching around Fort Nelson a couple of days, they were ordered to continue their flight on to Watson Lake. Fortunately for us, we had crashed between Fort Nelson and Watson Lake at a spot about 20 to 30 miles north of the flight path between these two locations.

"On the day that these P-40s (and their accompanying C-47) spotted us, it was clear, cold, and still. You could hear for miles, it seemed. We were in the shelter when all of a sudden we heard this low humming sound and we looked outside. There, what turned out to be south, were four little dots, almost hidden by the treetops, going from left to right.

"Our crew had prepared for this and so let fly with flares, tracers out of the turret, etc.—a real Fourth of July display. Then we waited for results. Sure enough, they had seen us and I will never forget the tremendous thrill we experienced as those four little dots slowly turned toward us and flew over our location, as well as the location of the other two ships. We knew now that we were no longer lost!

"On the next day, two bush pilots, flying an old high-wing, single-engine Fokker on skis, came in with a Royal Canadian Constable and landed near us. Dancer and I were loaded on the Fokker and flown to Watson Lake and then to Ladd Field, Fairbanks, Alaska, for treatment. After about a week I was back flying our beloved monster. I do not know what became of Dancer, but understand that he was returned to the States.

"The Constable stayed with the rest of our crew plus the crews of the other two planes (no injuries) and led them to a lake five to six miles away, where they cleared a runway and in about a week were flown out by a C-47 on skis.

"The spot of our three-plane crash was to later become known as 'Million Dollar Valley' and is so referred to in various books on the Air Force in Alaska. Several months after the crash, the AF sent in ground crews to cannibalize the wrecks and those parts so removed became a major source of supply for our B-26 Aleutian Campaign maintenance problems.''

No details could be found on the other two Marauders that crashed in the vicinity of Smiley's ship (other than what he related), nor of the two others that were lost, but the remaining nine ships of the original air echelon movement finally arrived at Elmendorf on 27 January.

In February, the B-18s of the 73rd Bombardment Squadron, which had been in Alaska since March of 1941, were replaced with 17 B-26s. Transitioning from the old Douglas B-18 "Digby" to the Marauder must have been quite an experience for the pilots of the 73rd, but at least they had some twin-engine time under their belts as a starter.

The 406th Squadron of the 42nd Bomb Group of Marauders, training at Gowen Field, Boise, Idaho, also moved to Alaska eventually. These squadrons flew the Marauders until B-25s began replacing them in September 1942. By the end of February 1943, all their '26s were gone. Their combat lifespan was the shortest in any theater of operations.

Combat conditions in Alaska were just as bad as, if not worse than, in the South Pacific, but on the opposite end of the thermometer. The weather was marked by almost continual rain and fog, not to mention the snow and ice of the winter months. Ceilings ranged from zero to 500 feet maximum, with visibility seldom over five miles. Most of the flying was done just above the surface of the water. Navigation was all done by dead reckoning because the necessity for radio silence, with the Japanese in such close proximity, precluded the use of radio for homing.

These weather conditions made takeoffs and landings extremely hazardous. On return from a search mission on 6 June 1942, Marauders flew for four hours over water at 50 feet altitude or less, in fog. Upon landing, the far end of the runway could not be seen!

Both personnel and airplanes were maintained during the early period under extremely difficult conditions. Combat crews had to set up their own tents, and, until 5 June, cook their own meals. The bivouac area for the crews was a sea of mud, and water covered the ground inside many of the tents. Airplane maintenance was performed largely by the officers and enlisted men of the combat crews. Gas was pumped from 50-gallon drums and oil poured from five gallon cans. Not even the Spartans had it so rough! As in the Pacific, squadrons operated sometimes on an individual basis from remote airstrips where, if it can be imagined, conditions were even worse.

1942

May: Twenty-four Marauders joined the 28th Group in Alaska and carried torpedoes in search of the Japanese carrier *Ryuko* that attacked Dutch Harbor. They found her, but no hits were scored.

In late May, 17 B-26s of the 73rd and 77th Squadrons were moved to Cold Bay and Unmak, in the Aleutian chain, in preparation for an anticipated Japanese attack which actually came in late June. At various periods Marauders were also based at Adak, Attu, Amchittka and Shemya.

15 June: Capt. George Thornbrough landed a torpedo on the deck of an aircraft carrier in an attack on a Jap task force, thereby helping to dislodge it from Attu and Kiska in the Aleutian chain.

17 Oct.: B-26s sink one Jap destroyer, damage another, and set afire a cargo ship at Kiska.

19 Oct.: Marauders sink two Jap destroyers of Hibiki class in a flight at near deck level, dropping five bombs on one and four on the other near Kiska. One B-26 was shot down by destroyer AA fire.

24 Nov.: Telegram from Lt. Gen. Arnold to Martin: ''The bombers you build are proving themselves today in the Aleutians, in North Africa, and in the Southwest Pacific. At Kiska, a formation of Marauders sank two Jap destroyers in one raid.''

25 Nov.: A flight of B-26s sink an 8,000-ton Jap collier in Holtz Bay, Attu.

13 Dec.: Three B-26s bomb Jap ship aground west of Trout Lagoon at Kiska and pound shore installations.

As had happened in the Pacific, by this time B-25s were being assigned to the B-26 squadrons, torpedo operations were discontinued altogether, and in early 1943 the '26s were pulled out of this theater. Finally, in August 1943, the Japanese gave up trying to maintain beachheads in the Aleutians and withdrew their task force. The Marauders, although few in number, had played a significant part in the actions that forced the Japanese to change their war plans in that theater.

It had been an entirely different type of operation from that in the Pacific, aside from the fact that the weather conjured up conditions normally associated with the lower end of the Celsius stick. Ground targets were few and disappeared entirely after the Japanese evacuated their few bases in the Aleutian chain. Naval targets and shipping were the prime targets throughout the campaign. While mission distances over water were not as great as in the Pacific, the low ceilings and the miserable weather conditions made them equally horrendous. As in the Pacific, the B-26 crews in Alaska had pioneered the combat scene with no replacements, miserable maintenance conditions, sporadic and unreliable supply provisioning, and against sometimes overwhelming odds. In these two theaters, through no fault of its own, the B-26 was extremely vulnerable to attacks by relentless critics!

Since so few B-26s were assigned to the three squadrons, it was difficult to pick out any credible statistics as to their operations alone, but only three were lost to enemy action between 3 June 1942 and 10 March 1943—not too bad, considering!

Lt. Howard F. Smiley had been flying out of airstrips at Cold Bay and Unmak Island since 3 June 1942 and in September of that year was ordered to fly B-26 40-1376 (the 16th B-26 to come off the Martin production line) back to Anchorage

Fig. 4-9. *Navy painting officially captioned: "Cooperation—On the puddled runway at Kodiak, an Army B-26 refuels and a Navy gas truck supplies it. Beyond the cluster of officers' quarters rises Woman's Mountain, whose massive form and pelt-like surface suggests some prehistoric monster, while in the distance lies Devil's Creek Canyon." (photo courtesy LTC Howard F. Smiley, USAFR Ret.)*

for extensive repairs. He took off from Unmak Island (Otter Point) and flew east, intending to stop at Cold Bay for refueling. However, that base was closed in by weather, so he had to stretch his fuel and made it into Kodiak to refuel.

While waiting for the fuel truck, a Navy combat artist, Lt. William F. Sraper, USNR, came over and made sketches of the airplane from which he finally painted the scene shown in Fig. 4-9. Shortly thereafter, Smiley took off and continued his flight to Anchorage. Back in the States the following year, Smiley was surprised to see a full-color, full-page print of the painting in the August 1943 issue of *National Geographic* magazine. He contacted the Navy Department and was given a color photo of the painting.

It just so happened that when Smiley was rotated back to the States in early 1943, he was assigned to ferry the same 40-1376 to Avon Park Army Air Field, Florida. When he landed at Avon, the Engineering Officer took one look at the ship with its flat struts (landing gear), cracked right wing main spar, rusty control cables, leaking seals, patched holes in the plexiglass nose, four missing slinger ring bolts on the engine mounts, etc., etc., and ''red-Xed'' the tired old gal on the spot! She became a source of mock-ups for the ground school there. A glaring example of what the Aleutian B-26 pioneers had to endure—40-1376 had flown combat in that condition, but she wasn't fit nor safe enough to use as a transition training ship in the States!

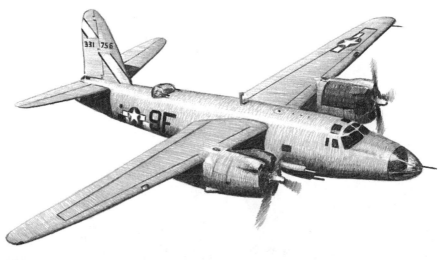

5

COMBAT, PHASE TWO:
Desert Jackals Harass Desert Fox

While only five squadrons of Marauders had been sent to the South Pacific and just three squadrons to Alaska, the Air Force sent three groups to Africa, beginning in late 1942, where they were assigned to the 12th Air Force. It was here that the Marauder was "born again" after the Truman Committee fiasco and began redeeming itself on the comeback trail.

Even though it was finally more extensively used as a medium-altitude bomber in this theater, the Army still hadn't learned its lesson and continued low-level operations off and on. But it was here that tactics were tried and proven on a massed squadron formation bombing a single target for maximum effectiveness.

The desert terrain of North Africa on which the hastily constructed temporary airfields were located afforded the opportunity for a change in take-off and landing procedures in order to save time and fuel—by one group, at least. It was not uncommon to see their Marauders taking off six abreast, raising clouds of sand and dust in the process (Fig. 5-1). Landings were also accomplished with three or six abreast on the final approach. In actuality, this multiple takeoff routine produced too much dust and was finally discontinued in Africa, but was resumed again in Sardinia later on, where a 1200-foot wide harder surface runway was available with oiled-down takeoff lanes (Fig. 5-2).

The 319th Bomb Group was the first to become operational, on 28 November 1942, and followed the land battle with successive basings at

Fig. 5-1. *Aircraft of the 17th Bomb Group taxiing out for takeoff at the Telergma airdrome. One can imagine the dust generated on takeoff with this much being generated just taxiing! (photo courtesy Jack Gordon)*

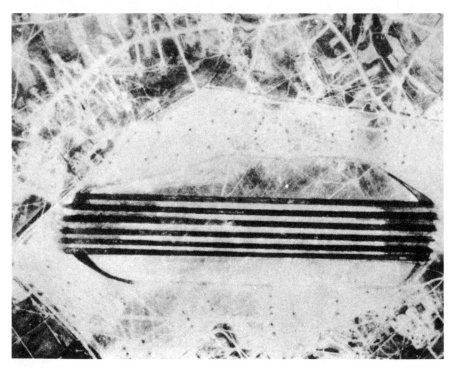

Fig. 5-2. *Aerial view of Decimomannu airfield in Sardinia, showing oiled-down six-lane runway. (photo courtesy Charles O'Mahony)*

airdromes in Tafarouri, Maison Blanche, Telergma, and Biskra, Algeria; Dujda and Rabat-Sale, French Morocco; Sedrate, Algeria; Djedeida, Tunisia; Decimomannu, Sardinia; and Serragia, Corsica. This was Tactical Air warfare at its ultimate—direct air support of the ground troops—and nowhere in the world did medium bombardment groups move from base to base to give close support to the ground forces as many times as those in the MTO.

Around 26 December 1942 Commanding General Doolittle issued orders instructing the MTO B-26 units to operate at medium altitudes (around 10,000 feet) on all but sea sweeps against enemy shipping. The 3l9th was equipped with D-8 bombsights, so the few missions it did fly at medium altitudes before being equipped with the Norden bombsight were not too successful. The aircraft of the 17th Group had left the States equipped with the Norden, and later on the 320th would also come over with one out of every four aircraft allotted a Norden. The D-8 was adequate enough for low-level work, but at medium and high altitudes the sophistication and accuracy of the Norden were required.

It was here in North Africa that standard bombing procedures for the mediums were born, using the Norden, and these would later on carry over and be refined in the ETO. Only the lead ships of each flight carried the Norden bombsight. Other wingman bombardiers in the flight would open their bomb bay doors on the leader and toggle their bombs out as the leader dropped.

Wingmen bombardiers became jokingly known as "toggleiers" and many became bitter over the fact that they never got to put their many months of training on the Norden to practical use—and rightly so.

Behind the scenes of Doolittle's dictate could be detected the influence of Capt. Vincent W. Burnett, whom Doolittle had taken with him to Africa as his technical adviser, accountable only to the General himself. Once again Doolittle and Burnett were instrumental in championing the Marauder.

As mentioned before, General H. H. Arnold, Air Force Chief of Staff, had faith in the Marauder and merits accolades in the "Save the Marauder" exercise for his wisdom in not only assigning Doolittle to find the cause of the troubles and get them corrected, but then designating him to command the units in combat to develop the correct battle tactics for the airplane.

1942

18 Dec.: B-26s of the 3l9th Bomb Group (M), 12th Air Force, round out eight successive days of air assault on Axis positions with a sharp raid on railroad yards at Sousse, south of Tunis. They also put out of commission an Axis radio station at El Aouine and pounded Gabes. Flak brought down two Marauders.

The 17th Bomb Group became operational on 30 December 1942 and it was successively based at Telergma and Sedrata, Algeria; Djedieda, Tunisia; Villacidro, Sardinia; Crete; Corsica; and Dijon, France.

6 Jan.: B-26s pound airdrome for third successive day at Kairouan, 36 miles southwest of Sousse.

9 Jan.: B-26s shoot down two and a probable third Me-109s in air combat over North Africa. B-26s bomb Kairouan air base with excellent results.

11 Jan.: Flying through heavy flak, B-26s attack railroad yards and oil storage tanks at Gabes, North Africa. Twelfth USAAF, mainly composed of B-26s, attacks airfield 10 miles south of Tripoli, scoring direct hits and damaging three Me-l09s attacking the force.

12 Jan.: After downing an attacking Me-109, Lt. W. W. Watkins, of Galveston, Tex., pilot of a B-26, rides with a bouncing bomb in the bomb bay, and keeps it steady enough to land safely in North Africa.

13 Jan.: Marauders score hits on a highway bridge at La Mencha and a railroad bridge at Chaba between Sousse and Sfax, North Africa.

On 19 January a secret document entitled "Miscellaneous Instructions and Suggestions for Inspection and Operation of B-26 Medium Bombardment Airplanes" was issued in the 12th. It was authored by Capt. V. W. Burnett, 12th Air Force Combat School Operational Engineering Section, La Senia, Algeria, North Africa, a school he had set up.

A formal "Pilot's Information Manual" on the B-26 hadn't been officially issued by the Air Force yet, so this was a sorely needed treatise. While it would be redundant to quote verbatim all ten and a half pages of this document, some comment on it is in order. The introduction was particularly pointed and is quoted herewith:

1. These instructions and suggestions have been prepared for the use of those responsible for the operation of B-26 type aircraft in this theater. They do not supersede or replace formal bulletins and/or technical orders published by the U.S. Army Air Corps but are issued to emphasize the importance of certain procedures and techniques that experience has dictated are of extreme value in minimizing ground delays and operational inefficiencies.

2. It is extremely important that every member of the crew be thoroughly familiar with the mechanical details of this airplane and its accessories in order that the maximum operational time can be realized.

3. If all crew members are thoroughly familiar with the operational functions of the equipment, it may be possible to bring back a disabled aircraft even though some of the crew members are not physically able to perform their assigned tasks.

The various sections of the pamphlet covered "Daily Inspection," "Pre-Flight Instruction," "Combat Mission Suggestions," "Inspection After Attack," and "Miscellaneous Instructions and Suggestions," which covered Ground

Handling, Flight Characteristics, and Proper Use of Brakes.

In order to convey an appreciation for what a pilot was faced with when learning to fly the B-26, the second paragraph of the subsection on Flight Characteristics is quoted here: "Bear in mind that the B-26 is being operated at from 58 to 60 pounds wing loading and that stalls can be produced very easily up to 160-180 mph by trying to change the longitudinal direction of the ship too fast, or by tightening up a steep turn too much. Unfortunately, due to the heavy wing load and relatively short wingspan of the B-26, quite a bit of altitude is required to recover from stalls, and, should they occur at high speeds, the airplane will have a tendency to snap-roll. This is particularly important to guard against if the airplane is being flown on instruments and recoveries from indicated losses of altitude must be made smooth and gradual."

No one was more qualified to write such a booklet than Burnett, and the extent of his technical knowledge, as well as his many hours of flying the B-26, was very evident in its "no nonsense" contents.

23 Jan.: B-26s destroy single and twin-engined Nazi aircraft by bombing airdrome at Ben Gardane in southern Tunisia.

28 Jan.: Six members of a B-26 crew, shot down behind Axis lines in North Africa, destroy aircraft instruments. Next day they were spotted from a nearby busy highway by enemies in a German and Italian command car. They were captured, but while rounding a corner, jumped their guards, threw them from the car, and escaped. A week later they returned to the Allied base.

2 Feb.: Lt. Wm. F. Irwin, Houston, Tex., pilot of a B-26, lands safely in a North African swamp following attack by 12 Me-109s, which fired 20 cannon shells into his bomber.

4 Feb.: Marauders, attacked by Me-109s in a 40-minute running battle, down two Nazis and continue on to bomb communications and air bases at Gabes.

6 Feb.: Capt. Thomas C. Griffin, Chicago, Ill., navigator of a B-26, tells of sinking an Axis ship carrying tanks and 1000 troops near Bizerte. The aircraft was damaged by flak.

Ira S. Guldin, now of Kutztown, Pennsylvania, was an armament flight chief with the 95th Bomb Squadron of the 17th Bomb Group and relates that there was a shortage of coal for their heating stoves in the underground huts, built thus to help ward off the night cold (Fig. 5-3). They lived in these holes from February to May 1943 and supplemented their coal supply by throwing rocks at Arabs who had hitched a ride on passing freight trains. The Arabs naturally retaliated by throwing chunks of coal from the cars back at the troops—more Yankee resourcefulness and improvisation at work!

Not only were the living conditions rugged but working conditions were equally so, and most maintenance—even the advanced echelon type—had to be performed in the open (Figs. 5-4 through 5-6).

12 Feb.: Marauders spray "knockout drops " (2000-pounders) in a terrific blasting (hundreds of tons of bombs) of Axis docks and supply lines in Tunisia.

Fig. 5-3. *Rain-soaked living quarters of the 95th Squadron of the 17th Bomb Group at Telergma, Algeria. This hut is undergoing renovation. (photo courtesy Ira S. Guldin)*

Fig. 5-4. *This shot and the next show the difficulties under which engine changes and other maintenance was performed on the desert air bases. (photo courtesy Jack Gordon)*

Fig. 5-5. *These mechanics are with the 37th Squadron of the 17th Bomb Group. (photo courtesy Jack Gordon)*

Fig. 5-6. *Photo of an unidentified 37th Bomb Squadron crew at Djedeida, Tunisia, illustrates the parched condition of the earth. Mechanics had to spread tarpaulins under the aircraft to keep from losing tools and parts in the large cracks in the sun-baked earth. This condition could also create nosewheel strut failures if taxiing wasn't done properly. (photo courtesy Jack Gordon)*

14 Feb.: Two waves of B-26s attack Tunis airdrome; shoot down four Me-109s.

16 Feb.: B-26s attack Kairouan, dropping bombs into concentrations of enemy planes. Two enemy aircraft attempting a takeoff ran into bomb bursts. The B-26s shot down 11 Me-109s attempting to fight off the bombers.

17 Feb.: S/Sgt. Dolon Hinson, gunner of a B-26, is credited with downing an Italian Macchi 200 over Decimomannu airdrome in North Africa.

Feb. 24: B-26s aid in forcing Rommel's troops back into Kasserine Gap. Also bombed Sheitla and Feriana areas. Marauder crew of *New York Central* B-26 sets good record on 13 combat missions in seven weeks, during which they shot down six enemy planes.

The reader will note that in spite of these dispatches being excerpts and not all-inclusive of those in the Martin testimonial, missions were flown much more frequently in the MTO than in either the Pacific or Alaskan theaters. This can be explained with these reasons: 1. The weather conditions were much better; 2. Target distances were not as great; 3. Enemy targets were more than plentiful; 4. Air Force planners had benefited from experience gained in the Pacific and Alaska; and 5. More accurate intelligence regarding enemy movements, strengths, etc., was possible.

1 Mar.: Capt. Gernsy Carlisle, San Antonio, Tex., piloted a defenseless B-26 through antiaircraft fire and attack by five Me-109s. The Marauder's guns had jammed and three of the crew were killed or wounded. After 20 minutes, the aircraft arrived safely at home, honeycombed with bullet holes.

2 Mar.: Escorted B-26s bomb a railroad bridge at La Mencha near Sfax, skimming the ground at 60 feet. Blew up another bridge, and in a 30-minute battle with Me-109s and FW-190s, the Marauders downed four.

11 Mar.: B-26s help advance of French ground forces near Gafs in North Africa by pounding enemy positions.

19 Mar.: A gunner in B-26 *Angel From Hell,* S/Sgt. Henry Corsch, Brooklyn, N.Y., shoots down an Me-109.

23 Mar.: B-26s drop bombs among more than 40 Nazi aircraft on the ground at the airfield at Djebel Tebaga between Gabes and Sfax.

28 Mar.: Marauders and other types drop 16,496 bombs on enemy troops in one week ending this date. Result: 9 Axis ships sunk, 60 damaged.

Jack Gordon, now of Greenville, Mississippi, was a crew chief in the 37th Squadron of the 17th Bomb Group in its WWII infancy. He recalls wondering if the 17th would ever get overseas intact. First, the crews for the Doolittle Tokyo raid were pirated from them, and subsequently the Air Force began pulling cadre crews away from them to form the 319th and 320th Groups. That's why the 17th adopted the monicker "Daddy of Them All" (WWII medium bombardment groups) when they finally moved to the MTO.

Gordon's first B-26 was a short-winged, stubby-ruddered B-2 model picked up at Baer Field, Ft. Wayne, Indiana. It wasn't until the 17th had been in Africa for quite some time that he finally took over the care and maintenance of a B-10 model, with the longer wing and taller rudder. This one had come from the Martin Omaha plant and was to become his favorite airplane.

In March of 1943 Jack was bestowing tender loving care on a B-3 model, Serial Number 41-17970, which became part of a task force that conducted special bombing tests on a lake near Biskra. The Germans had taken a beating and were expected to evacuate Africa in possibly the same manner as the British had left Dunkirk earlier on and the Allies were determined to foil the attempt.

An Army Air Force Captain named Pace had come up with an idea that he maintained would wreak havoc upon the Germans in a Dunkirk-type evacuation, and his plan was tested at the lake. Along with the group conducting the test was an observer, Army Air Force Colonel Campbell, who was a personal friend of President Roosevelt's and who had formerly operated the largest wheat-growing business in the U.S. He was then in service as a dollar-a-year man and one of Roosevelt's many confidants who reported directly to him from on-the-scene actions. Gordon remembers him as being "a very good guy."

Special bombs were built by attaching tail fins to one end of a 55-gallon drum filled with waste oil. To the nose was welded a 100-pound practice bomb casing filled with seven pounds of black powder and a mixture of crude rubber soaked in 100 octane gasoline.

Two of these bombs were carried in the B-26 and dropped on the lake from about 2000 feet altitude. The resulting fire was a conflagration that spread across the waters of the lake in a frightening whoosh of flame, a forerunner to the napalm bombs used by our Air Force in Korea and Vietnam.

Gordon remembers Doolittle flying down one day to observe the tests (Fig. 5-7). Jack was in the bomb bay of 41-17970, watching the bombs fall out from the 2000-foot height, and the next thing he knew here was Doolittle's B-26 buzzing along the lake under his ship and on the deck to get a close look at the wall of fire! Leave it to Jimmy to check effectiveness all the way.

Someone had chalked "Today's Menu—Fried Kraut" on one of the practice bombs, but as it all turned out the scheme was never used, as the Germans smuggled their high-ranking officers out of Africa by air and the majority of the troops surrendered on Cape Bon before any large-scale evacuation could be mounted (Fig. 5-8).

11 Apr.: Marauders drop bombs on eight Junkers transports and 25 other aircraft at Oudna Field near Tunis. Enemy fighter formation already in the air refused to fight.

22 Apr.: Marauders pound enemy shipping at Arbatax Harbor, eastern Sardinia. Hit shipping piers and shipyards at Carloforte Harbor in southwest Sicily.

The last Marauder group to become operational in the 12th Air Force was the 320th, which ran its first mission on 22 April 1943 and occupied bases at Tafforaoui and Montesquieu, Algeria; Massicault and El Bathran, Tunisia; Decimomannu, Sardinia; Alto, Corsica; and DiJon and Dole-Taveux, France.

Fig. 5-7. *Maj. Gen. James Doolittle, third from right, conferring with officers of the 17th Bomb Group on a North African Air Base in 1943. No fancy uniform for Jimmy—he dressed down with the troops. (photo courtesy Jack Gordon)*

Fig. 5-8. *The "napalm" task force lined up in front of 41-17970 at the Telergma airdrome. Capt. Pace is Number Five, Col. Campbell Number Six, and Gordon Number Ten. (photo courtesy Jack Gordon)*

As the 12th moved through North Africa, then on to the Mediterranean islands, and finally to the French mainland, they occupied many former Italian and German flying fields.

2 May: Marauders hit merchant vessel steaming north from Cape El Mebah on the east coast of Cape Bon; shoot down 18 Me-109s, FW-190s, and Macchi 200s and score direct hits on six aircraft on the ground at Elmas & Milas fields in Sardinia.

7 May: Marauders participate in 2000 sorties on the Medjerda River Valley between Madjes-El-Bab and Tunis. Marauders assist in blazing path four miles wide and three miles deep for British First Army. In these attacks they sink one destroyer and eight other Axis vessels in heaviest 24-hour raid of the war in Africa.

9 May: 400-plane raid on Palermo, including Marauders. The target was one square mile, packed with docks and war industries, such as the Fiat Automobile Works, ship-building yards, an arsenal for shell cases, a chemical plant, and an iron and steel works. (*Author's note:* The mediums of the 12th often hit strategic targets, such as mentioned in the 9 May dispatch, merely because they were within their range and the aircraft were available. The heavies concentrated on strategic targets on up into the Balkans—the Ploesti oil refineries is a good example.)

10 May: Marauders sink three troop-laden motor barges 30 miles west of Marrittino Island near Sicily. They were planes from Major General Doolittle's forces. Marauders attack enemy tanks on Tunis-Bizerte road near Protville, and sink two Axis ships and a probable third near Cape Bon.

12 May: For the third successive day Marauders hammer Marsal and Catania, Sicily, in sequel raids to that on Palermo; 125 tons of bombs were dropped on Catania.

15 May: Marauders blow up ship in Cagliari harbor; start fires in oil tanks, freight yards and naval berths.

The Burnetts had taken an apartment in Washington, D.C., when Squeek was first assigned to Doolittle, and this later proved to be a boon to them, especially after he left for overseas duty.

Beginning with the 12th Air Force's short stint in England, and later on when they moved on down to Algeria, Burnett (Fig. 5-9) acted as an "Ambassador without portfolio," carrying secret documents and dispatches between 12th AF Headquarters and General Arnold's office in the Pentagon and vice versa.

Being one of only a hundred or so military pilots to hold a "Green Card" instrument rating at the time, Squeek could write his own clearances, and therefore operated pretty much on his own schedule when on these courier flights. To Evelyn's delight, he usually managed to RON (remain overnight) in Washington, and although he was stationed halfway around the world, they had

Fig. 5-9. *Glamour photo of Major Vincent W. Burnett taken soon after his promotion, 1 April 1943, while on duty with Doolittle in Africa. (photo courtesy Evelyn Burnett)*

the unusual opportunity of being together from time to time, even if only for a night.

The members of Burnetts' flight crew also enjoyed the benefits of escaping the combat area. He would bring them to the Washington apartment for a home-cooked meal, then give them the keys to his car for a night on the town, the only stipulation being that they pick him up at 0700 the next morning ready to fly the Atlantic again. After stopping by General Arnold's office to pick up documents, they'd proceed to Bolling Field to fly back overseas again.

20 May: Marauders bomb 73 Axis aircraft on the ground at Elmas, Moserrato, Villacidro, and Milo Airdromes in Sardinia. B-26s shoot up and bomb 15 small boats and three enemy gun positions on Pantalleria.

21 May: Marauders bag six Axis aircraft over Decimomannu, heavily damaging radio and airfield buildings and barracks. Pounded Villacidro airfield, bringing to 285 the three-day total of enemy aircraft destroyed in the air and on the ground, including six six-engined Me-323s, giant transport planes.

23 May: Marauders clean up in Tunis, Bizerte, and Cape Bon area and blast Axis forces into submission. Allied forces mop up, capturing 433 German and 125 Italian aircraft abandoned on the ground.

24 May: B-26s attack and demolish five small vessels at Pantalleria. Strike at Carloforte harbor in Sardinia, also smash airfield buildings, dispersal areas, and a bivouac area at Pantalleria. (*Author's note:* The reader will note that mention is never made of hitting the *runways* on various Axis airfields. This was strictly intentional on the part of the 12th AF so, if need be, they could be used immediately upon evacuation by the Axis air forces and occupation by our own.)

25 May: Marauders again raid Pantalleria, dropping a store of bombs. Blew up one supply ship, four small vessels, and damaged seven other ships. Also conducted heavy raids on Carloforte on southern tip of Sardinia, Arbatax on east coast, Inglesias on west coast, and Alghero airfield to the north. Another unit pounds Sicily, hitting docks, sheds, and quays at Licata, sulphur works and a powerhouse at Empedocle, a supply vessel and power station at Portoscuso, and the airfields at Bobba di Falco and Terranovar (Fig. 5-10).

26 May: Marauders attack Alghero airfield, cover hangars with bombs and set afire a fuel dump. Pound the fortress of Messina, hitting the ferry slip, railroad yards, supply dumps, rail shops, power stations, and military buildings. In one week, Marauders contribute to destruction of 357 Axis aircraft, the majority on the ground.

28 May: Marauders unload over 4,000 fragmentation bombs over Decimomannu, smashing numerous aircraft on the ground. Down seven Axis fighters in 18-minute air bout.

31 May: Marauders attack Pantalleria, the 84 square-mile former prison of ancient Rome, for second week without fighter opposition. Hit docks causing fires and explosions.

2 June: Marauders pound supply vessels, railway docks and dock installations in Sardinia.

5 June: Marauders bomb Pantelleria for sixth time in 48 hours and play important part in the heaviest bombing of any Italian base during war.

7 June: Marauders and Baltimores (Martin A-30 attack bomber) help down 11 Axis aircraft in a Pantelleria raid. In another attack on a naval base for submarines and torpedo boats, Marauders shoot down two attacking Me-109s.

103

Fig. 5-10. *B-26s of 17th Bomb Group's 34th Squadron returning to Sardinia from a bombing mission after Allied Forces had taken the island. Ship in foreground is on one engine. Note ammunition belt being jettisoned to reduce weight, and receptacle under tail turret to catch spent shells from the tail guns to prevent them from hitting aircraft underneath in the flight. (photo courtesy Ira S. Guldin)*

Marauders attack Proto Pone Romano in southern Sardinia, scoring a direct hit on the stern of a 500-foot merchantman and other hits on a quay and coal dump. (*Author's note:* Although the Baltimore belonged to the RAF, it entered into these communiques now and then because, to repeat, the list had been compiled by the Glenn L. Martin Company to help justify the Marauder's worth when production cancellation was being threatened in early 1944—just another little innuendo as to the fact that "Martin builds rugged and dependable combat bombers." Also, no doubt noted is the generous use of words and phrases such as "aided," "helped," and "along with other aircraft" when the dispatches described bombing results or numbers of enemy fighters destroyed. Besides the 17th, 319th and 320th Groups of Marauders, the 12th Air Force also contained the 47th Bomb Group (L) (A-20 Havocs) and the 321st Bomb Group (M) (B-25 Mitchells). In the newly-formed 9th Air Force were the 12th and 340th Groups, flying B-17s and B-24s, not to mention the RAF and Free French Air Force with their complement of bomber types. This may have been a bit of literary license on Martin's part, but there were still plenty of dispatches describing the Marauder's individual exploits to prove that it was doing a good job.)

10 June: Marauders and Baltimores cover attack of troops landing on Pantelleria.

12 June: Pantelleria capitulates. Capt. Henry P. Van Lear, Lynchburg, Va., was a flight leader posted to attack that isle again and upon receipt of the surrender turned off to be among the first to bomb Lampedusa, 80 miles south. Dock areas and gun positions were battered after the lead flight, led by Capt. Harold B. Lamson, Finleyville, Pa., bombed a merchant ship and eight small boats. Other Marauders were in at the finish of Pantelleria, protecting the British Navy, which had come in from nine to three miles to shell the coast. The 20-day assault on Pantelleria resulted in a 39-to-1 aerial victory ratio.

13 June: Marauders commence solid assaults on Milo airfield, near Trapani, Sicily. They helped riddle 150 Axis aircraft on the ground there, and at Castelventrano and Bocca di Falco (Fig. 5-11).

As technical adviser to General Doolittle, Vincent W. Burnett's duties were many and varied; message courier and personal pilot for the General were two of the official ones. An *unofficial* but vital one went as follows:

Burnett was at his desk just outside Doolittle's office one morning when General "Jim" stopped on his way in and said, "Squeek, it looks like we won't

Fig. 5-11. *Twelfth Air Force B-26s encountering flak over the mountains of southern France, 20 July 1944. (photo courtesy Glenn L. Martin Co.)*

be getting a liquor supply for a while, due to higher priorities for badly needed supplies. We're about out, but I understand there is liquor to be had at Gibraltar. So what are you going to do about it?''

Squeek replied, ''I'm leaving in a B-26 just as soon as I can round up a crew!''

He then hurriedly collected around $1000 from his fellow officers to pay for the booze and took off for Gilbraltar. Since it was around 800 miles across the Mediterranean from Algiers, they stopped in Oran to refuel. They knew the Luftwaffe would be patrolling the sea lanes for shipping, so all crew members kept a sharp lookout for enemy aircraft after leaving Oran.

About 200 miles out, the Sergeant in the dorsal turret called attention to two specks in the sky off to one side. Squeek held his heading, altitude, and airspeed until the specks grew into Ju-88s—which dove on the B-26 with guns blazing. The Jerries figured they had a sitting duck lined up, with two on one, but didn't realize what they were up against.

As the Marauder gunners returned the fire, Squeek racked the ship into violent evasive action reminiscent of his old airshow days, and the crew could hardly believe they were actually performing some of these maneuvers in a B-26! The encounter lasted only a few minutes; one Ju-88 was hit and disappeared in a cloud of smoke over the horizon and the other turned tail and ran, never being able to get Squeek in his sights. The Marauder came out without a scratch.

The balance of the flight to Gilbraltar was uneventful, and they loaded the ship with liquor and headed back to Algiers unmolested. Mission accomplished in support of the 12th AF Axiom: ''You can't fight a war on K-rations alone—gotta have something to wash the stuff down!''

Maybe Squeek wasn't entitled to have a swastika painted on the ship since there was no other Allied aircraft along to verify whether it was a kill or a probable, but Doolittle's ship probably would have looked like any other combat Marauder had it been kosher to paint miniature diplomatic pouches, B-4 bags, and whiskey bottles on the side to designate the many respective courier, personnel ferrying and whiskey runs it made in the MTO.

The first ever B-26 to complete 50 combat missions was *Hell Cat*, Serial Number 41-1787s, A B-26B-2 of the 17th Bomb Group (Fig. 5-12). The event occurred in the late spring of 1943 when the group was based at Djedeida, Tunisia. Subsequently *Hell Cat* and her crew, including the crew chief, were sent back to the States to participate in war bond tours all around the country.

18 June: S/Sgt. Clifford W. Wherley, Elmwood, Ill., honorably discharged from the Army as underage at 16. He had been awarded the Air Medal with three Oak Leaf Clusters as a turret gunner on a B-26 in North Africa, having participated in 100 hours of combat time on 21 missions; he had one Me-109 to his credit.

21 June: Marauders battle their way through swarming enemy fighters to batter airfields at Castelventrano, Borizzo, and Milo. They downed two enemy

Fig. 5-12. *Crew Chief Glenn M. Wilson poses proudly before his 50-mission* Hell Cat *as the squadron artist spreads his legs, the better to apply his brush on a special inscription. He's already added the 50th bomb symbol to the 49 others and three swastikas. Note fixed gun barrel protruding from lower right of nose, but no package guns installed at that time. (photo courtesy Jack Gordon)*

aircraft in aerial combat and destroyed numerous grounded planes. Barracks, administration buildings, and dispersal areas were smeared at Castelventrano.

25 June: Marauders help destroy 19 Me-109s and one Macchi 202, maintaining an aerial victory ratio of better that three-to-one since Pantelleria.

9 July: A B-26 unit, created shortly before the fall of Tunisia, completes a 33-day record of amazing caliber. Since Tunis, it made 50 trips over enemy territory, dropped 600 tons of bombs on Pantelleria, and shot down 46 Axis aircraft. Marauders bring to 23 their two-day raid total on Sicily, keeping five landing strips at Garbini under a constant hail of bombs. Burning runways, revetments, and dispersal areas were left behind. (*Author's note:* This dispatch referred to the 320th Bomb Group.)

10 July: Marauders and Baltimores participate in the Sicilian offensive. One B-26 pilot, Lt. N. B. Robins, Wappinger Falls, N.Y., describes the landings: "It was the greatest mass of ships I've ever seen, with 40 miles of boats of all sizes everywhere." The Marauders, in a free-for-all fight, bomb Piozza Ameria, barracks at Palazzollo, and Caltgirone in southeastern Italy.

12 July: The famed Marauder *Coughin Coffin* came to its end after 50 combat missions piloted by Capt. Wm. Pritchard, Mobile, Ala. The plane had

107

its landing gear blown off and fuselage torn to shreds over Sicily, but made a safe belly landing and all its crew walked away from the plane unscathed. Not a single crew member was ever hurt in the 50 missions, although the *Coffin* suffered 120 hits from flak. Its record: Destroyed eight Messerschmitts and three Axis ships, including a cruiser.

An amazing coincidence concerning Pritchard's *Coughin Coffin* was revealed while the author was researching his WWII memorabilia scrapbook. Among the many items pasted in the yellowed pages was a small pamphlet sent out each month by the Lutheran church to its members in the service, called *The Messenger.* It usually contained a couple of stories of religious experiences of service people that were unusual, plus *Reader's Digest*-type quotes of humor, wisdom, etc. This particular issue was saved, after it was received by the author while in B-26 OTU training in October 1943, because the lead story concerned a B-26. This is how it went:

God Bless The Crew

The Stirring Saga of a Providentially Protected Plane

At a war plant in the Middle West, a worker stood watching the final inspection of a Marauder bomber. His thoughts turned to a distant battlefront and to the valiant young Americans who one day soon would claim that plane as their own.

Overcome with emotion and longing in some fashion to help those faraway heroes, he picked up a bit of chalk. In a bold, clear hand he wrote on the side of the plane: "God bless the crew of this plane. I will say a prayer for your safe return."

At length, on the field of an aerial base in North Africa, a Marauder bomber alighted. It was one of many just delivered, but to a certain little group of men it was something very special—their plane. They went over it inch by inch. Presently someone saw the chalked inscription. He beckoned to a companion. Soon the entire crew had gathered. In the awkward silence, the pilot self-consciously removed his cap. The others followed his example. To that sincere supplication each man may well have added his own silent prayer.

The bomber went out on its first mission—and returned safely. It went out again. And again. And again.

The story of the "baptized bomber" spread. An inquiring newsman interviewed the crew. They told him how they had gone into one hazardous exploit after another, always protected as by some spell. "We think," concluded Captain William T. Pritchard, "there's something to that little prayer. Our bomber has successfully completed 19 perilous missions without injury to the crew. If it were just luck, the law of averages would have ruled us out long ago."

In the North African Theater during the stirring weeks that followed, disaster tagged plane after plane. And yet this Marauder bomber kept right on going out—and coming safely back. Twenty-five missions were recorded . . . thirty-five . . . forty-five . . . fifty. No plane faced greater hazards. No crew took longer chances. Yet always the Marauder came back, its crew unscathed. The charmed inscription, now carefully covered with a protective lacquer, stood bright and clear.

Finally came the invasion of Sicily. Our Marauder was among the first to attack. Antiaircraft fire ripped its fuselage to shreds, riddled it with bullet holes, blew off its landing gear . . . Mortally wounded, its mission completed, the bomber turned for home. Somehow, as if in fulfillment of that humble workman's prayer, the great ship held together to bring home its consecrated crew. It made a belly landing at its base—injured beyond repair. But the men jumped out unscathed. So even in the final hour this Marauder was true to its trust.

15 July: Marauders in a 200-plane attack from Lt. Gen. Carl A. Spaatz's North African Air Force pound Messina, Sicily, in relays, hitting railway yards and an antiaircraft position.

19 July: On this beautiful day, Marauders formed the second wave in the two and a half hour attack on Rome, the first ever in Rome's 2697 year history, and the heaviest single raid on any Italian city. Bombs hit military installations (the pilots having been particularly briefed so as not to hit religious or cultural shrines), causing a mustard-colored smoke to rise and be seen from 30 miles. Marauders concentrated on Campino airdrome, eight miles southeast.

24 July: Marauders score numerous hits on parked aircraft and railroad buildings on a heavy raid on the airfields of Aquino, north of Naples. Aquino is the birthplace of St. Thomas Aquinas and Juvenal.

Joe Kingsbury, now of Santa Clara, California, was a bombardier in the 441st Squadron of the 320th Bomb Group and a close friend of pilot Charles O'Mahony. Joe flew 65 missions with the 441st, and was one of the very few combat fliers to have taken color photos during WWII. Some of Joe's best slides are reproduced on the following pages in Figs. 5-13 through 5-21.

29 July: Off the Italian coast, one Marauder fights off eight Me-109s and downs one in a 15-minute running battle. The other seven were downed later by an RAF squadron of Marauders.

1 Aug.: Marauders of the coastal command destroy an Me-323 in running flight off Cape Corse in northern Corsica; 120 enemy troops killed in the German six-engined transport. Other Marauders from same command attacked nine Junkers 52s, damaging three.

6 Aug.: Marauders in battle with 30 enemy aircraft over Catonzaro, downed eight. Blast railway and oil tanks there. Bomb bridges at Augitola in southern Italy.

21 Aug.: Marauders bomb Aversa and Benevento and aid in shooting down 14 enemy aircraft while losing several B-26s. Trains set afire, warehouse and

Fig. 5-13. *A tent on Corsica, 1944—not necessarily the one from the novel of the same name, but indicative of the Spartan living quarters of 441st Squadron's pilot Bill Robinson, on the left, and bombardier Jim Murray. Note pierced steel planking floor scrounged from runway construction engineers. (Joe Kingsbury photo courtesy Charles O'Mahony)*

Fig. 5-14. *Bombardier Joe Kingsbury, second from left, and his combat crew on Corsica, 1944. Because of the short runways on Corsica, the crews removed the package guns to reduce weight. Since German fighter opposition had markedly decreased by then, lighter loads of machine gun ammo were also introduced to save weight. (Joe Kingsbury photo courtesy Charles O'Mahony)*

Fig. 5-15. *Pilot Charles O'Mahony in the cockpit in Corsica, 1944. (Joe Kingsbury photo courtesy Charles O'Mahony)*

111

Fig. 5-16. *Ships of the 320th Bomb Group lining up for takeoff on Corsica, 1944. (Joe Kingsbury photo courtesy Charles O'Mahony)*

Fig. 5-17. *320th on the way to the target on the coast of Italy, 1944. Formation is a bit loose at this point, since no fighter opposition is imminent. (Joe Kingsbury photo courtesy Charles O'Mahony)*

Fig. 5-18. *An excellent shot of the lead ship taken from the Number One wingman position. Notice slight nose-high attitude of the B-55 model in level fight. (Joe Kingsbury photo courtesy Charles O'Mahony)*

Fig. 5-19. *Approaching the target, the formation begins to close up. Note three-ship flights used on this particular mission. (Joe Kingsbury photo courtesy Charles O'Mahony)*

freight sidings destroyed, gas works and public buildings damaged. Lt. W. Hines, Somerset, Ky., navigator-bombardier, brings home a B-26 after pilot has been killed. It was Hines's first landing as a pilot. (*Author's note:* This was one of a number of documented cases of a crewmember other than a pilot bringing home a bomber. Many of the navigators and bombardiers were washed-out pilot cadets before taking up their sextant and bombsight skills. During OTU or RTU training, cross-country, ferry flights, and the like, some of the pilots would give them ''stick time'' in the cockpit. It all paid off in the end.)

23 Aug.: Marauders continue remarkable week-end activity by blasting Salerno rail lines and downing 31 enemy fighters. Today's battle was against 80 enemy fighters, of which the Allied escort shot down two. The B-26 losses were five for the 48-hour period.

Fig. 5-20. *At the IP (Initial Point), the Number Two man of this flight is tucked in close. While a package gun pod is intact on this ship, there is no gun barrel protruding from it. (Joe Kingsbury photo courtesy Charles O'Mahony)*

Fig. 5-21. *Bombs away! Bombs falling from the lead ship clearly show the intervalometer separation. Number One wingman must have been a recent replacement with few missions under his belt, as he is lagging behind.* (*Joe Kingsbury photo courtesy Charles O'Mahony*)

27 Aug.: Marauders raid Grazzinise, destroying enemy fighters in the ensuing air battle. Runways, dispersal areas, hangars, and barracks on the field were destroyed. (*Author's note:* Evidently the intelligence and logistics brains of the 12th AF had decided that this airfield wouldn't be worth occupying, so they went ahead and bombed runways and all.)

31 Aug.: Marauders pummel Aversa, dropping tons of high explosives and scoring many direct hits in the maze of tracks and warehouses. Large fires were seen among freight and tank cars parked on the sidings. Attacked by 25 German fighters, six Marauders down four, and four more probables, and damage two over the Mediterranean. B-26s concentrate on rail junction at Torre Annunziats, near Naples, and in ensuing combat shoot down 16 enemy aircraft along with fighter escort. B-26s accounted for 15.

During August and September the 12th and 340th Bomb Groups and their B-25s were transferred to the 12th Air Force. This left the 9th Air Force with no aircraft, and its headquarters was moved to England to take command of all the medium and light bombardment groups in the ETO as the buildup of air power progressed there.

1 Sep.: Seventy-five enemy fighters jump Marauders and escorts in raid on Aversa and 17 enemy planes were downed. This brought to 360 the total enemy loss since the fall of Sicily—a ratio of better than three to one in Allied victories. Marauders continue to whiplash at Italy's toe, striking La Mazia, Sapri, Pallaro, Peala, and Cantanzaro Marina and in all activities were responsible for a major share in downing 21 enemy aircraft.

11 Sep.: Playing a new role, Marauders help escort and lead Italian Fleet from Nazi-held bases in northern Italy to Allied ports and bases in Sicily and Malta. A lone RAF Marauder, piloted by Wing Commander H. Law-Wright, witnessed the stiff fight in which German bombers finally sank the Italian battleship *Roma*. The ship split in half and sank after putting up a good fight, according to Law-Wright.

12 Sep.: Marauders cut main interior highway from Naples at Migano, 40 miles to the northwest; also strike the Benevento railway yards and a highway near Isernia.

27 Sep.: Continuing the bridge-blasting campaign in central Italy, Marauders blast a bridge at Cancello, another at Ponte, and a third at Ciazzao, all along the Volturno River. Also destroyed a junction at Maddaloni and a bridge at Mignano.

This was as far as the Martin-compiled combat record of the Mediterranean Marauders went. Evidently Martin figured this was more than enough to tell the story. And so it was.

As German fighter opposition began to slack off somewhat, the Maraudermen of the MTO felt that the four package guns were more of a hindrance than they were useful, so they began removing them in order to save weight in the aircraft. Some removed the entire installation, while others only removed the guns and left the pod housings intact.

Jack Gordon supplied Fig. 5-22, an unusual photograph of a 17th Bomb Group Marauder that ended up on its back after a crash-landing in North Africa. No details were available as to how the ship ended up in this position, nor whether or not the crew escaped uninjured, but from the skid marks in the photo, it appears that the ship must have slid along on its back for quite some distance before finally coming to a halt.

Former 17th Bomb Group Armament Flight Chief, Ira S. Guldin, reminisces about a few of his experiences among the devil-may-care B-26 drivers in the MTO:

"Of course, in those days we were all young and nuts. I saw our Squadron CO, a Captain, knock down a pyramidal tent in Sardinia with his prop. He didn't just blow it down on that low pass over the squadron area; his prop actually hit it. He stayed on and I believe made brigadier later.

"I went back to a former airbase in North Africa to check the guns on a plane left there. Coming back to our base, a pilot and an engineer Sergeant flew the plane. On landing, the pilot took his hands off the wheel and let the sergeant land. A perfect landing! You never knew what would happen.

"When we were stationed at Villacidro, Sardinia, they asked me to go along to pick up a new plane at HQ in Cagliari, a 40-mile flight, and check the guns, turrets, etc.

Fig. 5-22. *This unidentified 17th Bomb Group B-26 turned turtle during a crash landing. Note skid marks and rear turret ammunition belts hanging down. Most of the salvageable items have already been stripped from the wreck, including the main landing gear, which was apparently undamaged. The cannibalizing crews are still at it. (photo courtesy Jack Gordon)*

"We got into the new plane to return and going down the runway, at near flying speed, the pilot cut the engines and braked to a sudden stop. I didn't even wait for them to check out what was wrong, but got into the one we came down in to fly back to home base. There was a big poker game scheduled for that evening, and I didn't want to be late for it.

"After takeoff, I was sitting in the navigator's seat and noticed that the pilot was on the deck and he stayed that way. I got up between him and the copilot to watch, and soon we saw a large towered electric line in our path. We climbed over it and then went down on the deck again. He wiggled his wheel left and right and up and down and said something felt funny, but we continued to fly okay.

"Upon landing, I crawled out the navigator's hatch and sat up there going back to our parking spot. When we got there, everybody was looking at the back of the ship and what do you know—no top turret glass! When they got up into the ship to investigate, the guns and the ammo boosting motors were all filled with dead blackbirds! They had come up out of the trees he flew over so low!

"Like I said, we were all nuts back in those days!"

1944-45

Even though the supply lines were somewhat shortened as the Marauder Groups moved from North African bases to the Mediterranean Islands of Sardinia and Corsica and finally to the French mainland, the maintenance problems for aircraft continued to be a detriment, and even some advanced echelon maintenance had to be performed out in the open.

Although living conditions were still on the Spartan side in the islands, at least the troops felt that they were in more civilized territory if only for the fact that the language of the locals was more pleasant to the ear than the guttural Arabic they had been used to in North Africa.

Civilization aside, the realities of combat flying were still with them, and occasional crashes on takeoff still plagued the outfits. An excerpt from a log in Ira S. Guldin's memorabilia states: "On the second mission of 29 February 1944 40 aircraft took off at 1115 hours to bomb active dispersal areas at Veterbo, L/G, SCT #2. *Sweet Sue,* battle number 88, of the 432nd Squadron of the 17th Bomb Group, developed mechanical trouble on takeoff and crashed, killing all seven on board." (Fig. 5-23)

Pierre G. Borodine, now head of an International Marketing Engineering firm in Centerville, Massachusetts, was attending the French college in

Fig. 5-23. *The remains of 17th Bomb Group's* Sweet Sue *after the crash on 29 February 1944. (photo courtesy Ira S. Guldin)*

118

Casablanca when the American forces landed at Fedala (now Mohamedia) in North Africa. A French citizen, raised in Morocco, he soon after joined the Free French Air Force and was stationed at the fighter base in Mecknes just before being sent to the USA for pilot training in 1943.

He received his flight training at Tuscaloosa, Alabama, and wound up becoming a P-47 pilot. Many of his 78 classmates went on to B-26 transition and ended up flying Marauders in North Africa with the Free French Air Force (Figs. 5-24, 5-25). Pierre's fondest memory of Tuscaloosa is summed up in this quote: "The Promised Land was found to be in Tuscaloosa, since 78 lively and frisky Frenchmen found themselves in the midst of 1000 equally frisky coeds of the University of Alabama!"

While American airmen were known for their wild and crazy deeds, they were not exclusive in this aspect by any means, as Borodine attests. While stationed at Mecknes, he saw an FFAF squadron of A-20s land there for refueling and rest. "They had just flown in from Dakar, where they sat the Armistice. The CO had with him a pet lion that was quite accustomed to flying and was, at the time, about eight months old—almost full-grown, you might say.

"Upon landing and having found that his lion was asleep in the airplane, the CO and his crew just left the cockpit canopy open and went to lunch. At some point the lion woke up, smelled the steaks frying in the kitchen of the nearby O club, and decided to investigate. One jump on the wing, another to the ground in front of an astonished and terrified refueling crew, and that lion made a memorable entrance in the O club.

Fig. 5-24. *A couple of Pierre Borodine's flying school classmates and their OTU aircraft at Craig Field, Selma, Alabama in early 1944. (USAAF photo courtesy P. G. Borodine)*

Fig. 5-25. *A Free French Air Force C-45 model B-26 on a combat mission over southern France in late 1944. This was one of the ships transferred to the FFAF from the US 12th Air Force, probably after they'd moved to Corsica, as evidenced by the one package gun in place. (photo courtesy P. G. Borodine)*

"One of the problems was that the Base Commanding General, a stuffy old bird, had just sat down with his staff for lunch. In the ensuing commotion, all except the bomber crews fled through the windows. The General found a youth that he didn't know he possessed, beating several younger officers to the relative safety of a nearby guardhouse.

"The next day, the bomber squadron was ordered to Casablanca to deposit the lion in the local zoo and then on to Marrakech. I heard later that the squadron ended up in Algiers, where eventually it was converted to B-26s. Some of the pilots were assigned to a newly organized P-38 photo squadron serving in the Italy, Rumania, Yugoslavia, Albania, and Greece theater. One of those pilots was Antoine de Saint-Exupery (*Wind, Sun, and Stars*), and the other was my cousin, Commandant Jean Leleu. As for myself, I shortly after that was shipped out to the USA for my own pilot training in Alabama."

The silver FFAF Marauder shown in Fig. 5-25 prompted Jack Gordon to recall that the first F model B-26 in the natural finish to arrive in the Mediterranean theater was for the 37th Squadron when the 17th Bomb Group was based at Villacidro, Sardinia. He remembers listening to the radio on the night after the ship flew its first mission and hearing Axis Sally* declare: "If you boys in the 37th Squadron at Villacidro airdrome want to keep that nice shiny airplane, you had better leave it at home or it won't be coming back to you!"

---

*A British traitor who broadcast propaganda from Berlin during WWII.

Jack says they enjoyed listening to Sally's good music, sexy voice, and usual banter, but when she pinpointed them with that remark, she got their attention for sure. Sally was wrong about the silver ship though, as it finished out the war with around 140 missions (Fig. 5-26).

Strikes against the Italian mainland increased in intensity from the island bases and the 12th Air Force, operating during a good share of its missions in a true tactical role since North Africa, became more involved with close support of the ground troops as the Italian campaign progressed (Figs. 5-27, 5-28).

While still back in Africa, one of the original airplanes of the 17th Bomb Group had blown a tire on takeoff in Liberia and the resulting gyrations had sprung her out of line. Repaired and put back into service, the pilots all complained they had to work their butts off flying her in formation because of her ''dog trot'' flight characteristic. There was no way the mechanics could correct her sprung condition. Flown by itself, it performed very well but trying to hold it in tight formation with other ships wore the pilots to a frazzle.

Jack Gordon relates that when they started receiving replacement aircraft and no longer needed the ship for combat, they removed the turret, guns, armor plate, and other heavy equipment and converted it to a transport ship for the 17th. Being stripped down, this short-wing B-2 would really get out and move

Fig. 5-26. *The silver B-26 that made a liar out of Axis Sally. S/Sgt. Matlock is standing before* Starduster *in May 1944. (photo courtesy Jack Gordon)*

121

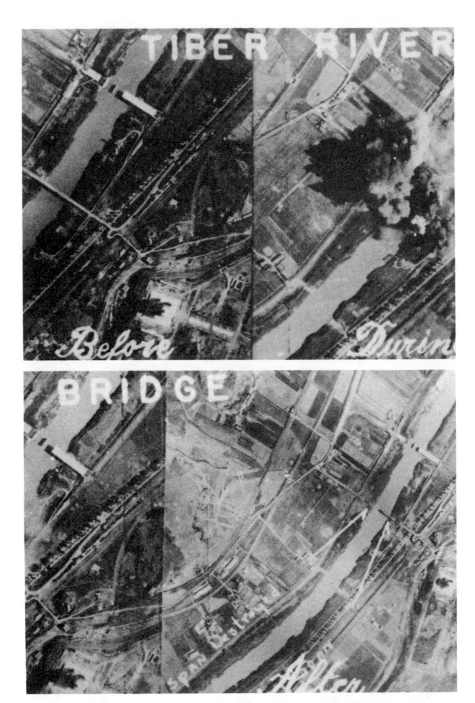

Fig. 5-27. *An example of the precision bombing results achieved by Marauders from medium altitude. Before, during, and after sequence of a Tiber River bridge hit by the 17th Bomb Group. (photo courtesy Ira S. Guldin)*

Fig. 5-28. *320th bomb Group Bob Dinwiddie's ship on single engine returning from a 1944 bombing mission. They didn't make it all the way back to the base, but ditched off the coast of Corsica. All survived. (Joe Kingsbury photo courtesy Charles O'Mahony)*

but was exceedingly noseheavy and Jack says the service squadron "had to keep fixin' the nose gear."

Even though she was no longer flying combat, she still had to have a name and was called the *Flagship* of *The Fryjack Airlines, Inc.* (Fig. 5-29). The airline name was a combination of the names of two 37th Squadron Captains—Frymire and Jackson. In the summer of 1944, she was given to the French for use as a trainer.

Dave Mickelson, now of Sunnyvale, California, didn't join the 444th Squadron of the 320th Bomb Group until 27 August 1944, but amassed a total of 61 combat missions in the eight months before being rotated back to the States three days after V-E Day. His experiences were nonetheless as traumatic as those of the old-timers in the outfit, and the excerpts from his diary quoted here and the photos from his album add just another personal touch to the Marauder saga in the MTO.

Dave's airplane (combat No. 75) was distinctive in the fact that she carried three different names. While flying the ship to Sardinia over the southern Atlantic route, the right engine started cutting out over the South American jungles and an emergency landing was made at Zandery, Dutch Guiana. A change of spark plugs solved the problem, and the ship continued on its journey with the crew naming her *Jungle Happy.*

Soon after arriving in Sardinia, *Donna Deloris* was painted on the right side of the nose, with the shark's teeth logo of the 444th Squadron added under the nose (Figs. 5-30, 5-31).

In October, the official squadron nose art painter, Vernon Prince of Heath, Ohio, received permission to paint his girl friend's picture on the left side of the nose of #75 and added the name *Maria* (Fig. 5-32).

123

Fig. 5-29. *Captain "Smiley" Newbern poses at the nose of the 17th Group's transport ship in May 1944, just before she was turned over to the French. (photo courtesy Jack Gordon)*

Fig. 5-30. *Mickelson's crew on the* Donna Deloris *side of his ship. Standing, L to R: Tail gunner Silas A. Ross, Engineer Raymond V. James, Pilot Mickelson (displaying typical mission lunch of V-8 juice and peanut butter sandwich), Copilot Everett Liebenderfer; kneeling, L to R: Radioman John Pozniak, Bombardier Vernon Larrabee, and Cameraman Charles Bennet. Corsica, Sep. 1944. (photo courtesy Dave Mickelson)*

Fig. 5-31. *Old "Three-Name" #'75 taxiing out for takeoff on a mission to bomb a fuel dump near Cremola, Italy. Some crewmembers liked to ride emerged from the navigators astrodome hatch while taxiing. This was their equivalent of some pilots' practice of taxiing with one arm hung out the opened window of the plane in a "hot pilot" drape. Corsica, 30 Sep. 1944. (photo courtesy Dave Mickelson)*

Fig. 5-32. *#75 flying over the Brenner Pass in Northern Italy on Mickelson's 13th. Princess Maria sits atop the shark's teeth on the nose. October 1944. (photo courtesy Dave Mickelson)*

125

Mickelson describes his sixth mission:

"Flak is fascinating and today we found out how much so. Junior, Larry, Jesse and I flew again in old *Jungle Happy* on an afternoon mission to take out a couple of bridges on the north side of the Po Valley, about 20 miles from the Adriatic Sea. We had a formation of four squadrons—36 planes—to bomb two bridges, a two-track railroad bridge and a road bridge. We were briefed on two batteries of flak guns—one of four guns which we had to fly right over on our bomb run, and a battery of eight heavy guns to our left just beyond the target, and if we made a sharp break we would only be in range of the eight guns for a short time, maybe 30 seconds.

"The mission went like all the rest except it was a little longer. Right after we opened the bomb bay doors on the bomb run, those four guns opened up on us and did they show us some shooting! We were in the second squadron, following the first by about 200 or 300 yards, and 200 to 300 feet lower. Those four guns threw up shells at us, and they all went off at once in a small patch about 50 feet apart just midway between the first squadron and us.

"Right in front of us those black little puffs were appearing—four of them coming out of nowhere every four to six seconds. Innocent little things they seemed to be. We would fly right through the black cloud with no effect except the smell of gunpowder. All down the run those guns kept tracking us with amazing accuracy, except they didn't actually get mixed up in the squadron.

"I had my camera out and for a while didn't know what to do. I wanted to take a picture of the bombs coming out of the lead ships, but wanted to get a picture of some flak, too. I only had three exposures left, and it suddenly dawned on me to take some pictures of this amazing spectacle we were witnessing (Figs. 5-33, 5-34). I quickly snapped one of some flak, wound it like mad and got one of the lead squadron dropping their bombs, then I wound the camera again, our squadron dropped, more flak, and what I did with the camera then I don't know. Maybe I will know when I develop the film, but I know I did have my finger on the switch that closes the bomb bay doors and I did see three flak bursts quite close. The fourth burst that I didn't see, which would have completed the patch, and which I figured from the position of the other three should have been right on top of us, for some reason or other or by the Grace of God or something didn't go off.

"With our bombs away, we broke and broke fast! They knew we were going to break, which way, how fast, and how much altitude we were going to lose, because all through that 180-degree diving turn those four flak bursts kept coming up at us. They weren't quite as close, but they were still up there. After we completed the turn, we were out of range and could relax. It was then that I looked back and saw what they shot up at us. I must have seen 250 black clouds of what once were flak bursts. Those eight guns added to it, but all those bursts were behind us so they didn't thrill as much. One plane's engine was smoking a bit, and one fellow was leaking gas, but that was about our extent of damage. We thought sure we had some holes, but didn't find a one after

Fig. 5-33. *Mickelson's first shot, on the mission described in the text, caught the flak bursts between the first and second box on the bomb run. Fourth burst is out of sight to the left. 9 Sep. 1944. (photo courtesy Dave Mickelson)*

Fig. 5-34. *Second shot shows first squadron dropping bombs on the Nervessa RR bridge and the flak bursts getting closer to the second squadron. Dave never did reveal how his third shot came out. 9 Sep. 1944. (photo courtesy Dave Mickelson)*

landing. We hit the bridge good and did a 100 percenter except for one ship. He toggled a little late. The other two squadrons, who had the other bridge, got a 100 percent mission. When you are on two 100 percent missions you get an Air Medal, and a cluster for every one after that. Jesse has three already, with me none.''

Author's Note: Criteria for the awarding of the Air Medal in the MTO was based on bombing accuracy, as Mickelson states, while in the ETO it was awarded strictly on the number of missions flown—after five, the Medal was awarded, and for each five flown thereafter an Oak Leaf Cluster was awarded.

For a look at the off-duty side of life on Corsica, we're privileged to read this little squib from Dave's diary: ''I finally got to Bastia Wednesday night with B.H., who had talked his way into getting a Jeep. Bastia is the largest city on the island, about 20 miles north along the ocean and similar to Cagliari of Sardinia except it is French and not Italian. Both are harbor towns with part of the city extending up into the hills. I never did eat in Cagliari, but food is hard to find in Bastia. You can eat at the Army mess if you are in town on official business and have orders. The PX hasn't much at all, so it doesn't pay to go there for that. You can get ice cream, cookies, and coffee at the officer's Red Cross Club, which is one of the few places to go in town if you don't want to go into a bar, of which there are several. The Red Cross also has a barber and reading and game room.

''To eat, we found a black-market restaurant which was located in the front room of one of the homes of Bastia. It was on the second floor. The food was fair, but the change of eating at a table with chairs, instead of off the ground, and being served, was well worth the $5 it cost us.''

Regardless of the theater of operations they were in, Maraudermen who weren't scheduled to fly a mission often went down to the flight line to sweat out the return of a mission on which their buddies had flown. Mickelson relates one such incident: ''It was becoming twilight and quite cold, with no wind. Maybe it was the stillness, but the cold crept through one's body at a much faster rate than it should have. We just came down from the Squadron area to sweat out the late afternoon's mission, as someone heard Poling's ship was kinda shot up. This was the first time I ever sweated out the mission's landing, and as we stood in front of the control tower watching the planes rounding the pattern, waiting for the first one to come in, I began to realize how different it was watching the show from the ground than in on the flying of it.

''I don't know if I was scared or if it was the cold or maybe it was the fact that these planes, as they came in on their final approach just ready to set down, passed over what used to be a B-26 and a good crew, which earlier in the day had a little trouble and never took off, but I shivered as I watched.

''As each plane hit the runway with a roar—not from the engines, but from the impact of the plane's tires and the steel mat runway at 130 mph—I thought about the other plane and crew that should have been coming in and landing on this mission.

"Down they came, one, two, three, hitting that runway with a roar and holding that roar most all the way to the end, making no other noise except the muffled backfires of the engines letting off steam or personal satisfaction after putting on quite a piece of work during the afternoon. The planes completed their run down the runway, an okay wave to 'Doc,' who is always down there in a Jeep to see his boys return and then forgotten, off the stage and out of the show they go in the eyes of the audience, who now switch their attention to the next landing."

Author's note: "Doc" was the group chaplain. It was common practice for these dedicated men to be at the takeoff end of the runway at the start of each mission to give their charges a "thumbs-up" sign as they started their takeoff roll, and then to be at the opposite end of the runway upon their return to greet them. As Dave intimated, it was unfortunate that this was probably the only time some crewmembers saw their chaplain.

Evidently Dave wasn't as superstitious as some, because the entry in his diary for his 13th mission calls it just that and not #12-A, as many called it. The account of this milestone goes like this:

"This day started off just like any other day, with better weather, but just as cold. Hard to get out of bed, get to the mess hall, then down some black coffee and toast, butter, and marmalade, and then lay around a half-hour until briefing or until the mission was called off. The day before I predicted this one would go, and go it did. We hadn't dropped bombs on the enemy for two weeks.

"Briefing went off as usual and we got down to our planes in plenty of time before engine starting time. Fighters might be expected, so we talked over our defense until time to crank up. About this time, Jesse sees a column of black smoke coming from the 319th Field, immediately followed by an explosion, which meant but one thing, a plane going up in smoke. That column of smoke rose from that spot until we took off and left the island, but that was all we knew about it. Later, I found out it was a Beaufighter that burnt up on takeoff.

"Our target was the vulnerable railroad line that goes up the Brenner Pass, the only link from Germany to Italy. Things went mighty smooth except for a couple of incidents on our bomb run.

"At the tip of Lake Garta there is a town, and outside of that town the Germans have set up a new battery of flak guns. Little did I know what I was looking at until I saw some orange flashes on the ground. Immediately I thought, 'I wonder how close they will come?' Eight long seconds of waiting and I had the answer. We were just outside the range of that battery. Those little black puffs were on our altitude, but about a half-mile short.

"A little farther down the run, Number Two ship's right engine started to smoke to beat hell, and for an instant it looked like he would break out of formation, taking one or two planes with him. A little engine trouble, but Ramage held his position, losing only a little ground while he babied the engine along and got the kinks out of it. The smoking stopped and he and the right side of the formation were just able to get into position before bombs were away. The rest of the mission went off without a hitch, except for the Me-109 Jesse thought he saw 7,000 feet below us."

It may seem odd to connect a G.I. latrine with an aircraft crash, but the connection appears in Mickelson's diary. In this case the latrine had to be the most widely traveled one in the entire MTO. The 444th Squadron built it in North Africa, moved it to Sardinia, took it with them to Corsica, and finally moved it to France, where it was located in the middle of the front lawn of a chateau in which Dave and some squadron mates lived—nothing like giving it a place of honor! The chateau was in the village of Besse, near the DiJon airbase, where the 320th and 17th groups were stationed.

From Fig. 5-35 it is difficult to understand why this particular creature-comfort device was selected for extensive transfer, but selected it was! Maybe the fact that this particular "eight-holer" was considered to be deluxe from an engineering standpoint had something to do with it.

The latrine-crash connection appears in Mickelson's diary just after his description of his 13th mission on an October morning in 1944:

"It was just 2:30. I remember it well, as I had just left Larry at the PX tent to sweat out a line for rations. I was going back to help him carry our stuff home at quarter to three, but was delayed and never did get there until 4:15.

"I had just come from the tent where I had picked up a roll of toilet paper and was headed for the latrine. I don't know how I said it or why, but I remember

Fig. 5-35. *The intercontinent-hopping 444th Squadron latrine on location some 50 yards from Mickelson's tent on Corsica. The three occupants seem to be enjoying their call of nature. October 1944. (photo courtesy Dave Mickelson)*

saying in the tent that I wished we were stationed at the field up the way that was used in this area for crash-landings, as it had no steel matting and so I could take some pictures of the crashes.

"For some reason or other while going to the latrine, I turned and looked back at the tent and then at a column of smoke coming up from the end of the runway or thereabouts. I walked back to the tent, laid down the paper, picked up my camera and said, 'I think we have a plane at the end of the runway that didn't make it.'

"Off I started in a walk toward the pillar of smoke. One block from the tent was a road and on it, as I reached it, was a truck that had stopped to pick up a few fellows who had the same idea as me—to get to the smoke to see what was making it. The truck was about to start when a muffled thud was heard. It was the plane at the base of the column of smoke and that was its gas tanks going off. I snapped a picture of it and off we went.

"All heads were turned toward the pillar of smoke, which now wasn't a column but an ever-increasing billow of smoke like a giant colorful flower—but, under the circumstances, not so beautiful. We drove to a position about even with the control tower, which is located halfway down the runway. We were about three quarters of a mile away. We stopped by instinct as we came over the crest of the hill as everyone we saw there was like statues, standing on top of planes, trucks, hills, and all over with their eyes in one direction, not saying a word.

"Then, again, the base of the smoke suddenly blossomed out in a majestic mushroom of orange flame. I snapped a picture (Fig. 5-36) and then the noise hit us. It was the bomb load going off. Everybody hit the ground, but I took another picture. The driver was crying and wanted to get out of there quick.

"The pilot of the ship was Schane from Class 25 at Lake Charles. Didn't anyone get out? No one knew. How did it happen? No one knew. After about three minutes the crowd got braver and started approaching the scene of the accident. I walked, but most of them rode by me like hell on some kind of transportation or other. I wasn't in too much of a hurry, as there might be another 500-pounder laying around ready to go off. One of the eight bombs never did go off.

"As I drew near, I could see the tire marks where the plane left the runway and went to its final resting place (Fig. 5-37). The left tire had blown out a little past the tower and Schane cut the throttles and tried to stop before the end of the runway. The plane, with its load of bombs, didn't stop but went off the runway, hit an embankment about four feet high, and then traveled about 50 more yards and stopped amid flames.

"The pilot and copilot were thrown clear and Doc had raced into the plane to drag out the engineer. The other two men went with the plane. That's the second time Doc ran into a burning plane to save a man. Too much cannot be said about him!

Fig. 5-36. *One of the bombs exploding in the crash, creating the lighter colored mushroom-shaped cloud. The darker smoke at upper left is from the fuel tanks, which had exploded a few minutes earlier. Corsica, October 1944. (photo courtesy Dave Mickelson)*

Fig. 5-37. *Tire skid marks are visible in this photo showing approach to the crash site. Corsica, October 1944. (photo courtesy Dave Mickelson)*

132

"The ammunition was still going off when I got to the remains of the ship. The crash crew was on the ball though, and stopped the remaining fires in short order. All that was left intact of the plane were two pieces of wing and a part of the tail section. There were three holes in the ground about four feet deep and 10 feet in diameter, but for some reason the holes were four feet apart at the edges (Fig. 5-38).

"The two props were way down the field, mangled in the dirt. I saw one cylinder head and part of the auxiliary section of one engine; the pilot's armor-plated seat was in one piece, but down the field, kinda twisted.

"When the armorers came to remove the live bomb, the people went home, some to eat and later to go to a movie in the bright moonlight. The show was good and funny, but ended, and the fellows slowly and quietly ambled home as the moon gave off its last welcomed light before disappearing behind a cloud."

Three more of Mickelson's wartime photos are shown in Figs. 5-39 through 5-41.

Howard R. Baxter, now of Marion, Indiana, was a T/Sgt. with the 444th Squadron of the 320th Bomb Group and had a unique experience in the MTO. Here's the story in Baxter's own words:

Fig. 5-38. *Mangled wreckage at the crash scene, with one of the bomb craters behind the man running at the left center. Corsica, October 1944. (photo courtesy Dave Mickelson)*

Fig. 5-39. *A flight of the 444th Squadron crossing the coast of Italy on 8 November 1944 to bomb the San Astasia railroad bridge. The lead ship is a B-10 model that still had the flexible tail gun installation. (photo courtesy Dave Mickelson)*

Fig. 5-40. *A P-47 of the 86th Fighter Group joins a 444th flight headed for home in Corsica after bombing the Ala, Italy, railroad bridge on 10 November 1944. Mickelson states that there were a few Me-109s in the area at the time. The lead ship is a new one that hadn't yet received the 444th's distinctive shark's teeth paint job. (photo courtesy Dave Mickelson)*

Fig. 5-41. *The 444th Squadron Headquarters at Besse, France, about five miles from the DiJon air base. Mickelson says this shot was taken in December 1944, and in January the mud finally froze up for a month or two. (photo courtesy Dave Mickelson)*

"Headquarters 12th Air Force at Bari, Italy, contacted the 320th Bomb Group in late 1943, asking for a B-26 for Maj. Gen. Doolittle's temporary use as Commanding General of the 12th Air Force. Since I, as crew chief and flight engineer, had gotten a new plane from the States, Headquarters asked me if I would be interested in going on detached service to the 12th Air Force for a few days—which turned out to be nine months. I also flew this plane as copilot or engineer with Brig. Gen. Earl Partridge, Doolittle's Chief of Staff." (*Author's Note:* Evidently Doolittle's regular B-26 was out of commission or out of pocket at the time. Maybe it was off on an extended booze-finding junket.)

"After General Doolittle left the 12th Air Force and went to the 8th Air Force in England, the B-26 stayed in Bari. It was flown to Sardinia in early spring of 1944. On takeoff we experienced a runaway prop and had to return to the base for repairs. We left Sardinia late, and due to thunderstorms in the area were forced to fly south and come up through the southern tip of Italy, further delaying us.

"The Bari airfield had no landing lights, and with dusk upon us we were forced to land short of our destination, somewhere in southern Italy. We located what we thought looked like a paved strip, but after committing ourselves to landing, discovered it was a plowed field. I believe it was an act of God that we, and the plane, survived the landing in the soft soil.

Fig. 5-42. *Baxter's B-26B-10 stuck in the mud. Note that, like a good crew chief, Baxter had tied on the nose and pilot's compartment protective cover until the ship was ready to fly again. This model still had the old flexible tail stinger. (photo courtesy Howard R. Baxter)*

"The aircraft sat in this field, as shown in the photo (Fig. 5-42), for approximately six to eight weeks, when the Army engineers laid down a steel mat runway approximately 2000 feet long in order to fly the plane out. After some coercion by a 1st Lt. (name unknown), he and I flew the airplane out and returned her to Bari.

"About three weeks later it was flown to North Africa by an Army Air Force captain (pilot) and a captain of the infantry (copilot), (names unknown). On landing and taxiing down the strip, the pilot called for flaps up and the infantry captain pulled the landing gear out from under the plane, and that was the end of B-26 41-18295."

In December 1944, the 319th Bomb Group was changed over to B-25s and was finally rotated back to the States in January 1945. December also saw the 17th and 320th Groups, along with two French B-26 Groups, formed into the 42nd Wing of the First Tactical Air Force, Provisional. They had played a major role in the invasion of southern France on 15 August 1944, and now were flying in direct support of the 7th Army. This left the 12th Air Force composed entirely of A-20s and B-25s (Figs. 5-43 through 5-51).

Performance reporting methods had changed somewhat from those in the South Pacific, but the statistics represent each group's complete battle record from start to finish. The only figures found in their entirety at the Maxwell AFB archives were those of the 319th Bomb Group (B-26 only):

Number of Missions	469
Number of Sorties	10,518
Target Types Hit	
Railroad Bridges	246
Road Bridges	72

Road Targets	28
Marshalling Yards	35
Railroad Targets	10
Airdromes	34
Shipping	12
Dock Facilities	9
Gun Positions	44
Command Posts	17
Dumps	9

Aircraft Losses

Flak	50
Enemy Fighter	27
Other	23
Percentage	.0073

Victories

Enemy Aircraft Destroyed in Air	119
Enemy Aircraft Probably Destroyed in Air	55
Enemy Aircraft Damaged in Air	71

Last Mission Flown on 31 December 1944.

Fig. 5-43. *A flight of the 441st Squadron, 320th Bomb Group, heading back to their DiJon base after a mission in southern France. (Joe Kingsbury photo courtesy Charles O'Mahony)*

Fig. 5-44. *A P-47 escort ship playing around the 320th formation on a mission in late 1944. Note the droppable belly tank on the '47, an early "Razorback" model. (Joe Kingsbury photo courtesy Charles O'Mahony)*

The losses due to enemy action had decreased considerably from those experienced in the Pacific, and this was due in most part to the change in tactics, improvements to the airplane, and better defensive armament. The latter no doubt also accounted for the increased victories over enemy aircraft in the air.

The 320th had similar successes and bombed the same type of targets, but the only figures found were these:

Number of Missions	583
Aircraft Losses (All due to enemy action)	80
Victories	
Enemy Aircraft Destroyed in Air	84
Enemy Aircraft Probably Destroyed in Air	37
Enemy Aircraft Damaged in Air	52

Last Mission Flown on 1 May 1945.

The amazing fact about these figures is that while no accounting is made of aircraft lost on takeoff crashes, there were evidently no losses due to mechanical failure or weather.

Last but by no means least is the record of the "grandpappy" of all medium bomber groups in WWII, the 17th, the oldest medium group in the AAF. Not only was it famous for this distinction, but, as mentioned before, the crews for the Doolittle Tokyo raid came from its ranks, cadres for both the 319th and

Fig. 5-45. *First Tactical Air Force Marauder from the 95th Squadron losing an engine from a direct flak hit near Toulon, France, in December 1944. There were only two survivors. (USAAF photo)*

320th were pulled from it, and various other members were transferred to newly forming bomb groups that eventually ended up in the ETO.

Why, with all this going for it, its records in the archives at Maxwell are the skimpiest is not known. Probably its biggest accomplishment was racking up a total of 606 combat missions during its tour in the MTO, more than any

Fig. 5-46. *34th Squadron ships of the First TAC coming off a smoke-laden target in southern France, December 1944. (USAAF photo courtesy Glenn L. Martin Co.)*

Fig. 5-47. *A four-ship flight of the 444th Squadron, 320th Bomb Group at point of "bombs away" on a mission over France in the spring of 1945. Note seventh bomb of the string of 500-pounders just emerging from the Number Four ship's bomb bay and the intervalometer spacing of the lead ship's bombs. (photo courtesy Howard R. Baxter)*

Fig. 5-48. *Late in the war the Luftwaffe launched cannon-firing Me-262 jet fighters against Marauder groups as well as the heavies. This shows the damage inflicted on the wing of a ship from the 320th Bomb Group. Fortunately, the shells were duds and passed through without exploding. Had they exploded, they could have blown the wing off. (Joe Kingsbury photo courtesy Charles O'Mahony)*

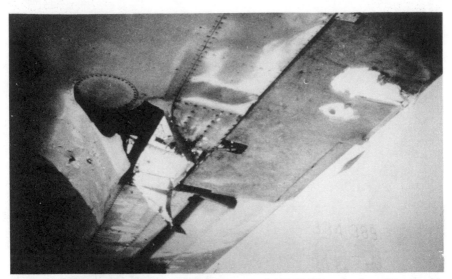

Fig. 5-49. *View of the Me-262 cannon shell damage to the 320th Marauder from the underside of the wing. (Joe Kingsbury photo courtesy Charles O'Mahony)*

Fig. 5-50. *This 441st Squadron, 320th BG, Marauder was not so fortunate and lost most of a wing from a direct flak hit while attacking a northern Italy railroad bridge in late 1944. Note right aileron in "full up" position. Evidently the pilot was making a valiant effort to right the ship. Besides knocking off the tip of the left elevator, the outer wing tore off most of the rudder as it flew by. There were no survivors. (photo courtesy Charles O'Mahony)*

Fig. 5-51. *Crash-landing result of the last plane to be shot down from the 320th BG at the end of the war. Copilot Paul Ramsey is standing beside* Lady Lynn, *which he landed when the pilot's injuries were serious enough to render him incapable of landing. May 1945. (photo courtesy Charles O'Mahony)*

other Marauder group in WWII. Most assuredly that unknown Marauder with 336 missions had to be in the 17th. Their last mission was flown 1 May 1945, and not only did they fly one that day, but they went out in a blaze of glory by flying *two*.

At the annual reunions of the 17th Bomb Group, Jack Gordon, the 37th Squadron's representative, is given the red carpet treatment by all the other members and this is the reason why:

Jack has been a model airplane builder and enthusiast for many years and has built many gas-powered flying models, which he still flies occasionally with his flying club at the site of the old WWII Greenville, Mississippi, Army Air Field Basic Flying Training base.

Probably the pride of his fleet is a one-inch-to-the-foot-scale model of one of his favorite 37th Squadron B-26s, *Package for Adolf,* combat number 28 (Fig. 5-52). This model is on display at each year's unit reunion and is shipped to the site knocked down, in a specially designed two-by-three-by-five-foot box which has the fuselage, wings, tail section, engines, props, and landing gear all cradled separately in shock-resistant mounts.

Jack often meticulously reassembles her and she occupies a place of honor at the reunion for all his old buddies to admire. Many faraway looks develop in their misted-up eyes as they lightly run their fingers over her surfaces.

Fig. 5-52. *Jack Gordon's display model on the Greenville runway. 17th Bomb Group vets have difficulty determining that this photo is not of the original ship. (photo courtesy Jack Gordon)*

Jack had originally intended her to be a flying model and she is built to do just that, special engines and all. However, after the first showing at a reunion some years back, his 17th BG pals threatened to shoot him at sunrise if he ever subjected this beauty to the possibilities of a crack-up!

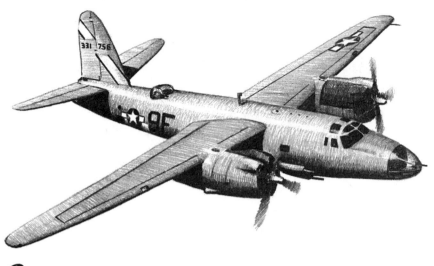

6

COMBAT, PHASE THREE:
Maturity as a Fighting Machine

The Marauder was really to come into its own in the European Theater with the eight medium bombardment groups of the 9th Air Force, but the second mission run was a disaster. Why the top brass didn't heed the lessons learned in the Pacific, where low-level missions were marginal at best, and from the Mediterranean operations, where medium altitude bombing was highly successful, will forever remain a mystery, but it was decided to send them on their first ETO mission at low level.

1943

17 May: Lt. Clayton F. Allen, Binghampton, N.Y., participates in B-26 raid on Antwerp, Belgium. This was the first news of Marauders going over the English Channel from British bases.

This press dispatch was not entirely true. Maybe it was the first time the press was allowed to *report* a Marauder operation out of England, but the Air Force knew better. Considering what had taken place on the first two missions, it's just as well the Air Force kept the events under wraps. Here's what actually happened:

On 14 May, 12 Marauders of the 322nd Bomb Group, then based at Bury St. Edmunds, Essex, were sent to attack the Velsen generating station at Ijmuiden, Holland, the location of the big German sub pens. They flew through heavy flak at from 100 to 300 feet and placed their 20-minute delay-fused 500-pound bombs on the target with no loss of aircraft at the drop point. However, one ship had to abort due to 20mm cannon hits on the way in and headed back to England, jettisoning his bombs in the sea and making an emergency landing at a British base still under construction at the time.

The 20mm cannons also damaged two other ships in the target area, one of which made an emergency landing at the Nonington Air Depot after orbiting for an hour while the crew repaired the emergency landing gear system, which had been damaged when the main system was shot out. Only the nosewheel of the other ship's gear would come down and, after orbiting the home base for around half an hour with no success in improving the situation, the crew elected to bail out. Five men made it down safely, but before the pilot could get out of the ship, it went into a spiral. It crashed and burned, killing him.

A low-altitude attack had been chosen for the mission for two reasons: to take advantage of the element of surprise to escape detection, and for accuracy in the placement of the bombs on the target. Even though the group was now equipped with the greatly improved B model of the B-26, the famous Norden bombsight was not being used. They were relying on a modified N-6 gunsight mounted in the cockpit for the copilot to use in releasing the bombs. This sight had been used in Africa for zero-level attacks because the D-8 bombsight required an altitude of at least 500 feet to be effective, preferably 1000 feet. Since no bombardier was required, a compass was installed in the plexiglass nose of the 322nd ships and the navigator rode up there for more positive recognition of landmarks and the target area.

Conjecture has it that the only reason this first mission had in fact escaped detection by the Luftwaffe fighters was because they had been distracted by an intense air battle between their interceptors and the heavy bombers of the 8th Air Force over the German Bight at the time.

Intelligence reports from subsequent recon flight photos indicated that the delayed fuses of the bombs had probably enabled the Dutch workers to escape and allowed the Germans time to defuse or remove the bombs before any appreciable damage had occurred. Consequently, a second mission was scheduled for 17 May, again at low level. Group officers' objections of extreme danger because of the now-alerted German defenses were overruled, and the mission took off as scheduled.

Eleven aircraft took off and only one—which had aborted over the channel on the way out due to electrical failure—came back! Heavy flak was encountered, and the lead ship, flown by CO Colonel Robert M. Stillman, was the first to go down. Another ship took a direct hit and collided with a third, with both going down as a result. A fourth went down from flak and two more were downed by flak near Haarlem. On the return flight, the remaining four ships were jumped by Me-109s and all were shot down (Fig. 6-1).

After this tragic beginning, operations were discontinued, Norden bombsights were installed in the lead ships, and the group was put through

Fig. 6-1. *A painting,* Lowland Dutch, *shows B-26s on a low-level raid over Holland. This does not depict the strike at Ijmuiden, however, as the ships in the painting carry the tail insignia of the 344th Bomb Group, which did not fly its first mission until March of 1944. (painting by Emmett Lancaster)*

intensive training for bombing at medium altitudes, the purpose for which the airplane had been designed. Even so, B-26s in OTU training at MacDill Field and its satellite bases were still practicing skip-bombing and strafing on Mullet Key in Tampa Bay!

As a portent of what was to come, no news was heard of the ETO Marauders until this dispatch came out:

6 Aug.: Eighth Air Force headquarters disclose that all American medium bomber operations from England to Western Europe since May have been achieved by B-26 Martin bombers. First raid in May over Velsen at "zero" altitude—just skimming the treetops—and no planes lost but 10 lost on second raid. On 16 July resumed operations over Abbeville, at medium altitude from 10,000 to 15,000 feet, and since have made raids on 11 targets and have lost two planes. B-26s carried bomb loads of 2,460 pounds and have a speed of 330 miles per hour. Low-level operations with violent zigzagging makes them comparatively safe against enemy radar, but makes them vulnerable to flak.

At the time of this dispatch, the 9th Air Force Headquarters had not yet moved to England from North Africa and Marauders were still assigned to the 8th. It was a feeble attempt at brushing over what had happened at Ijmuiden, but now maybe Magruder could breathe easier after seeing the 10,000 to 15,000 foot altitude factor become a reality in print as well as in practice.

147

The last sentence in the dispatch had to be the understatement of the year, and the "330 miles per hour" speed was purely a figment of someone's imagination. Perhaps a Martin technical representative assigned to the 322nd and some high-ranking general who truly believed in the B-26 had influenced the reporter in order to tout the airplane. They couldn't be faulted for this, if it happened, because at that point the airplane needed all the support it could get.

Maybe those early B models with less armor plate than later ones, and with less than a full load of bombs, ammunition, and fuel could attain 330 mph after dropping their bombs and diving away from the target. In actuality, when the 9th Air Force was at full strength the following year, the groups bombed at a standard 185 mph and maybe would reach 200 to 250 mph at best in a diving turn off the target. Even these higher speeds off the target were discouraged in order to assure maintaining a tight formation for defense against fighters.

Of course, they were then carrying bomb loads of 4,000 pounds, in addition to full loads of fuel and ammunition. Depending upon the target, bomb loads were either two 2000-pounders, four 1000-pounders, eight 500-pounders, or 16 250-pounders. When the special 200-pound fragmentation bombs were carried, 26 were hung on the bomb racks, which brought the maximum load up to 5200 pounds.

Elaborating on the portent of what was to come, the 8th Air Force, being the larger of the two USAAF Force-size units in the ETO, and participating in more spectacular raids deep into the German heartland later on, received the lion's share of the publicity. It always galled Maraudermen to read a full-column account of the 8th's activities in the London *Times* or the U.S. Army *Stars and Stripes* newspapers that ended with a short, one-sentence squib: "Mediums were also out," or "Marauders and Havocs of the 9th Air Force also bombed airfields and rail junctions in Northern France."

Hopefully this account will prove that the 9th played a significant and important role in the ETO as well. Ask any ex-ETO infantryman what boosted his morale more, a Marauder group bombing enemy ground positions and P-47s diving down to bomb and strafe the Wermacht, or a gaggle of Forts or Libs making beautiful contrails in the blue on their way to bomb a ball bearing plant.

Meanwhile, three more Marauder groups became operational in July and August—the 323rd at Earls Cone, the 386th at Great Dunmow, and the 387th at Stony Cross, all in county Essex. They were still assigned to the 8th AF, as the newly transferred 9th didn't take over until September. At that time all medium bomb groups in Great Britain, future groups to come over, as well as three light bombardment groups of Douglas A-20 Havocs still to come and the various and assorted fighter groups involved were transferred to the 9th (Fig. 6-2).

13 Aug.: Marauders attack German airdrome at Poix, France, 35 miles inland south of Somme. Attack St. Omer airfield in France and railroad yards at Abbeville.

Fig. 6-2. *First B-26 (a B model) to be delivered directly to the war zone from the factory taxiing out for takeoff at the Martin Baltimore airport 13 November 1943. This one could have gone to either the MTO or ETO as a replacement aircraft; ferry pilots of the Air Transport Command usually flew these replacement aircraft over. Note fixed gun still in place in lower right of nose and ammo box just above it. (photo courtesy Glenn L. Martin Co.)*

19 Aug.: Marauders raid airfield at Woensdrecht, Holland, and near Lille, France. These were among eight daylight raids made in four days over European targets without the loss of a B-26. Men who fly B-26s in England call it "the sweetest airplane in the air" and say "we're the ones who are flying them and we like them." Col. Lester Y. Maitland, former Clark Field Commander in the Phillipines and now a leader of B-26s in England, says, "The B-26 in skilled hands is no more dangerous than any other aircraft. Statistically, the B-26 has had a remarkably high record in operations. In combat, these airplanes are able to take severe punishment from flak and still get home." Other Marauder pilots say, "The B-26 is a go-to-battle son-of-a-gun; sure, she needs a little attention and upkeep, but you can't feed Man-O-War* on potatoes, either."

If Magruder didn't put this testimony in a gilt-edged frame and hang it on his office wall at the Martin Middle River Plant, he should have! At least the Air Force was utilizing the power of the pen to keep the wolves at bay.

20 Aug.: Marauders blast airfields at Poix and Amiens-Ghissy, downing one enemy aircraft. Marauder losing altitude rapidly dumps extra load into English Channel. After dropping 8000 feet to 1800-foot altitude, the B-26 was leveled off by pilot James A. Gianatisis, New York. It returned safely to base.

---

*A famous race horse of the period.

28 Aug.: A B-26 piloted by Lt. Floyd A. Blackbury, Denver, Colo., downs two Me-109s over France while participating in a raid on Poix airfield.

31 Aug.: Marauders attack St. Omer in France and return without a loss. Blast German airfield at Lille-Vanderville and a power station at Manzigurbe with loss of one aircraft.

After it had been definitely proven that the Marauder performed best at medium altitude, various group formations were tried to determine what number of aircraft could attain the maximum results and afford the best defensive configuration. Boxes of 18, 21, and 24 aircraft were tried, and finally, in August, a 36-plane formation became the standard group operational battle configuration. Two boxes of 18 each were composed of a lead flight of six and a high and a low flight of six each flying in a line echelon with the lead flight. The Number One box led the mission, and the Number Two box followed it into the target.

3 Sep.: Marauders attack Manzigurbe power station near Bethane, France, and other targets in Pas de Calais Department "with good results." "Marauders strike at heart of Paris," according to Axis radio.

6 Sep.: Marauders attack railway marshalling yards at Ghent, Belgium, with "good results" and destroyed three enemy fighters in an ensuing air battle.

10 Sep.: B-26s pound Boulogne on northern French coast so severely that the concussions and reverberations were felt along the Cliffs of Dover.

16 Sep.: Continuing daily assaults, which have occurred from England since mid-July, the Marauders bombard German airfields near Paris in occupied France. The Hispano-Suiza and Caudron-Renault aircraft plants and ball bearing works were pounded. (*Author's note:* Even though the mission of the 9th Air Force was to strike tactical targets while the 8th concentrated on the strategic ones, every once in a while B-26s attacked strategic targets such as these ball-bearing plants merely because they were conveniently within the Marauder's range and the heavies didn't want to bother with them. Many strategic targets were bombed by the B-26s of the 12th Air Force as well, primarily on the Italian mainland.)

20 Sep.: Marauders pound Nord airfield at Lille, France, carrying the new nonstop offensive to the fifth consecutive day and maintain a five-to-one ratio in enemy aircraft downed over France and Holland. In two articles by Bob Considine and Lee McCardell, a summary of the two months of daily assaults from England over western European bases was disclosed. According to McCardell's dispatch, Marauders had participated in 2500 sorties since mid-July and had suffered only 11 losses—the safest and best combat record by percentage of any Allied aircraft in the theater. An intermediate period of the 60-day record, described by Considine, revealed how 892 Marauders thundered over enemy bases on various missions with the loss of only two. He writes: "Their losses after just two months in England made the lowest record of any type of plane. They are coming back riddled with holes, sometimes on one engine (which makes the rate of descent for landing 2000 feet per minute) and sometimes they come sliding in on their bellies—safe at home plate. And they are systematically driving the Germans crazy.''

23 Sep.: B-26s penetrate deep into Northern France to hammer Nazi airdromes at Conches, 60 miles west of Paris. In an article from England, William Randolph Hearst, Jr. says Marauders are a ''new and fierce headache for the Germans. While Liberators and Flying Fortresses suffer an average loss of five percent per mission, Marauders lose only one-half of one percent per mission.''

These glowing September reports—on events that took place some time earlier—show the expertise of the 8th Air Force public relations staff. They realized that the best way to get the Marauder success story across to a news-hungry public back home was to have renowned and credible reporters such as Considine, Hearst, and McCardell tell the story. After all, they had already made ''Flying Fortress'' a household word.

Whether the 9th AF's PR men just didn't have the pizazz when they took over, or whether it just became too boresome to wax eloquent over their B-26 groups going out day after day, relentlessly bombing targets and coming back with minimal losses in aircraft and personnel, is a matter of conjecture. At any rate, the Marauders doing a job became so routine that what little press they did receive was usually ''ho-hum'' in both wording and length. Even Gabriel Heatter's famous opening line, delivered in a terse and foreboding manner in many of his radio broadcasts—''There's bad news tonight!''—seldom was followed with a commentary on Marauder exploits.

24 Sep.: Marauders operating on seventh mission in seven days in northern France raid Evreus-Fauville, and hit Conches again. Also smash Beauvais-Lille airbase.

27 Sep.: Participating in their 19th raid of the month, Marauders blast Beauvais-Lille Airfield. It was the eighth attack on that field in the month. Raiding Conches airbase, Marauders down four enemy fighters.

It was evident from these dispatches that the Marauders had to return to bomb certain airfields repeatedly. While it's true that less-than-desirable first-effort bombing results were sometimes the reason for this, along with the different areas of a base being selected for demolition on different missions, the main reason—and the one most frustrating to Maraudermen—was the Germans' tenacious ability to repair the damage and put the field back in operation again. Of course, having to weather repeated attacks, never knowing precisely when or where they would occur, must have had a demoralizing effect on the Luftwaffe, and certainly contributed to the decline of its effectiveness.

In one of the last official dispatches from the Mighty 8th before the 9th began issuing its own, this appeared:

1 Oct.: According to the monthly figures released by the 8th Air Force, Marauders and their fighter escorts downed 200 German fighters in September. This was in round-the-clock cross-channel raids on German bases in France. In an Associated Press dispatch from London, Marauder activity over western Europe from mid-July through September was summarized. Marauders were credited with 4,000 sorties on 75 missions (one per day average), with a loss of only 13 planes. The B-26s bombed docks and railroad centers, and smashed permanent enemy fighter bases in France, thereby cutting their effectiveness and driving them further east. This was done by destroying hangars, barracks, and radio control towers instead of easily repaired landing strips. Thus the path was cleared for heavy bomber missions into the industrial heart of Germany.

This report was just a bit misleading in content. A few night Marauder missions were tried but were quickly abandoned. Round-the-clock bombing was in effect, but not by Marauders. The Allied strategy was to bomb Germany into submission from the air; the RAF bombed strategic targets at night while the U.S. 8th Air Force hit them in the daylight hours. The U.S. 9th Air Force was committed strictly to the destruction of Luftwaffe bases and other tactical targets.

In the December 1943 issue of *Air Force* magazine, the following article, by the leading proponent of medium altitude tactics for the ETO Marauders, appeared:

The Marauders Came Through

By Col. Samuel E. Anderson

CO of a Medium Bombardment Wing in England

On a fine summer afternoon in July, a B-26 formation roared over the English Channel at 12,000 feet toward the railroad marshalling yards at Abbeville, France.

Above the formation hovered a watchful escort of RAF Spitfires, ready to nail the German fighters that already were rising from their home bases to meet the attack.

Below the formation was the enemy coast—hard-shelled rim of Western Europe that must be smashed for full-scale invasion.

And behind the formation were hundreds of hopes, plans, and doubts that the Marauders would bomb the target and return—all of them—to base.

For this raid was an experiment. It was the first time that B-26s had been sent across the invasion front at medium altitude. They were travelling at a height within range of not only the heavy flak defenses but also the many light flak emplacements near the target area. They were flying into a territory dotted with Nazi fighter bases that protect the great German industrial areas.

I say there were doubts behind this experiment, because the first one had failed. That was a low-level attack by a B-26 formation two months earlier in which disastrous casualties were suffered. Regardless of the reasons for the failure of the first experiment, everyone from the pilots down to the grease-marked mechanics waited in tense expectancy for the results of the new tactics against the Luftwaffe and the heavy German ground defenses.

There were some who even doubted whether the Marauder could operate successfully at any altitude, or under any conditions, in the European Theater. And that attitude was applicable to all types of medium bomber. The RAF had only a handful of Venturas, Bostons, and Mitchells, alternatively stabbing the Nazi defenses at both medium and low level. Maj. Gen. Ira C. Eaker, commanding the 8th Air Force, Brig. Gen. Robert C. Candee, commanding the 8th Air Force Support Command, and we of the Medium Bombardment Wing did not agree with this attitude. Today's mission was our attempt to disprove all doubts.

Thus it was that there was considerably more than just the bombing results riding on this formation of B-26s as they opened their bomb bay doors over Abbeville.

We were back at home base an hour later—and we all returned safely. The Spits had taken care of the FW-190s and the Me-109s that had attempted to intercept and, while some of the planes suffered damage from flak, direct hits were avoided by evasive action. A few planes, though heavily damaged, came home without great difficulty. Since that mission, B-26s have come back with one engine shot out, with rudders almost shot off, with flaps and landing gear rendered inoperative—conclusive proof that the B-26 is a tough plane which can take a lot of punishment.

This mission—this experiment—had been highly successful, and as General Candee said after our return: "It's just the beginning of continued operations to crush the German Air Force."

Within the next two months, taking time out only for extremely bad weather, the Marauders entered into a shuttle relay across the English Channel and North Sea that totalled 60 announced raids, an average of one a day. They flew more than 2470 sorties with a loss of only 11 aircraft and dropped more than 2800 tons of bombs.

Our objective has been two-fold; first, the destruction of the German fighter force in Western Europe, on the ground and in the air; secondly, the building of a battle-seasoned force to support our ground forces when they invade Europe. Although we rarely have caught the Hun on the ground, we have blasted the airdromes guarding German industries until photo reconnaissance had definitely established that many of the landing fields had been abandoned.

St. Omer, Poix, Tricqueville, Bernay St. Martin, Woensdrecht, Beaumont Le Roget, Caen/Carpiquet, Lille/Nord, Lille/Vendeville, Bryas Sud, Merville, Amiens/Ghissy—these Luftwaffe fighter bases have been under continuous attack, and the wearing-down process has shown good results.

Although we have given about 75 percent of our attention to German airdromes, marshalling yards and an occasional industrial target have been on our schedule, too. One of the best jobs of precision bombing ever recorded was the raid on the Le Trait shipyard August 4, when a fairly small formation of B-26s placed their bombs into a target 330 by 650 yards and almost completely destroyed it (Fig. 6-3). Additional hits were scored on a submarine and a tanker in the slips.

The biggest day of operations came in coordination with the "amphibious exercises" held in the English Channel on September 9. That morning we threw our Sunday punch. Our targets were coastal defenses near Boulogne which contained heavy guns ranging up to 16 inches. Every 15 minutes for two hours, the Marauders were hammering the gun positions, and the effectiveness of the saturation was apparent not only in the fact that the landing craft in the exercise were not fired on, but also in the strike photos. One photo showed at least 42 bomb craters in one emplacement containing six guns.

Aside from the obvious conclusion as to what may be expected from the medium bombers supporting a possible invasion of Western Europe, that day offered a perfect example of what may be expected from the combat crews. One of our airdromes was shut in by weather that ordinarily would give pilots

Fig. 6-3. *Strike photo of the raid on the Le Trait shipyards on the Seine River. Note near-perfect concentration of bomb burst. (photo courtesy Ralph G. McConnell.)*

a restful morning in their bunks. It was a heavy ground fog about 400 feet thick, with 100-yard ground visibility. But the crews had learned during the briefing that an Allied fleet was approaching the French coast. Although they later learned that it was an "amphibious exercise," it seemed like the real thing at the time.

Up from this fog-bound field shot the Marauders, plowing through the murk until they broke out on top when they formed into boxes and went to Boulogne. In this extremely hazardous takeoff, only one bomber was lost.

The total for the morning of the "amphibious exercises" was 216 sorties. We lost three, in addition to the one on takeoff, which was our heaviest loss on any one mission to date, bombing at medium altitude.

Because of the magnificent support from RAF Spitfires, which have taken care of nearly all enemy fighters, a medium bomber's biggest worry over Western Europe has been the flak. It comes in big doses, but it isn't nearly as tough as the B-26 and the combat crews who fly through it. However, the proportion of bomber to escorting fighters has risen steadily. The same number of fighters which escorted Marauders on their first medium altitude sortie now ordinarily escort many times that number.

Many of the 26s have limped back to base looking like a sieve, and I have lost count of the ones that have come home safely on only one engine. On one occasion a B-26, piloted by Captain Donald L. Weiss, was badly crippled by flak before it reached its target. Instead of jettisoning his bombs, Captain Weiss decided to make his run over the target on one engine. Losing altitude, he had fallen out of formation, but he fulfilled his mission.

After putting his bombs on the target, Captain Weiss turned again toward England and took evasive action all the way out past the coast—still on one engine.

And there was once a time when people believed the B-26 could not fly on one engine!

The Marauders raiding Western Europe have had just enough encounters with FW-190s and Me-109s to keep their 12 .50-caliber guns from getting rusty. The few enemy fighters that have slipped through the Spitfire's screen have been given a hot reception. Claims against them over a two-month period are 10 destroyed, four probables, and 11 damaged.

Out of the extremely low loss record of the Marauders and the gradually apparent results of their precision bombing against Nazi airdromes, there has grown in the combat crews a spirit of quiet confidence in themselves and in the ability of their bombers to deliver the goods (Fig. 6-4).

"I wouldn't want to take one home to use after the war as a family airplane," they admit. "But when it comes to combat, I'll take a Marauder every time. It's a hell of a fine fighting airplane!"

If Peyton M. Magruder happened to read Sam Anderson's *Air Force* article, one can imagine the satisfaction he must have derived therefrom. His "Submarine

Fig. 6-4. *Crash-landing of a 387th Bomb Group Marauder due to flak damage. Many times the control tower would dictate that the belly landing be made on the grass so as not to obstruct the runway for any length of time in case removal of the aircraft proved to be difficult. In this landing the waist windows were probably clogged with dirt, so all the crew had to exit through the pilot's opened canopy hatches or the navigator's astrodome hatch just aft of the cockpit. (photo courtesy A. Jackson Lawrence, III)*

with Wings'' had finally surfaced after proving herself in the depths of the skies over Western Europe (Figs. 6-5 through 6-14).

1944

This year brought the 9th Air Force up to full strength, comprising a Bomber Command, Fighter Command, Troop Carrier Command, and Service Command. The Bomber Command contained the 97th, 98th, and 99th Combat Wings; Fighter Command consisted of P-38, P-47, and P-51 aircraft, which performed escort duty, fighter sweeps, dive-bombing missions, and photorecon flights. The fighter sweeps and dive-bombing really began in earnest in the post-D-Day period. In the beginning, since 8th AF fighters were committed to escorting their heavies, the Marauders were escorted by RAF fighters. When the 9th developed its own Fighter command, it took over the job. Troop Carrier Command was equipped with C-47 tugs or troop transports and Waco C-4A gliders. The Service Command had maintenance depot facilities located on the various airbases used by the 9th.

Maintenance and service was quite a different story in England as opposed to the Spartan conditions in the Alaskan, South Pacific, and Mediterranean theaters, and this naturally contributed to the improved performance of the Marauder. The airfields on which the 9th AF medium and light bomber groups

156

Fig. 6-5. *This Momma didn't need a pistol to get her points across!* You've 'Ad It! *was a popular British expression quickly picked up by the Yanks. Author chokes on his pipe as he gazes at the artwork on Lt. William Harrison's ship of the 497th Squadron, 344th Bomb Group, in spring of 1944.*

were based in East Anglia (the majority of which were concentrated in the county of Essex north and northeast of London) were either former RAF bases or newly constructed ones with hard-surface runways; many had substantial metal hangars. Shorter supply lines also aided the effort, along with the fact that crews and all other personnel were housed in either Nissen huts or concrete barracks as opposed to tents.

The unsung heroes of all combat aircraft organizations were the crew chiefs and line mechanics who serviced and repaired the airplanes. An article appeared in the April 1944 issue of *Air Force* magazine that described the tireless and dedicated efforts of these valuable men:

24-Hour Job

Major Bernard W. Crandell

He's always cursing the B-26 and praising the B-17, which is explainable only because a man is sometimes critical of a thing he loves most dearly.

He swears he isn't interested in the four Marauders that he and 11 other mechanics must maintain. Not the least bit attached to any of them, he insists, as he carefully watches 18 specks in the sky approaching the airdrome. Crew chiefs may take a personal interest in their '26s, but a flight chief treats them like a big, cold hunk of machinery, he repeats as the Marauder formation swings around on the approach leg.

Fig. 6-6. *Marauder of the 387th Bomb Group's 556th Squadron dropping a maximum 5200-pound load of 26 200-pound fragmentation bombs over France in early 1944. Yellow and black diagonal rudder stripes identify the Group and large white letters on aft fuselage denote the Squadron (FW) and the aircraft (K). Serial number shows this to be a B-50 model. (photo courtesy Glenn L. Martin Co.)*

"Watch this one," he suddenly gasps. "Watch it now. It's *Pistol Packin' Momma!* She's coming in right there. You got to take a look at that ship. Damndest picture on it you ever saw. Old 'Nap' is paintin' it on, and it's an old gal leaning against a rail with a big gun in her hand. He hasn't painted her head on yet—hasn't had time since the last Amsterdam raid. Been patchin' the

Fig. 6-7. *A painting of a Marauder on an Essex hardstand after one of the frequent rain showers that complicated the work of maintenance men. Titled* Reflections, *the painting is by Emmett Lancaster.*

Fig. 6-8. *This nose art depicts some crew's penchant for recording each mission, regardless of its type. The bombs, of course, represent a regular bombing mission. The duck represents a diversionary mission, the donuts indicate a mission that was called back before bombing (but after which the crews still enjoyed the Red Cross donuts and coffee provided for returning airmen after each mission), and the candy canes represent missions on which no bombs were dropped for some reason or other. Taken of Capt. Emanuel Schifani's ship on a 495th Squadron hardstand at the 344th Bomb Group base at Stansted-Mountfichet, Essex, in the spring of 1944.*

159

Fig. 6-9. *The line crew is taking a coffee break in the midst of extensive work on the engine accessory section of the famous* Flak Bait *of the 322nd Bomb Group on its Great Saling hardstand. (photo courtesy W. J. Johnston)*

Fig. 6-10. *Marauder crew officers could look like gentlemen when prepared to go to London on pass. Combat crews (enlisted and officer alike) were entitled to more passes than ground crews, so the more caring and conscientious ones brought items back from "Big L." L. to R: Copilot Author, Bombardier J.W. Curley, Copilot Hollinger, and Bombardier Jacobs, in 497th Squadron area of 344th Bomb Group at Stansted-Mountfichet. Early summer 1944.*

Fig. 6-11. *Lt. Al Frieburger's* Rum Buggy *on 496th Squadron hardstand, 344th Bomb Group. Note fixed gun in lower nose has been removed. Bomb dollies and racks clutter the background. Spring 1944.*

Fig. 6-12. *Another unique nose art design. The aerial gunners posing by this 322nd Bomb Group ship look as glum as the bombardier in his outhouse. (photo courtesy W. J. Johnston)*

Fig. 6-13. *Typical squadron area Nissen huts on an Essex Marauder base. Note bicycles parked outside. Contrary to what Hollywood may have led movie-goers to believe, not every American airman had a jeep—95 percent rode bicycles, which were issued to all flight crews, maintenance, armament, supply, engineering, and communications personnel. (photo courtesy Ralph G. McConnell)*

damn thing up . . . turret dome busted, hydraulic system shot out, conduit in engine hit, oil dilution line hit by same piece of flak, hits on two leading edges, holes in two pieces of cowling, hole underneath pilot but it didn't come through, holes in the fuselage . . . *Pistol Packin' Momma!* What a ship! Damndest picture you ever saw! Come and take a look at it!''

Fig. 6-14. *Nose art shot of Capt. J. C. Maffry's 497th Sqdn. 344th BG partially paint-stripped Marauder. Inscription below name reads: "The wings are coming by ATC." Spring 1944, Stansted-Mountfichet.*

Master Sgt. Jack Loving, the Marauder flight chief who looks at his ships in that coldly impersonal manner, also has the reputation at his base in England for being the "bitchiest" man on the line—"Which is an indication," observes the group air executive, "that he's doing some thinking and feels fairly happy over the state of repair and maintenance on his ships."

Loving is an ordinary man from Beauregard, Miss., with an important job. The job consists of keeping four B-26s, each capable of dumping 4,000 pounds of bombs twice daily on Hitler's western fortress, in shape for such destruction of the enemy. It's up to Loving and 11 other air mechs to ensure 32,000 pounds of bombs daily for Nazi Europe.

Grooming $1,000,000 worth of bombing machinery is a responsible business for a 21-year-old from Beauregard—responsible enough to make it understandable that he might have a worry or two and a fairly vivid way of expressing himself when his four Marauders, looking more like sieves than flying machines, droop pathetically on the hardstands only 12 hours before their next mission.

Those next 12 hours, and the preceding 12 just spent sweating them through the last mission, are called the "24-hour jobs." This means it takes 24 hours of work, most of it under the feeble rays of worn flashlights, all of it through the penetrating cold of the English winter, to patch holes, to mend hydraulic lines, to replace electrical conduits, to hope and fret over four battle-damaged airplanes. Loving is never sure that they'll be ready for the next mission, and

163

his eternal pessimism often disgusts his squadron engineering officer, who tries to figure how many bombers can go down the runway the next morning.

The "24-hour job" is a misnomer for a night of wrestling with 34,000 pounds of intricate machinery. Because even after the mechanics have won their 24-hour match with the machines, they still have another eight or ten hours to sweat them out from the mission, and perhaps a repeat performance of the night before.

"We spent 30-hour stretches on the line during the first days of October when they were going out every day," Loving recalls sourly.

The only Marauder on the field that was properly named, Loving thinks, is *Flak Happy* of his flight. They've had some lively times with *Flak Happy* on the ground as well as in the air. "One night after *Flak Happy* came home with the leading edge shot up in three places, and an elevator and rudder smacked by flak, we had an air raid," he relates. "We had to get the ship back in condition so we stayed over there with our flashlights, helped considerably by the light of the flares the raiders were dropping. *Flak Happy* got off the next morning all right.

"On the last Amsterdam raid it came back full of holes. One piece of flak went in above the bombardier's head, cut the cables to the bomb racks and the line from the airspeed indicator. There was only a small strand left of the right aileron control cable and one large hole where the top of the left wingtip should have been. That time the ship had to go to the hangar for four days while the service squadron did the sheet metal work on the wingtip. At the end of four days everything was fixed, too, and *Flak Happy* with its left wing nothing but patches went back for more action."

Patching is a fairly simple job, according to Loving. If the flak doesn't damage a structural member, a piece of aluminum is riveted over the hole. And if the hole is a small one, a patch of cloth is slapped on. Although these patches are called "temporary," Loving says they're permanent as far as he is concerned.

When flak hits the highly sensitive leading edge of the wing where hundreds of wires and conduits are embedded, the repair becomes a major job. Birds are Loving's pet peeve because they do nearly as much damage as flak when they strike the tender leading edge. Similar touchy points in the B-26 are the hydraulic system, and, of course, the powerplants, Loving explains.

Loving says he and his 11 mechanics are seldom told what the target is the B-26s are attacking, but they can usually tell where the ships have been by the amount of battle damage they bring home. "Amsterdam and the Calais—Boulogne area are the toughest on the ships," Loving adds. "Amsterdam always means another 24-hour job for us.

"*Pistol Packin' Momma* got it worse than *Flak Happy* on the last Amsterdam mission. As for the other two ships, 739 had only a few holes in it and 906 didn't get off the ground because the oil dilution solenoid stuck open and let fuel run into the engine—another damn 24-hour job. After we'd drained the engine and changed plugs and started her up, a cylinder head blew out and that was about the limit. We changed it, though, and had it ready by next morning.''

Loving figures that, on the average, the crew chiefs and other mechanics in his flight spend between 15 and 20 man-hours daily on each B-26. ''But after a hot raid, much more than that,'' he quickly adds. ''If we have the necessary parts we stick with the repairs until we're finished. Those 24-hour jobs wouldn't be so bad if it wasn't so damn dark and cold.''

The speed of repair and maintenance of the B-26s in England recently drew a commendation from the Air Force on the general condition of the bombers, a recognition that Loving and his flight were glad to get after having both Bomber Command and Air Force inspectors snooping around for three weeks. Loving says the combat crews were as happy over the commendation as the ground crews, which was proof enough that the boys who fly take an interest in what the mechanics are doing. On that point, Loving is emphatic.

''The pilot on 739 and his crew take an unusual interest in what we do,'' he explains. ''He is Lt. Frank S. Barrett of Dallas, Texas, and the crew chief is Tech. Sgt. William L. Whitton of Austin, Texas. You might know what happens when you get two Texans together. Every time one of the combat men goes to London, he always asks the ground boys if there's anything he can get them.

''We've put an awful lot of patches on old 739. It's been out on 29 missions and always gets back somehow. Lt. Barrett won't give it a name because he figures it will change his luck.''

The name *Pistol Packin' Momma* was selected by the bomber's crew chief, Tech. Sgt. James T. Ratliff of Tylertown, Miss., and his assistant, Sgt. Dominic G. Naplitana, of Brooklyn, N.Y. Although Marauders are usually christened by their pilots, occasionally the honor is taken by the crew chief because, Loving explains, the crew chief is as much the ''boss'' of the bomber on the ground as the pilot is while the plane is in the air.

''The crew chief can red-line his Form 2-A at any time to keep the ship on the ground,'' Loving says. ''And that's a matter that would take a command pilot to declare otherwise. The crew chief can red-line the ship, but I'm always there when he's ready to take it off again. I'd never turn a ship back to a pilot until I am ready to go up in it myself.''

Since May 14, 1943, when the Marauders made their first attack against Western Europe, Loving has seen a complete turnover of the bombers in his flight. He lost two ships on that disastrous May 17 raid, and one since then. The latter was 817, the B-26 that carried him across the Atlantic to England. The loss of 817, along with its crew and one of the most popular pilots in the group, hurt the crew chief, Tech. Sgt. Antonio I. Vendrame, of Santa Barbara, Calif., considerably, Loving says. ''Tony hardly believed it when I told him 817 had been shot down. He now has 906, the ''command'' ship that the squadron operations officer or the CO fly. Everyone likes Tony on that job.''

Some of the other B-26s formerly in Loving's flight have gone to training or replacement centers. One of them was the *Silver Streak*, a B-26 without paint that had extra speed but at a distance either was invisible or reflected a blinding flash from the sun. *Silver Streak,* an old-type Marauder with the 65-foot wing, made only one mission at medium altitude and had to be rolled into a hangar every night to conceal its brilliance, but it was held in high regard because it had gone for 350 hours without an engine change.

"That might not seem so much as when compared to some other airplanes," Loving says, "but a year ago we would have thought it was wonderful for a B-26."

In addition to repair and maintenance, the ground flight must make engine inspections every 25 hours' flying time and modify the new replacement aircraft. Modifications always bring another 24-hour job, for the bomber may be scheduled for its first mission the following day.

As flight chief, Loving finds his overall job only begins with his store of technical knowledge. Coordinating the work of four crew chiefs and the other mechanics into a well-balanced team requires more than technical knowledge, especially from a youngster who gives instructions to men eight and ten years older than himself. But Loving proved he had the respect of the men all along the line, according to the group executive.

"I first heard of Loving when the boys said he was the hottest aerial photographer in the business," the air exec recalls. "A few weeks later they began talking of Loving as being the best aerial gunner they'd seen. The next thing was how good this Loving was at navigation, and then I heard he was an expert on radio. Finally they told me he was a top-ranking air mechanic. I decided to go out and get acquainted with him."

Loving's brief but rare background runs from his enlistment, May 20, 1941, as a photographer—"because I was interested in chemical solutions"— to April 1942 when his squadron was given its first Marauders and he decided to be an air mechanic. He learned it all on the line and takes some pride in the fact that he never went to air mechanic's school.

A flight chief can live a decent life—less than 15 hours a day on the line— only when there are few missions during a month, Loving admits. The day a mission is run, however, is fairly easy. On the morning the bombers are to go out, for example, Loving and his ground flight will leave their Nissen huts as late as 0550, eat breakfast—"We've learned not to wait"—then go to the hardstands.

"We preflight the bombers, checking everything and giving their engines a run-up and then top off the gas tanks," he says. "If the wings have frost, we scrape it off with defroster fluid. Then we might talk with the combat crew until they climb in. Someone starts the energizer, and that's about the last we do."

The last thing, of course, is the cool, indifferent stare of the flight chief as his four B-26s trundle off the hardstands and swing around the track to the runway. Then he might sneak over to a shed where old Nap is mixing paint to finish the picture on *Pistol Packin' Momma* when she returns.

166

While this article tells about some of the trials and tribulations of the maintenance men, the armament section and communications section—both working in direct and close support of each bombing mission—experienced similar working conditions and were seldom if ever recognized in print. They carry equal status as unsung heroes.

Beyond this were the dedicated personnel in the intelligence, supply, security, medical, motor pool, and administrative sections who all made it possible for the combat crews to carry out their day-to-day blasting of the Nazi war machine and its facilities. In a manner of speaking, each bomb dropped had one of these men's signature on it.

The combat crews received all the glory, but without the efforts of the entire group organization there would have been none—nor could even the first bomb have been dropped on the enemy.

As the year progressed, the following additional medium bomb groups became operational in the ETO on the dates and at the locations shown:

15 February:	391st;	Matching
6 March:	344th;	Stansted-Mountfichet
13 March:	394th;	Holmsley
20 April:	397th;	Hurn

History was to repeat itself when the crews of Col. R.F.C. Vance's 344th Group began stripping the olive drab and grey camouflage paint off their aircraft during their aerial movement from the States to England via the South Atlantic route. While not all chose to do it, there were enough stripped either wholly or partially to give the group the nickname "The Silver Streaks." The squadron-sized "Silver Fleet" of the South Pacific was reborn at group size in the ETO.

It had been determined that camouflage paint was of little or no use at medium altitudes, and since there was no longer an urgent need to make the aircraft less discernible on the ground—the Luftwaffe very seldom ventured over the East Anglia portion of England on nuisance bombing raids on airdromes any longer—camouflage was gradually phased out. Eventually all replacement aircraft came to the ETO in the natural aluminum finish.

By spring, Col. Samuel E. Anderson, who wrote "The Marauders Came Through," was a Brigadier General in command of the 9th Air Force Bomber Command. Brig. Gen. Herbert Thatcher had taken over as CO of the 99th Bombardment Wing. Anderson, probably more than any other commander in the ETO, championed the B-26 and was most influential in convincing the higher brass of its true capabilities at medium altitudes.

Pinpoint bombing became a day-to-day reality with the Marauders of the 9th and their accuracy at altitudes in the 12,000 foot range became legion. Prior to D-Day, typical targets were bridges, airfields, marshalling yards, gun positions, ammunition and oil storage dumps, and the infamous V-1 flying bomb sites.

The tight formation flown by the Marauders (Fig. 6-15) accomplished a twofold purpose: It provided a close pattern of bombs on the target, and strike

Fig. 6-15. *Formation join-up of Marauders of the 599th Sqdn., 397th BG over the Essex countryside in summer of 1944. Note some have no camouflage while others carry the olive drab only on the top surfaces. (photo courtesy Major Paul Gardella, USAF Ret.)*

photos of hits on narrow bridges proved the accuracy to be nothing short of miraculous!

The other advantage to tight formation flying was the protection it afforded against fighter attacks. In the South Pacific and Mediterranean Theaters, Marauders did not enjoy the luxury of a fighter escort on every mission, nor were there the number of fighters available for escort duty as in the ETO. As a consequence, bombing results were varied and too many bombers were lost to enemy fighters. The Air Force did learn from this experience, and once full-scale medium bomber operations were in effect in the ETO, a fighter escort accompanied each mission.

Seymour B. "Buck" Feldman, now of Albuquerque, New Mexico, was an American volunteer who flew fighter aircraft with the RAF from 1941 to 1948 and was then repatriated to the USA. While flying the Hawker Typhoon with No. 3 Fighter Squadron based at RAF Station Manston, he said he had the pleasure of escorting Marauder groups on several missions during 1943 and early 1944. In a communication to the 387th Bomb Group Association a few years ago, he stated:

"I should like to express my personal admiration for a job well done during World War II. After rendezvous with your Marauder formations, accurate navigation brought all concerned to the target area, and it was the precise bombing carried out that impressed me to no end. The fast cruising speed of the B-26 made escort missions a piece of cake for the Typhoon pilot, and we found it no task to practically fly off your wingtip when providing close escort.''

During his RAF tour, Buck flew Hurricanes, Typhoons, Spitfires, and Tempests, and shot down 11 V-1 flying bombs that had been launched against London. He was decorated by the late King George VI with the RAF Distinguished Flying Cross (Figs. 6-16, 6-17).

Fig. 6-16. *Dashing RAF pilot "Buck" Feldman, 1944. From the smile on Buck's face, he must have just pranged a V-1. (photo courtesy S. B. Feldman)*

Fig. 6-17. *"Buck" Feldman's V-1-busting Hawker Typhoon. (photo courtesy S. B. Feldman)*

Because of their tremendous defensive concentration of firepower, the Luftwaffe was reluctant to press home attacks on Marauder formations and usually only picked on flak-crippled stragglers that had dropped out of formation. The only area that could not be covered by the B-26's guns was a small cone directly below and to the rear of the tail turret. Most of the few Luftwaffe attacks came from this quarter, and the enemy fighters would come up in trail from below and behind to fire a short burst and then half-roll down and away, thus avoiding most of the guns of the flight they were attacking.

Even a crippled Marauder was not exactly fair game for the Luftwaffe because our fighter jockeys were very protective of their "Big Brothers" and, whenever it was possible, one or two would break formation to shepherd a crippled B-26 back across the channel, zigzagging back and forth above the Marauder in order to stay with him.

As a result of the tight formations and concentration of defensive firepower, an infinitesimal number of Marauders were lost to enemy fighter attacks. The greatest loss occurred during a single day late in the war.

It was 23 December 1944 and the Marauder groups flying out of airfields in France had been briefed to expect heavy enemy fighter opposition on the missions of the day, which were to give support to our troops trapped in the Battle of the Bulge. No missions had been flown for a week previous because of bad weather stand downs, and intelligence had surmised that the Luftwaffe would take advantage of this to regroup for one more big defensive attack of a suicidal nature.

It materialized all right, and was made even more effective by the fact that the Allied fighter escort scheduled for the missions didn't arrive on time. The Luftwaffe, using their newest armament and tactics, including the new Me-262s of General Adolph Galland's jet fighter JG-52, fiercely pressed their attacks on the unprotected Marauder groups. As a result, 39 Marauders were listed as missing in action, two abandoned over friendly territory, six crash-landed or were written off as beyond repair after landing, and over 120 sustained major battle damage. Although no German fighters actually rammed Marauders, this was the closest thing to a "kamikaze-type" attack ever made in the ETO.

Regrettably, the first news reports filed that evening, stating that 200 Marauders had been lost to enemy action, reached the States. The many ships that were forced to make emergency landings at bases all over northern France made it impossible to tally the exact losses that day, and it wasn't until Christmas Eve that the final and correct figures became available.

By that time, the damage to the Marauder's reputation had been done, and Maraudermen had a rough time convincing their families back home that this was just a rare and isolated incident and that the "Widow-Maker" tag some sensation-seeking news writers had pulled out of the closet was completely unjustified (Figs. 6-18 through 6-27).

To offset the absence of fighter attacks during normal operations was the fact that the German 88mm flak guns were most accurate at the altitude at which the Marauders operated. It was determined that a straight and level flight for as little as 30 seconds gave the German radar gun detectors sufficient time to track the formation and to place shots right in the midst of it. Consequently, evasive action of changes of heading and/or altitude every 15 to 20 seconds was employed to minimize flak damage. Of course, once committed to the bomb run, there was no evasive action permitted, and runs of 25 seconds or longer took their toll.

If a mission leader took more than a minute for his bomb run, his crew team was considered to be either suicidal, guilty of brown-nosing, or just downright crazy by the other crews in the formation. It was nothing short of miraculous

Fig. 6-18. *Brand new B-50 model, Serial Number 42-95960, received by author's crew at Hunter Army Air Field, Savannah, Georgia, in January 1944, while 344th BG was staging to fly enmass to England via the southern Atlantic route.*

171

Fig. 6-19. *Wheels just coming up on a 344th B-26 during acceptance check at Hunter Field. Even then there were still runaway prop problems on takeoff (author's ship included), but no aircraft were lost as a result. Trial and error remedies had finally produced a fail-safe answer to the emergencies. Bomb bay tanks were installed at Hunter for the overseas flight.*

Fig. 6-20. *Captain Lucius D. Clay's 495th Sqdn. Marauder flying alongside author's ship on first leg of overseas flight, January 1944. Note camouflage already stripped from Clay's ship at this early date. Package guns hadn't yet been installed, nor was the flexible .50 in place in the nose.*

172

Fig. 6-21. *It was tradition for all aircrews to purchase flight boots in either Belem or Natal, Brazil, as a distinction of flying the South Atlantic. Here the author sports his new "Belem boots" outside the PX at the third stop on January 1944 overseas flight.*

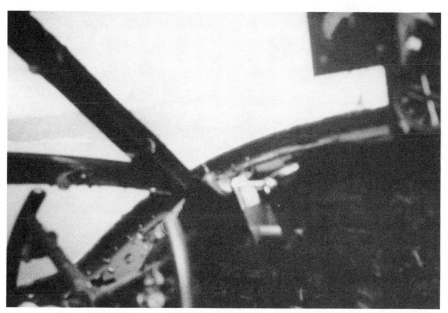

Fig. 6-22. *Probably the most welcome sight to all aircrews flying the southern route to England was this one of the approach to Ascension Island from Natal, Brazil. The sign over the briefing room door at Natal read: "If you miss the Ascension, your wife gets a pension!"*

Fig. 6-23. *During a 22-day delay Marrakech awaiting favorable weather for the final hop to England, the 344th crews took in the sights of the city. Here's a pair of Jacks—the author on top.*

Fig. 6-24. *The 344th became operational on 6 March 1944; this shows pilot Capt. R. E. Wilson and bombardier 1/Lt. R. F. Humes in author's ship after fourth mission. April 1944, Station 169, Stansted-Mountfichet.*

Fig. 6-25. *The space taken up by the bombsight and .50-cal. nose gun in the greenhouse is shown here. Bombardier 2/Lt. Geary is in the pilot's seat of this 497th Sqdn., 344th BG Marauder just after landing from a mission. Hydraulic fluid leaking onto tire from nosewheel strut is the result of a hit from a flak fragment severing a line. Crew chose the name because they said pilot A. J. Wood resembled Chicken Little, and the ship always bounces back. Late spring 1944, Stansted-Mountfichet.*

Fig. 6-26. *A flight of the 456th Sqdn., 323rd BG losing tight formation due to pinpoint flak as described in the text. The ugly black puffs were fearsome enough to observe, but when crews could distinguish orange or yellow flame inside the black, they knew they were close enough to receive fragment hits from the bursts. (photo courtesy Ralph G. McConnell)*

that effective bombing results were attained with a 30-second to one-minute bomb run, but it happened every day. Cool, calculating navigators bringing the group to the Initial Point and the target, in spite of visibility of one-half mile down-sun in the haze; steel-nerved pilots keeping the PDI needle centered on the bomb run despite flak bursting all around; and—probably the bravest member of the crew—the bombardier out in front, with no protection in that plexiglass nose, managing to lock onto the target and keep it in his sights, especially with a navigator squeezed up against his back in the nose, as was common with some groups—they, by the grace of God and the Marauder, made it possible!

The tenacity and raw courage displayed by the bombardiers, as they faced death each mission, was vividly described in an article that appeared in the Stars and Stripes during August 1944:

Bombardier—Warrior in a Greenhouse

In souvenir fragments are carved heroic experiences of the "Plexiglass Kids" who drop the bombs.

By Lt. Charles H. Franks, USAAF

These are the mementoes of men who fly in glasshouses and throw bombs.

The Marauder bombardier who had his eyelashes clipped by a plexiglass fragment, picks up the fragment and has carved from it a miniature heart or a set of wings. The bombardier who received a plexiglass fragment on his cheek places it among his souvenirs . . . next to the heavy steel flak fragment that hit him in the chest a few missions before.

Another proudly shows a bent insignia. "It was knocked off my collar by a flak fragment," he explains. One bombardier unfolds a map that had the entire target area clipped out by a fragment.

In these souvenir fragments are carved heroic experiences of the men who serve in the egg-shaped plexiglass noses of Marauder medium bombers. In each of them is embedded the personal story of a plexiglass kid who sits in a "greenhouse" and toggles the switches that send bomb after bomb crashing down on Nazi targets in Western Europe.

The "greenhouse" is the plexiglass nose of the aircraft. Part of it is the plate of glass through which the bombardier often sees the flak burst below and around him and many times hears the dull thud of a flak fragment as it pierces the glass in front of him.

There's reason enough for a bombardier to see too much. The nose, almost all transparent, includes the plexiglass three feet high and wide, three and a half feet long. There is no armor plating for the man who works in glasshouses

Fig. 6-26. *Bombardier 1/Lt. Ralph G. McConnell, in nose of his Marauder, clearly illustrates why the "greenhouse" was so named. (USAAF photo courtesy Ralph G. McConnell)*

other than his flak suit; the only armor is behind him to protect the instruments and the pilot from forward fire.

Of course, there is the Norden sight in front of the bombardier, over the 3/8-inch plate glass. And there is a gun and box of fifties. But they won't stop much flak. Nor will the bomb bay release controls on the right of his glasshouse walls (Fig. 6-25).

To complete the picture of loneliness—the loneliness which made one bombardier compare his situation to a man up a telephone pole, with kids throwing rocks at him—you have to remember that the physical layout of the glasshouse, whose only exit is by crawling back and through the copilot's position, almost certainly makes a bail-out impossible except under the most favorable conditions.

The armor-plate door half blocks exit and any violent movement of the ship (such as a spin or a steep dive when it's had it) pins the bombardier to his compartment. Anyway, he doesn't have his chute on; no room.

When a flak fragment crashes into the nose of a Marauder, it creates additional fragments from the plexiglass it strikes. All these fragments are usually thrown towards the bombardier, seldom away from him. This combination of flak and plexiglass fragments has been named "plexi-flak" by the bombardiers of the Marauder Group in England led by Col. Glenn C. Nye, of Raleigh, N.C., and it has won for them a score of Purple Hearts.

It was only a small piece of "plexi-flak" that hit 2/Lt. William E. Schuele of Milwaukee, Wis., but it took from him the sight of one eye. Quite often it has scratched some bomb-dropper's face like the claws of a frightened kitten. It comes up from the bottom, too, and has given several bombardiers the inclination to eat their supper standing up.

Although most pieces of "plexi-flak" are small, their terrific speed makes them dangerous. The blast force of the flak burst plus the air pressure created by the forward speed of the aircraft send the flak and glass fragments showering through the greenhouse with terrific velocity.

"They don't drift up at you," Lt. Ralph G. McConnell of Upper Darby, Pa., a bombardier with 35 missions to his credit, says. "Those pieces of steel travel with the speed of a bullet, and they smash through the glass before you know what happens."

McConnell contends that the bombardier sees too much through the walls of his plexiglass house. "You see the flashes of the guns on the ground and then you sweat the flak bursts out, wondering where in hell they're going to crack. You see the ships ahead of you going through a flak barrage and know that you have to go through the same thing," McConnell said.

McConnell and other bombardiers will tell that there are a few seconds on every mission in which they do not observe gun flashes, flak bursts, or fighters. It occurs when the Marauders are on the bomb run and the bombardiers are captains of their ships. In these few moments they strive to accomplish what every man in their bomb group from the personnel clerk to the armorer, from the adjutant to the pilot, works for . . . to place the bombs on the target (Figs. 6-26 through 6-28).

In these few seconds, the value of the work of several thousand men is determined by the success or failure of the men who fly in the glasshouse and release the bombs earmarked for a German airdrome, marshalling yard, or other installation in Western Europe.

It is also during the bomb run that the bombardiers are bothered the most by "plexi-flak." And because of it some of the true great stories of Marauder crews have been recorded . . . like those of *No Regrets* and *A WOL Kid.*

Captain Phillip Bridges, of Stephenville, Tex., fingered the release switch on his bombsight nervously. The ground defense Jerries down below were throwing up flak as if a miss meant a transfer to the Russian Front. A terrific

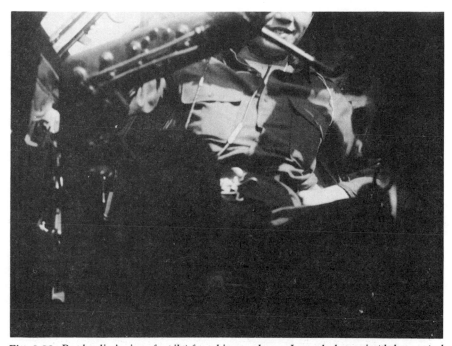

Fig. 6-28. *Bombardier's view of copilot from his greenhouse. Large dark area just below control column is copilot's right foot on the rudder pedal. The copilot must slide his seat backwards in order for the bombardier to crawl out of the nose. (photo courtesy W. J. Johnston)*

barrage reached out for *No Regrets,* and by the time the Marauder reached the target, it looked more like the "wreck of the old 97" than a polished aircraft.

The Captain felt the hit on the nose of the ship, heard the hail of plexiglass fragments as they showered his compartment. He picked the target in the sight, released the bombs and uttered "Bombs Away," softly over the intercom. His job finished, Captain Bridges slumped over his bombsight, a jagged hole in his steel helmet, his face peppered by a riot of plexiglass fragments.

The ship's navigator, Capt. Jack Tyson, of Albany, Georgia, mumbled to himself, "Boy, I'm going to see the Chaplain tonight if I get back from this one!"

The left engine of the Marauder had just cut out and a short message—"I'm hit"—over the intercom from the tail gunner was followed by a warning from the waist gunner: "Focke-Wulfs at five o'clock." At the same time a flak fragment thundered through the fuselage of *No Regrets* just behind the pilot, Major Irvin C. Wursten, of North Logan, Utah, and knifed the trim tab cables.

Then, ten seconds after it had cut out, the engine started again. Like a referee's whistle, it set a Marauder team into whirlwind action. Staff Sergeant Harold "Arky" Rice, of Mobile, Ala., relieved the injured tail gunner, Staff Sergeant Kenneth W. McKeague, of Rhinelander, Wis., grabbed the two .50-caliber guns, and waited for the "five o'clock intruders." But the Jerry playboys changed their minds and their course as well.

Captain Tyson pulled the wounded bombardier out of the nose and administered first aid while the copilot, 2nd Lt. Clarence F. Crosier, of Greeley, Colo., skipped the catwalk that leads over the bomb bay to the tail section and doctored the injured tail gunner.

And *No Regrets* came back home. Its left engine cut out momentarily again on the route back, and it left some of its structure—such as the nose and tail sections—back there in the Pas de Calais area . . . but it came back home.

The story of *No Regrets* is a prototype of many in which Marauder crews see more action in ten seconds than is usually found in a Sunday afternoon matinee. It is the narrative of men like Captain Bridges who cling to their positions until the job is done, despite wounds, enemy action, and battle-damaged aircraft.

The grueling experiences of the *AWOL Kid* start in the plexiglass nose just after the bombardier, Flight Officer Julius Szollosy, of Brooklyn, N.Y., had dropped 4000 pounds of bombs. Flak fragments tore through the nose of the ship and took off his left foot just above the ankle. He cried hysterically over the intercom that he had been hit and then groped his way out of the nose.

Halfway out of the nose he was aided by the copilot, 2nd Lt. Francis J. Rassiga, of Canaan, Conn., but in the nose his right foot caught the rudder pedal, throwing the ship out of control. The pilot, Flight Officer Robert S. Tate, of Nashville, Tenn., fought with the controls and finally prevented the *AWOL Kid* from being AWOL.

Lieutenant Rassiga moved the wounded bombardier into the radio compartment and elevated the left leg above the rest of his body in order to stop a rapid flow of blood from the leg. He then injected a shot of morphine.

At the same time the bombardier was hit, flak fragments broke the leg of the tail gunner. Hearing the cries of the bombardier and the tail gunner over the intercom, the top turret gunner, S/Sgt. Harold M. Michaels, of Montreal, Canada, stepped down from his turret to investigate. It was the most fortunate move he had ever made.

A flak fragment flashed through the plexiglass top of the turret with such speed that it could only be heard, not seen. Had Michaels remained in the turret, the fragment would have gone through his head.

Sgt. Michaels, aided by the waist gunner, S/Sgt. Russell E. Allen, of Wabash, Ind., applied a tourniquet to the tail gunner's leg.

After the English coast was reached, Flight Officer Tate headed for the first available airdrome he could find. He found a field but also discovered that his main and auxiliary hydraulic lines had been shot away. He succeeded only in bringing the nose wheel down in place. The serious wounds of two members prevented the crew from bailing out and also stopped any thought of prolonged attempts to bring the main landing wheels down. Tate decided to crash-land the ship. He tried to bring the nose wheel up but it wouldn't come, so the *AWOL Kid* headed down for a crash landing with its nose wheel down.

On the way down, Sgt. Michaels braced the wounded bombardier in the radio compartment, and Sgt. Allen braced the tail gunner in the tail section of the ship . . . braced him in such a manner that if the fuselage had cracked or sprung, Allen's arms and back might have been broken.

The tail of the *A WOL Kid* skidded in first, and then the nose wheel touched surface. The men at the Royal Air Force field who witnessed the landing sent a message to a Marauder bomber command general later. It read in part, "We have never seen a more beautiful landing."

But Flight Officer Tate is worrying somewhat about bent propellers. He brought the aircraft down without damaging the engines, but he bent the props. And the boys are warning him: "You're going to catch hell for that!" It was Tate's initial trip in the first pilot's seat! (Fig. 6-29).

The narratives of *No Regrets* and *A WOL Kid* are anecdotes of the men serving in glass cages, of how their injuries uncover the expert teamwork that lies behind a Marauder crew. Their experiences are not always sent out in words by radio or press. Many are carried in the Purple Hearts that are presented for wounds due to enemy action . . . some are carved into plexiglass pendants.

Retired M.D., Dr. Raymond C. Sanders, now of Lansing, Ill., was a radio-gunner on the author's crew all the way from OTU in Lakeland, Florida, through the combat tour in England and France. As was typical of so many of the 9th Air Force enlisted men in Marauder crews, he went on to greater things after the war.

Fig. 6-29. *Fuel being pumped out of 596th Sqdn., 397th BG's No. 43-34127 after a crash-landing similar to that of* AWOL Kid. *There was always a slight controversy over whether to crash-land on the runway or the grass beside it, due to the possible sparks generated during a runway belly landing causing a fire. Most pilots chose the grass. (photo courtesy Major Paul Gardella, USAF Ret.)*

Things in civilian life didn't prove to his liking after being separated from the service in late 1945, so he re-enlisted in the Air Force for another three-year hitch. Completing this, he then went back to college in his old home town, Louisville University, and continued to earn a degree in medicine.

He and the author had lost touch over the years but resumed contact again through the chance coincidence of Sanders reading a note in *Air Force* magazine that had been inserted by the author to request photos for this book. At a joyous reunion in the summer of 1986, after not seeing one another for 43 years, we two endeavored to catch up on all that had transpired during those intervening years. Scrapbooks, diaries, photos, and memorabilia were brought out, dusted off, and examined, and reminiscing ran rampant for a few days as our respective wives listened with awe—and sometimes disbelief—at some of the incidents recalled.

One in particular is worth repeating, and although it may lose some of its impact in the retelling, it does make a point.

The enlisted aircrew members in Sanders' Nissen hut in the 497th Squadron area of the 344th Bomb Group at their Stansted base in England were attempting to wind down after a mission on which excessive flak had been encountered. Nerves were on edge as these gunners, radio operators, and engineers tried to relax over a game of poker before their mess hall opened for evening mess.

At a crucial point in the game, just when four had dropped out and the two remaining were engaged in a duel of raising one another's bets, a ground officer from the armament section came in to inquire about the status of the guns on a certain airplane. Engrossed in the action at the poker table (two footlockers pushed together with a GI blanket covering them), no one even bothered to acknowledge the officer until he bellowed, "Well, what about it, Lipinski?"

Lipinski, the armorer-gunner on the aircraft in question, didn't even look up, but muttered: "Cleaned, oiled, ammo belts full, and in perfect working order, Lieutenant."

Maybe he was looking to find some negligence, or maybe he was just feeling his oats, but the Lieutenant wasn't satisfied and replied, "Okay, Lipinski, they'd better be because I understand you had a jamming problem on the top turret today and we don't want to have a reoccurrence now, do we?" Still not looking up from the game, Lipinski retorted: "Back off it, Lieutenant. I told you they were okay. Now bug off and leave us to our poker game!"

This popped the officer's cork, "Dammit, Sergeant Lipinski, stand up at attention when you talk to an officer!" Lipinski slowly rose to his feet and faced the Lieutenant with a halfhearted "Yes, sir." The Lieutenant then proceeded to chew him out for not having proper respect for an officer.

This caught the attention of the others, and midway through the tirade the glib-tongued guardhouse lawyer in the group interrupted with: "Begging the Lieutenant's pardon, but we've just come back from having our butts shot off and are just trying to relax. Lipinski's gun position on his airplane is the top turret and he, of all people, wouldn't tell you those guns were okay if they weren't, now would he?'' Then, a bit sarcastically, "Besides, Sir, our officers on our combat crews don't demand that we stand at attention when we talk to them, and we respect them anyway because they're right up there getting their butts shot off along with us!''

The Lieutenant was speechless for a moment, but he finally said: "As you were, men. I'll arrange it so you do have some respect for me.'' He turned on his heel and left.

The Lieutenant went straight to the Operations shack and asked to be put on temporary flying status to go along on the next day's mission as an observer. Although not entirely legal, occasionally non-aircrew personnel were granted a temporary flying status under certain conditions. Permission granted, the Lieutenant thought to himself: "By damn, I'll earn the respect of those guys the hard way. If this is what it takes, I'll do it!''

He chose to ride in Lipinski's ship and the mission turned out to be one he'd never forget! The target was a marshalling yard at Amiens, France, and the group caught hell with intense and accurate flak at the target. Two ships went down in flames, and his ship took hits that severed control cables and threw them momentarily out of control just after bombs-away.

The Lieutenant was riding in the navigator's seat, and all he could see out of the little side window was the horizon cocked at a weird angle as the ship left the formation and went into a shallow dive. Over the intercom he heard a rapid exchange of information between the pilot and the tail gunner regarding the severed control cables, and as he peered around the bulkhead to his rear, he could see the tail gunner crawling out of his position and groping his way to the bomb bay. Just then the pilot called: "You want to make yourself useful, Looie?'' The armament Lieutenant told him he sure would, so the pilot instructed him to go back and man the waist guns, as the radio-gunner was taking over the tail position while the engineer tried to repair the control cables.

By the time they had lost 9000 feet of altitude and were down to 3000 feet, the engineer had successfully spliced the cables, and they resumed level flight again. Everyone had just returned to their normal positions when the bombardier called: "We're approaching the Abbeville area and we're all alone, so keep an eye out for old Herman Goering's squadron of yellow-nosed FW-190s. Our P-47 escorts are with other stragglers from our box. They must have figured we were goners and didn't bother to follow us down.''

Looie double-checked his parachute and tightened the straps on his flak vest as he cowered down in the navigator's seat and wondered why he'd ever volunteered for this crazy venture. He looked out the window again and could just make out the French coast and the English Channel beyond and thought: "We're going to make it if nothing else goes wrong.''

Then:

"Bombardier to waist: I see an FW below us at twelve o'clock and he's headed in the opposite direction.''

"Waist to bombardier: Roger, I'll watch for him."

"This is the tail. He just went under us and is back at six o'clock and turning, turning—now he's coming up after us!"

"Pilot to all gunners: Keep an eye on him and let me know how to turn so you can get your best shot at him."

"Roger."

"This is the tail. He just zoomed up past me and didn't fire a shot! Watch for him, Lipinski."

"This is the turret. I saw him go up, but now I've lost him in the sun."

"Bombardier to turret: I see him now and he's diving down from two o'clock. Get on him, Lipinski!"

"Roger, I've got him now."

Just as Looie muttered to himself: "Those guns had better not jam, Lipinski, or your butt will be mud," the ship jolted with cannon fire hits and Lipinski's .50s chattered in return. The 190 passed over the ship and Lipinski swung his turret around, blasting away all the time as he kept the FW in his sights. As it headed on down, a wing came off and it began tumbling out of control. "You got him, Lip! Good boy!" called the tail gunner.

Over the channel a quick inspection of the cannon fire hits by the waist gunner proved that the shells had been duds and had just entered the fuselage in the bomb bay section and passed on through and out the other side—missing ribs, control cables, electrical conduits and all.

Back on the ground again, Looie left the ship without a word and hailed a ride on a passing Jeep. He didn't even bother to go to debriefing, but instead went straight to Operations and took himself off flying status.

That evening after mess he pulled two bottles of Scotch from the hoard in his footlocker and paid another visit to Lipinski's hut. Sanders recalls vividly the entrance he made and the little speech he gave.

As the Lieutenant opened the door and stepped inside, one of the men called "Attention!" but the Looie said: "As you were, men. I went on today's mission to gain your respect, but after what happened up there, you men have earned *my* respect. Take these bottles of Scotch and enjoy!"

The men were so surprised at this turn of events that silence prevailed as Looie turned to leave. Just as his hand reached the doorknob, they exploded with profuse thanks. The Looie raised his hand for silence and asked: "By the way, Lipinski, how many rounds did you fire at that 190?"

Nonchalantly, Lipinski replied: "Oh, just a few short bursts, Sir."

"Is that a fact? Well, for your information the barrels were so overheated they drooped like spaghetti, and my boys are changing them right now."

With that, he opened the door and left, getting the last word in—and saving a little face in the bargain.

Most of the Marauder targets were usually defended with batteries of 88s that contained from four to six guns each. The barrage-type walls of flak encountered by the heavies at their high altitude were frightening to see, but were not nearly as accurate as the pinpoint bursts of four to six gradually "walking" into a formation of Marauders if it didn't change course soon enough. The importance of the target to the Germans could always be determined by how many batteries they had defending it (Figs. 6-30 through 6-32).

The most feared and respected flak came from the German flying bomb launching sites in the Pas de Calais area of Northern France. In fact, the old rhyme from the Marauder's near-fatal days, "One a day in Tampa Bay," was resurrected in slightly different wording and crews could be heard muttering: "Two a day to the Pas de Calais!" with justified horror in their tone. With summer approaching, the daylight hours grew longer, and whenever possible each group was scheduled for two missions a day.

Marauders began bombing these sites in the spring of 1944, long before the first of Hitler's V-1 (Vengeance Weapon I) was ever launched against England. The sites carried the code name "Noball Target" and most crews had no idea as to what they were bombing. They were referred to as "secret intelligence" targets by the briefing officers, and only the top brass knew what they actually were. The map on the briefing hut wall showed the targets only to be a patch of woods at certain navigational coordinates.

Fig. 6-30. *The tragic result of a direct flak hit. Although of poor quality, the photo speaks for itself and illustrates the devastating effect of a shell exploding just aft of the bomb bay. (photo courtesy Ralph G. McConnell)*

Fig. 6-31. *Ninth AF publicity men eventually got on the ball in the late spring of 1944 and a rash of glamour photos were taken of aircrews and flying personnel. Most were of crews standing by their airplanes; others were of the "wild blue yonder gazing" type, such as these Pennsylvanians from the 497th Sqdn, of the 344th BG. L to R: Copilot E.F. Horn, Bombardier Frank Tidikis, Copilot Emmett Lancaster, Copilot Ed Borreson, and Copilot J. S. Hollinger. (USAAF photo courtesy Emmett Lancaster)*

Fig. 6-32. *1/Lt. Henry C. Woodrum was on pass in London and came back to Stansted to find his 495th Sqdn., 344th BG airplane in this condition. Capt. L. D. Clay, Jr., had flown it that day on a mission and couldn't get the gear completely down due to flak damage. Only injury was to Woodrum's pride for his ship. Spring 1944.*

However, Marauder crews knew they had to be something very important for the Germans to defend them with the most accurate and intense flak to be encountered over any type of target. Bombing these sites became the exclusive job of the 9th Air Force, and the Maraudermen's nerves grew frayed at not knowing what they were bombing at such great (in their minds) loss and damage to crews and aircraft.

All was revealed in mid-June when the first "Buzz Bombs," as the Yanks called them, or "Doodle Bugs," as the dry-humored British dubbed them, were launched against London. Continued bombing of the sites still produced the accurate flak, but at least the B-26 crews finally knew what they were attacking and it gave some degree of purpose to the effort, no matter how horrific the missions continued to be.

In spite of the repeated bombing of these sites, hundreds of the pulse-jet powered V-1s were launched against London. Resulting damage was negligible because many of those that weren't shot down by British fighters or antiaircraft guns got off course and dropped harmlessly in the countryside. Of course, this lack of precise guidance to the target produced a psychological terror among the English populace—they never knew for sure just where they would fall.

There's just no telling how many hundreds more would have been launched if the 9th AF hadn't begun bombing the launching sites as soon as they did (Fig. 6-33).

In spite of evasive action taken, many Marauders fell to flak; others came back riddled and damaged to such extent that by all laws of flight they shouldn't have been able to remain airborne. An entire chapter could be devoted to detailed accounts of these hair-raising and mind-boggling feats of airmanship (Fig. 6-34).

Other methods were used to reduce the flak damage, and the first of these was a British invention called "chaff" or "Window." Thin strips of paper with a tinfoil-type backing were thrown out of a formation of three "Window ships" that preceded the main bombing formation on the run to the target. Sometimes, each ship in the formation would also carry the stuff and the waist gunner would toss it out, the theory being that this would disrupt the German radar-controlled guns by creating false signals. How effective it was is debatable, but at least the Window ships never got shot at. The German gunners always waited for the main formation.

Later on, the P-47 escorts dive-bombed the gun installations prior to the bomb run. Half of the escort force would orbit above the bomber formation as top cover, while the other half peeled off to dive-bomb. Here again, results were sometimes less than desirable, but it was a great mental cushion for the Marauder crews to see the "Jugs" dive down and bomb or strafe the guns. In the beginning they did silence a lot of them, but, of course, the Germans soon wised up to this tactic and held their fire until the bomb run had begun. Without seeing the muzzle flashes, the P-47s had no way of knowing the exact location of the AA batteries. They couldn't risk being hit by the Marauders' falling bombs, so had to wait until the guns opened up again after the target was bombed—which they

Fig. 6-33. *General Dwight D. Eisenhower, Supreme Allied Commander, examines a V-1 flying bomb launching site late in the summer of 1944 which had just recently been captured by American troops in northern France. Lt. General Omar N. Bradley, commanding all U.S. ground forces in France, points out some of its features. (USA photo courtesy Major Richard C. Harris, USAF Ret.)*

always did without fail. The courage of these fighter jockeys diving right into the maws of 88s spewing out lethal shells is beyond description!

Much later on, the first crude attempt at an airborne radar-jamming device came into use under the code name "Carpet." It emitted three watts of noise when tuned to the German Wurzburg flak-control radar frequencies. Since there

Fig. 6-34. *This photo, taken in France in November 1944, shows 495th Sqdn. Operations Officer Major Lucius D. Clay, Jr., on right. Lt. Ted R. Broome is on left. Clay subsequently became CO of the 495th and after the war had the distinction of being the youngest four-star general to command the Pacific Air Forces. (photo courtesy Col. Wm. G. Ehart, USAF Ret.)*

were so many intangibles affecting any given flak experience, it was difficult to determine if this system reduced the amount of flak damage or not.

Leaving nothing to chance and covering all bases, the Marauder groups used all four systems right up to the end of the war—evasive action, Window, dive-bombing, and Carpet. Of course, two other systems were widely used, which have been employed by soldiers down through the ages and long before the introduction of science and technology to reduce losses—good luck talismans and prayer (Fig. 6-35).

Besides the accurate flak at the 10,000 to 14,000-foot medium altitudes for bombing, it was a fatiguing chore flying at those altitudes without oxygen, especially on a long mission of from four to five hours or longer. Flying a close formation from takeoff to landing is grueling enough without having to do it at altitude with no oxygen. True, most missions ran in the two or three hour range, but even that length of time, a great portion of it above the oxygen-critical altitude of 10,000 feet, sapped the energy and produced a lot of headaches and lightheadedness.

Why the Army had specified an original service ceiling of 26,400 feet will probably never be revealed, but one wonders what they were thinking of for the Marauder. A medium bomber does not fly at heavy bomber altitudes. The

Fig. 6-35. *Nose art on Marauders ranged from artistic to bizarre, and from humorous to sentimental. Typical examples are shown in this montage of some of the ships in the 344th Bomb Group. (official 344th Bomb Group photo)*

oxygen equipment required for operating at high altitudes would only have added more weight, thus reducing bomb load or performance, or both. Bona-fide superchargers would have been required, and this would have meant more weight also.

Evidently the planners weren't quite sure as to what role the Marauder was supposed to play in the overall war scheme, and it took the tragedies of trial and error in actual combat to determine just what she was best suited to do.

Next to flak, weather was the other hazard that made the sweat flow and the touchholes twitch on Marauder crews. Flying formation in the clouds? This was SOP (Standard Operating Procedure) with the 9th AF 26s. On numerous occasions a 36-ship formation would join up below the overcast and then bore on up through it in formation!

Retired USAF Major Roy E. Russell, now of Newark, Delaware, was flying a Marauder with the 391st Bomb Group and thought he'd topped everything when the British Army picked up him and his crew after they'd bailed out over France on 25 June 1944. They were back in England within two days to fly again. Russell, a Lieutenant at the time, should have quit when he was ahead, but the incident that surpassed the miraculous rescue came later on, during a climb through the overcast.

Russell was flying the Number Two wing position in a flight of six, and the clouds got so black with rain he lost sight of the lead ship's right wingtip. In the event this happened, the procedure dictated that you turn either right or left 15 degrees (depending upon which wing you were flying) and hold that heading for three minutes, then turn back to the group heading and continue your climb through the overcast, joining back up with the formation after coming out on top.

Before he could execute his 15-degree right turn, Russell had drifted left and his left wingtip hit the vertical stabilizer of the Number Four (deputy lead) ship. Russell's wingtip was sheared off outboard of the pitot tube, and Four's rudder was so severely damaged he had to abort, but successfully crash-landed on a farm near the Cliffs of Dover.

Not so with Russell. The collision had been so deafening they thought their bomb load had exploded, and the airspeed indicator went out due to pitot tube damage. Nevertheless, on orders of the gung-ho group commander, he continued to climb at full throttle—2700 rpm and 52 inches manifold pressure—through the overcast, subsequently rejoined the formation, and completed the mission minus the wingtip and airspeed indicator readings.

What makes a guy like this volunteer for a second tour after what he'd been through? Russell did, and flew a total of 70 missions in the B-26. He says he was "young, crazy and looking for glory" at the time, but more than likely it was confirmation of the usual dedication and determination common among most Maraudermen (Fig. 6-36).

Fig. 6-36. *1/Lt. Roy E. Russell sitting atop a 2000-pound bomb on a Matching airdrome hardstand waiting for his ship to be serviced and loaded for the second mission on D-Day. No Hollywood version of the "50-mission crush hat" for combat flying—just a raunchy old flight helmet and a GI pot for a flak helmet before regular flak helmets were issued. Note detached rear fin of bomb. (photo courtesy Major Roy E. Russell, USAF Ret.)*

Midair collisions even occurred when weather was not a factor, however rare they may have been. Col. James J. Crumbliss, USAF Ret., now of Bossier City, Louisiana, and then a 1st Lt. Marauder pilot in the 451st Squadron of the 322nd Bomb Group, recalls with sorrow that the nose of his G-5 model (43-34409) was completely severed in a midair collision at 1000 feet during a formation join-up over Beauvaix-Tille airdrome in France on 18 March 1945.

Fig. 6-37. *Number 409 in the air over Beauvaix-Tille before the fatal collision. Note upward cant of wing and engine nacelles on this G model. (photo courtesy Col. James J. Crumbliss, USAF Ret.)*

It was a perfect, clear spring morning, but the Number Six ship in the flight being led by 409 (Fig. 6-37) misjudged his join-up approach and hit the lead ship across the nose, taking out another ship in the process. All three crashed on the downwind leg of the takeoff join-up. The only survivor was the pilot of 409, who merely unfastened his seat belt and dropped out of the severed nose, popped his chute, oscillated one time (which broke his fall), and hit the ground. Luckily, Crumbliss was not flying his G-5 that day, but three of his original crewmembers were on board.

How could this happen on a perfectly clear day? Crumbliss (Fig. 6-38) believes that poor operational procedure and inexperience were the cause. The 322nd usually assigned the least experienced pilots to fly the Number Five and Six positions in a flight, when in reality those spots were the most difficult to fly and should have been flown by experienced pilots. The pilot of Number Six had fewer than 15 missions to his credit at the time.

Coincidentally, Crumbliss was from Baltimore, Maryland, at the time, and his wife worked at Martin for a while, spot-welding B-26 bomb bay doors, so Jim had a unique kinship with the airplane.

The 9th Air Force led the Allied air armada in to the beaches on D-Day, 6 June 1944. First came the Troop Carriers, hauling paratroopers and towing gliders during the night before; then in the predawn hours 486 Marauders (each group mounted a maximum effort force of over 54 aircraft each) bombed the landing areas on the Cherbourg Peninsula.

193

Fig. 6-38. *Crumbliss and his crew in front of 409 on a raw, wintry day at Beauvaix-Tille in early 1945. Crumbliss is standing on the right. (photo courtesy Col. James J. Crumbliss, USAF Ret.)*

Remembering the second mission to Ijmuiden, it was with no little degree of trepidation that the Marauder crews bombed when weather forced them to go down to levels between 2000 and 4000 feet in order to maintain visual contact with the targets. Fortunately, the Germans were taken by surprise and losses were minimal (Figs. 6-39, 6-40).

A two-page centerspread that appeared in *Life* magazine the following week depicted an artist's conception of the early morning strike against the beaches. It was awesomely as grandiose as the actual operation, showing flotillas of landing craft plowing through the choppy channel, ships of our Navy shelling the shore defenses, which were returning fire, and the sky filled with 9th Air Force medium bombers, fighters, and troop carriers heading for their targets. To the utter dismay of Maraudermen, the medium bombers shown were B-25s!

While it is true that a special unit of RAF Mitchells flew down on the deck to lay a smoke screen along the beaches to coincide with the Marauder's attack above, the artist had really goofed on this one! Those few B-25s on the deck were the only ones in the operation. The 486 mediums bombing the shore installations were all Martin B-26 Marauders!

Artistic license is sometimes forgivable, but this gross inaccuracy will never be forgotten by 9th Air Force veterans!

Fig. 6-39. *Marauders of 344th Bomb Group marshalling for takeoff on a pre-D-Day mission to France. Station 169, Stansted-Mountfichet, Essex, England.*

Retired Air Force Major James Lee, now of Huntsville, Alabama, was an armament specialist Staff Sergeant with the 497th Squadron of the 344th Bomb Group, and among his WWII memorabilia is a copy of a news dispatch by a reporter named MacKenzie who rode with the 344th that day. This is the dispatch:

Mackenzie Rides Marauder Bombing Path for Invaders

A B-26 Marauder Base in England, June 6: Riding in the van of American air spearhead which covered the landing of American Rangers on the coast of France, this reporter had a panoramic view this morning of the D-Day Invasion and saw the first Americans come ashore from smoking landing boats which had ridden through a curtain of German gunfire to reach the beach a few minutes before.

Deep behind the invaded beach, American paratroops and glider-borne Rangers were locked in battle along a wide irregular front. Airborne units had landed long before dawn and were engaged with the enemy when warships of the United Nations steamed in open order to within a few miles of the coast and commenced to pour in a steady fire.

Low wispy clouds down to 1500 feet mottled the battlefield and the Marauder crews could discern only fragmentary glimpses of the struggle etched by the flat, spitting fire of mechanized guns and the spurting bursts of tracer bullets.

The Germans had dammed or diverted waterways and flooded large sections of the countryside. Some sheets of water appeared to be anywhere up to 20 miles in diameter.

The run of the Marauders down the invasion coast just as dawn broke was one of the most dramatic and amazing single episodes in the history of air warfare. Some of the American bombers came down as low as 2000 feet to blast batteries of German guns with a rain of bombs in a little under 15 seconds.

Scarcely a man who began that run expected to come out alive. Although the crews were normally briefed to bomb a target from 10,000 to 10,800 feet, they were told before their takeoff in the dark that they must come down to

195

Fig. 6-40. *The lead ship of the 344th BG is airborne on the pre-D-Day mission. While some groups liked to hold the aircraft on the deck to pick up airspeed after breaking ground, the 344th favored attaining as much altitude as possible right after liftoff. This ship is only two-thirds of the way down the 8000-foot runway.*

5,000 feet or even 1,000 feet to get under a lowering cloud curtain, and they realized their assignment was a suicide raid.

At even 10,000 feet the Marauder has a tough time with flak. At 5000 feet, it theoretically has not even a 50-50 chance. At 2000 feet, carbines and machine guns can stop it, let alone 88mm anti-aircraft shells.

But this target was considered vital to the first assault. It had been ordered blasted. Behind the shore batteries, a target impervious to anything less than blockbusters sheltered hand-picked Nazi anti-invasion troops.

With airborne American troops fighting close to the target on the landward side and with others landing from barges to seaward, precision bombing was vital, unless large numbers of Americans were to be slaughtered. That is why the crack group of bombers known as "The Silver Streaks" were briefed to come right down on top of the target if necessary for deadly accurate aim.

General Omar Bradley's intent, apparently, was to button up the German troops in the shelters and by the concussion of the 250-pound impact explosive bombs to stun them into insensibility, so they would fall easy victims to the thrusting invaders, who were timed to arrive on the beach just as the Marauders passed over.

In order not to create fresh huge crater obstacles for the landing tanks, but instead to provide ready-made foxholes for our invading troops, 250-pounders were chosen instead of the 2000-pound bombs these aircraft usually carry.

196

To protect the landing forces from the enfilading fire and at the same time to mark clearly an invasion channel to the beach, American B-25 Billy Mitchell bombers of a special unit dashed right down on the water and began a run to the beach at right angles to the bomb run of the Marauders. The timing of their smoke barrage, the landing, and the bomb run was excellent.

As we cut the French coast, a red Me-109 dived to the carpet, raced under the formation, and zoomed to register our altitude for the gunners in the flak valley we were about to enter. But a tail gunner in the box behind us sent a few bullets skipping after him and he pulled off for an adjacent landing field apparently unhurt. Then the flak began.

We had dropped down so low that machine gun tracer bullets were flying up through our formation like sparks out of a factory chimney, curving redly over and into us. But the Silver Streaks, attempting no evasion, raced down on the target strip with advanced throttles.

The advance flights suffered heavy flak for the whole 15 seconds of their run, but with magnificent courage wavered neither to left nor right, laying their loads along the whole length of the target.

As the last Marauder element of our group was moving in for its run an FW-190 jumped it, got in a burst, and one of the Silver Streaks exploded. The stricken ship crashed in flames on the water's edge.

(Only two of more than 450 Marauders on the mission failed to return, the United Press reported).

While the Marauders were making their run, the guns of the fleet continued to pump metal, and the coast was being well saturated. At the other end of the duel, the German guns which we had watched heavily shelling the incoming invasion fleet seemed to have slacked about 75 percent.

At the end of our run, we turned inland to make a wide detour across the Cherbourg Peninsula and back to England. This route was necessary to accommodate the seven other Marauder groups following ours and the bomber stream of heavies coming behind them. A veritable one-way air traffic lane going south from England and another one-way return lane a few miles to the west going from the peninsula north to England. The traffic was heavy in both lanes.

As we turned away, the dive bombers of the 9th USAAF began to scream down, and the main body of the invasion fleet had drawn perceptibly closer to the beach.

High above, Allied fighters were milling around in the sky. Long before, a great mass of them had swept over northwestern France. As H-Hour drew near, the sky was black with them. With the exception of the two pinch-hitters which jumped our formation from the deck, we did not see a single German fighter.

All our way over the peninsula, isolated moderate flak pursued us, but we soon climbed above the machine-gun range and saw the tracers curving harmlessly away.

From this morning on, everyone who took part in this historic spearhead attack which opened the second front may consider that he is living on borrowed time.

The crewmen of the Marauders looked like Bactrian two-humped camels. The foundation of their massive clothing was a Mae West life jacket. Over that came a bulky parachute and over that the flak suit, which is a smock of iron plates that weighs 20 pounds. The whole is topped off with a steel helmet, and none of it seems thick enough when 88mm shells from the ack-ack guns are rocking and bumping the aircraft.

Our ship was captained and flown by Capt. Curt S. Seebaldt of Rochester, Mich. He said after we landed that he felt profoundly honored to have been in the first U.S. group to spearhead the invasion. His copilot, a tall youth from Cut Bank, Mont., Lt. Carlyle Webb, declared: "I'm no actor, but I believe I have just taken part in the opening scene of the greatest show on earth!"

The navigator was Lt. Edwin Freeman of El Campo, Tex., who described the mission as the greatest flight he had ever made. The bombardier, Lt. Edward Harrison of Tunstall, Va., summed up what all the combat crews thought of the sweep: "It's the first time I've been that close to the enemy!"

The wheels of the vast invasion machine began to turn for the cross-channel lunge last Wednesday. The last forward moves in the assemblage of the invasion forces were completed. Vast transport fleets were at their stations. Warships of the Allied fleets were moving in on the bases for their opening attacks. All the intricate machinery of the greatest invasion enterprise in history was accelerating quickly and smoothly to assault tempo.

For weeks, the corps of correspondents—each individual assigned to his D-Day post—had been drilled and versed in the part he was to play. They were called to Supreme Headquarters of the Allied Expeditionary Force by telephone on Wednesday morning and instructed to tell nobody of the summons.

From the moment they arrived at Headquarters they were under strict military law, forbidden all communications with the outside world. They were told D-Day was at hand, briefed for the assault, and assigned to their invasion stations. They left their hotels quietly and secretly carrying light combat kit and leaving their effects strewn about untouched so even their room maids would not guess that anything unusual was afoot. Their bills were unpaid and dates waited starry-eyed and forlorn.

The last section to move out were the radio, camera, and newsmen assigned to cover the 9th Air Force medium bombers. They were flown from a London airport to various command airfields and disembarked in parties of three. This correspondent was in the last party to disembark at the station of the famous Silver Streaks.

This crack outfit of medium bombers, who since March have strewn havoc and desolation among marshalling yards, airfields, highways, docks, and strategic bridges deep in France and the Netherlands, has an equally famous Commander, Col. Reginald F. C. Vance of San Antonio, Texas (Fig. 6-41).

198

Fig. 6-41. *Col. R.F.C. Vance, CO 344th BG, pins a medal on Major J. C. Maxwell, 496th Sqdn. Commander, in impromptu awards ceremony at Stansted base. Dapper Col. Vance still wears his olive-drab Class A blouse from his Phillipine days. 495th Sqdn. CO, Major Jens Norgaard, awaits his turn on right. Maxwell rose to the rank of Major General after the war and his last assignment prior to retirement was heading up the Air Force supersonic jet transport project. (photo courtesy Maj. Gen. J. C. Maxwell, USAF Ret.)*

Col. Vance was assessed by Gen. MacArthur to be more valuable to the U.S. than 200 pounds of bar gold. It happened like this:

Col. Vance, who had arrived in the Phillipines 17 days before the Japs, led U.S. dive bombers until there were none left. He then was attached to MacArthur's staff and fought down through Bataan, through the tunnel into Corregidor and into the last ditch. When the moment came for MacArthur to decide on indispensables to be evacuated to Java by submarine, 200 pounds of gold were thrown off to make way for him.

The Silver Streaks have made more than 67 missions since they arrived in England last January. The sons of three generals man ships. They are Capt. Lucius D. Clay, Jr., First Lieut. Jack J. Jones, and Capt. Charles E. Hardy. These and 13 other pilots of the Silver Streaks are West Point graduates.

Every man of every combat crew in the group has been decorated and are all now seasoned veterans of the flak alleys of the invasion defenses. In operation, they weave through shrapnel, dart over their targets, drop their bombs, and then race home like bats out of hell. Flak is their chief hazard. Fighters of the Luftwaffe seldom trouble them. The Silver Streaks are as heavily armored as either a B-24 Liberator or a B-17 Fortress and have much more superior speed and maneuverability.

A few days ago an Me-109 chose to attack a crack Marauder and finished at the bottom of the Channel. The Streak piloted by Capt. Clay was toiling home on one engine when the German pursuit far below zoomed up to cut down the isolated cripple. As he reared up with spitting guns astern the American ship, Staff Sgt. George R. Anderson, a Californian, turned on his twin "choppers" in the tail turret and blew the attacker in half.

Besides the career of the Colonel, the Streaks take pride in their association with Gen. Doolittle's famous Tokyo raid. Lt. Col. Bob Witty, 28, of Cleveland, Ohio, a former newspaperman and father of twin boys and second in command of the group, was among the original volunteers for and planners of the Tokyo mission, but to his eternal regret was one of the five of the historic group in a Minneapolis hotel who offered to go but he was turned down.

It became known on Monday that Col. Witty, who had been grounded for nearly two weeks for the special purpose, was to lead the Streaks over the invasion coast in the place of honor of the whole first invasion phase—the first American aircraft group over the beachhead and spearhead of the invading American forces.

As soon as we arrived at the advanced airbase from which we were to set out on D-Day the following Tuesday, all of us were warned not to discuss our assignment with the combat crews as they had not then any inkling of what impended.

On Sunday, the Silver Streaks took off from the airfield in the green wooded English countryside for their last run before the invasion. They were set to pound the 300-foot-high trestle railway bridge over the Seine just above Rouen, France. A magnificent placement of bombs cut the bridge in three places and sent it tumbling into the river.

Next day, the eve of D-Day, all machines of the Silver Streak group were grounded and all personnel on the field were confined to camp. Those of us who knew that the invasion was to take place on the morrow and that the paratroops would be landed behind the German lines just before dawn packed our kits and sat by drinking black coffee and eating massive cheese sandwiches waiting for reveille, which was timed for half an hour after midnight.

There was no air of ill-suppressed excitement. None of us outside the colonel and a few others knew at what spot the first American invasion was to land. We knew that we would find out at 2:30 when we were briefed, but we did know that perhaps thousands of lives depended upon the accuracy of the Silver Streaks' bombing; that the job was to stun into stupidity the horde of German troops crouching under the concrete shelters facing the beach where American troops were to spearhead the army of deliverance into France.

MacKenzie's account, in the typical "dispatchese" of the time, somewhat glamorized the "Johnny-come-lately to the ETO" 344th, but painted a vivid picture of the first strike and elaborated on the secrecy that surrounded the entire operation. With all the many people "in the know" other than the military, it's a miracle that none of the information was leaked!

It is interesting to note that the two ships lost on the initial strike on D-Day were from Emmett Lancaster's flight of the 344th. Emmett mentions the one blowing up, but he didn't realize at the time it was a victim of an FW-190 attack along with the ground fire. In the painting the second one is seen sliding under 7I★D with fire coming from the right engine.

To continue with the 7I★D story: They continued to lose altitude but were finally able to hold it at around 1200 feet. At this level they caught more small caliber ground fire and bullets shattered the windshield in front of pilot Schwaegerl, making his forward vision impossible. Lancaster took over the controls and they jettisoned flak vests, guns, ammo, and all other necessary equipment to keep from stalling out as they mushed back across the Channel all alone.

On one engine the Marauder took on an even more pronounced nose-high attitude, and the shorter Lancaster had difficulty seeing ahead over the nose. The copilot seat had no height adjustment—only backward and forward—and even an added cushion under him didn't improve the situation appreciably. As a consequence, Schwaegerl instructed the tail, waist, and turret gunners to all come forward into the navigator-radio compartment, but even this didn't bring the nose down sufficiently for Lancaster to see well enough. Bombardier W.J. Kammermeyer stayed in the nose and acted as Lanc's forward eyes, directing him to the first airfield he spotted after making landfall on the south coast of England in the Bournemouth area.

Schwaegerl made radio contact with the field and requested a straight-in approach for an emergency landing; flares were fired and Kammermeyer talked Lancaster onto the approach until he could nose down on the final to make his first combat single-engine landing! This crew teamwork saved them and 7I★D to fly again.

Flying copilot in the deputy lead ship of the box in which Lancaster's flight was the low flight, the author remembers seeing the one ship blow up but became too engrossed in the bomb run to have noticed the second ship leave the formation. However, I did witness another miracle that could only have been accomplished by a Marauder. One of the wingmen in the first box took a flak hit, did a complete snap-roll and came right back on his leader's wing to continue the bomb run as if nothing had happened!

The same S/Sgt. George L. Teague, who gave us a comparison of combat flying in the Pacific and ETO was a tail gunner, and his ship was flying the Number Three position in the lead flight of the first box of the 344th's maximum effort on D-Day. According to Teague's diagram of the first box in the following account, reporter MacKenzie was in the lead ship of the low flight of this box. Here's Teague's personal description of that memorable day:

"We knew that something was up and though we didn't know exactly what, the majority opinion had it that the invasion was at hand. We hadn't flown the previous day, which was the 5th. This was unusual; the Group flew every day, just about. Also, there were some new markings being put on the planes. These were put on for quick identification and to prevent the Germans from disrupting the formations by using captured Allied aircraft.

"Briefing was called for the 6th of June at a very early hour, too—one o'clock in the morning. Most briefings were called for about four or five o'clock. As a result, hardly anybody got any sleep as we were all wondering what was coming off. We rode to the briefing shack in the weapons carriers after eating midnight chow. The weather was bad, raining and windy, and we couldn't see flying in this kind of weather unless the weather was a whole lot different on the continent.

"We got to the briefing shack with its rows of chairs, some of which were already taken by early arrivals. The map was draped with a green cloth as usual, and the briefing officer with his wooden pointer was waiting for everyone to be seated. Finally we were all there and he started. It was as we expected—this was the invasion! We were told we would be bombing a coastal battery just a few minutes before the infantry was to hit the beach. We were told that this battery could sink anything afloat and that it was imperative that we knock it out (Fig. 6-42).

"Unlike other missions, we were told if for some reason we couldn't make a successful run the first time, we weren't to try it again because there were other groups right behind us and the schedule was arranged to the second. Don't try to make a second pass; forget it. We were also told that we might be going in at an altitude of under 1,000 feet, which meant we would suffer heavy casualties and losses of planes but that we had to go in anyway; the invasion was of all importance and losses of planes were to be expected.

"This briefing was greeted with what could be called mixed emotions. There was much cheering at the news of the invasion, but deep silence at the heavy casualties bit. There was a constant rumbling of low talk, which was unusual. Usually, briefings are very businesslike and quiet except for the coughing.

"The briefing finally over, we went to our planes. Our ground crews, having been also briefed, were extra-conscientious and helpful. The flak suit wagon

Fig. 6-42. *Scene in 344th Bomb Group briefing room for pilots, copilots, bombardiers, and navigators at 0230 hours 6 June 1944. Taken by author with no flashbulb at risk of being court-martialed for breaking security.*

got a big play. I think most planes carried several extra flak suits that day, and if the pilots hadn't stopped it, every ship would have had a few hundred extra pounds in suits, which were alleged to make fine protective floor mats. One tail gunner I knew had himself a regular 'cave' built in the back until his pilot made him throw out about five extra suits.

"At 0330 everyone had manned their planes and at 0354 the first box started its engines, second box at 0402, and third box at 0410. At 0402 the first box started to taxi out and soon one could see a long line of blinking navigation lights heading towards the runway. At 0412 the first plane took off and we were on our way.

"It was dark and rainy; very poor weather for flying, and I imagine under less pressing circumstances we wouldn't have gone, especially since the weather was just as bad the other side of the Channel. The roster of pilots flying that day for the 495th Squadron looked like this:

		Norgaard-Witty		
(My pilot)Glass			Foote	
		Johnson-Williams		
Courtright			Henry	
Seebalt			Bowers	
Baily	Cahill		Phillips	Nichols
Steen			Dixon	
Carrington	Kolberg		McDonald	Fitzwater

"One thing missing as we took off were the spectators along the perimeter fence at the side of the runway. It was too early for them. Usually in the summer, even at five in the morning, the English were there watching us. On an afternoon mission I've seen as many as 200 lined up waving to us as we took off.

"One who probably watched us that day, no matter the time, was 'Ma' Robinson of the Nag's Head pub, which was just at the bottom of the hill from the 495th barracks area. She was a widow of about 70 and had adopted the 344th, especially those of the 495th Squadron. We used to spend many an hour drinking beer and playing darts in her little pub. We could always see her watching us as we took off and again when we came back. If it was dark, we wouldn't be able to see her, but we knew she was there. When a crew didn't come back from a mission, she would feel worse about it than we would. When her favorite, a gunner named Hickey, was shot down over Brest she cried for several days. Tears would come to her eyes ever after when his name was mentioned. She was a nice old lady and we all thought a lot of her.

"We usually climbed to altitude immediately after takeoff, but today we didn't; we barely got to 1,000 feet and stayed there. It was still dark so we couldn't see anything beneath us except for the odd light here and there which had escaped notice of the blackout wardens. We left the English coast at 0545 and it had become daylight—a murky half-daylight. There was a solid cloud cover above us and rain squalls every few minutes. Almost immediately when we got to the Channel, we saw the ships. I've never seen so many ships before or since. They were everywhere. We had flown only a few more minutes when we could see the warships close to the coast firing on enemy positions.

"We had finally managed to get up to 3,500 feet, and we swung in formation towards the Cherbourg Peninsula, opening our bomb doors just as we hit the coast. We were getting a few bursts—not very accurate—of light flak, also a bit of machine gun fire. Three minutes after we passed over the French coast, we dropped our bombs. We gunners, not normally able to use our guns on ground positions because of our usual 10 to 12 thousand foot altitude, today opened up at every flash we could see aimed in our direction. There weren't very many of them; it appeared that everything that the enemy could bring to bear was leveled on the beach. They didn't seem to be worrying much about us this morning.

"That was D-Day for us—almost a milk run. If it hadn't been for the weather, which I'm sure must have been difficult flying for the pilots, it would have been a milk run. Far from the heavy casualties forecasted by the briefing officer, we were hardly hit. I think we did a good job on the coastal batteries we were supposed to hit. We could see the troops on the beaches and we realized that it was no milk run for them. This was one of the times I didn't envy the ground troops' ability to jump in a hole or trench; there weren't any for them today, and I was very happy to be where I was—in a B-26 heading back to England.

"We flew back to Bishops Stortford at under 1,000 feet altitude. As we went over the English countryside, I sat in the tail turret watching the scenery. I used to like to fly low; we rarely did, because it was more dangerous than at altitude, but low flying never bothered me. We landed at 0733 and that was the end of my 30th mission in Europe, a comparatively easy one, though the day was far from easy for the ground forces. The next one, though—a marshalling yard deep in enemy territory, flown in the same kind of weather—was not to be so easy. But that was the next one, and we didn't worry about the next ones till they had to be flown.''

Being in the lead aircraft of the low flight in the first box of B-26s to hit the beachhead targets, Teague had the advantage of the element of surprise, and the first box didn't catch as much flak as the second and third boxes of the 344th, as evidenced by Lancaster's experience quoted earlier. Likewise, the groups following the 344th in were subjected to more intense smaller caliber ground fire.

Lt. Roy E. Russell, flying with the 391st Bomb Group on the D-Day morning mission, took two 20mm cannon hits on his aircraft that chewed a chunk out of his rudder and left a gaping hole in the right wing just forward of the flap. Figures 6-43 and 6-44 show the metal-rending results of these hits.

All Marauder groups went out on a second mission on D-Day afternoon, and a variety of targets were hit adjacent to the beachheads. Joe Chiozza, now

Fig. 6-43. *Holes in the right wing of Russell's Marauder after returning to Matching airdrome from the first D-Day mission. (photo courtesy Major Roy E. Russell, USAF Ret.)*

Fig. 6-44. *The damaged rudder on Russell's 391st BG Marauder, a C-45 model. Trim tab is still intact, but hole made lateral control difficult. (photo courtesy Major Roy. E. Russell, USAF Ret.)*

of Memphis, Tennessee, was a 344th BG bombardier and furnished Fig. 6-45, a strike photo of the hits scored on gun emplacements on the tip of the Cherbourg Peninsula by the 344th on their second mission on D-Day afternoon. The early morning mission had been a maximum-effort-type for all groups, but due to flak damage received during the initial strike, not enough aircraft were available for a second mission of maximum effort, so the groups launched the normal 36-ship formations.

Now, as the 12th AF had done in the Mediterranean, the 9th would be concentrating on targets that were in direct support of the Allied ground forces. In addition to the actual target destruction materially aiding the advance of the ground forces, just the mere sight of the Marauders, Havocs, and fighters of the 9th in the sky above them was a terrific morale boost. Those who had been a bit weak on their aircraft identification soon learned that when they saw those black and white wing and fuselage stripes, "their" Air Force was in there blasting the enemy.

Regardless of the meticulous and precise planning and scheduling for the D-Day invasion, foul-ups did occur. None were of too serious a consequence, and in spite of the seriousness of the entire operation, some had a humorous

Fig. 6-45. *Strike photo of second D-Day mission for 344th BG showing bomb bursts among gun emplacements on tip of Cherbourg Peninsula. Clearing weather permitted bombing at higher altitude than on the morning mission. (photo courtesy Joe Chiozza)*

flair. One such incident was described in an article that appeared in a 1950 issue of the *Air Force* magazine:

That Was It

By Charles Cooke

"This is it!" was said at thousands of briefings during the war. But when the Commanding Officer of our bombardment group of B-26 Marauders—we were known as "The Bridge Busters"—mounted the briefing platform one morning nearly six years ago at the ungodly hour of 0208, he spoke the familiar words with a significant shift of accent. He said: "This *is* it!"

It was. The date was June 6th, 1944.

At the Commanding Officer's next words, there was a stir among the pilots, navigators, bombardiers, and copilots in the jam-packed briefing room: "You will probably have undercast at the target. If you do, you are to go down into the clear, no matter how low that takes you. You are to hit your targets today if you have to go in at treetop!"

"You are flying this morning in support of the First Army's landing on the Contentin Peninsula. Each of the three flights in each of our three boxes will drop its bombs at 0620 as briefed. You will then get the hell out of there because fifteen hundred Flying Forts are coming in on another heading to blast the beach defenses at 0625. The first men out of the barges will hit the shore at 0630 and the invasion will be on."

The Commanding General of the 9th Bomber Command, in an unexpected personal appearance, made us a short "I know you will not fail" speech. We felt flattered that he had chosen to come to our particular base that morning.

The Chaplain prayed—another unprecedented thing at a briefing.

Takeoff was set for 0402. It would still be full night at that hour.

When, at 0130, we had filed, cold and sleepy, into the briefing room, the weather was so thick and the night so black and rain-filled that nobody thought a mission would be possible, although everybody knew, of course, that this was D-Day. The Marauder was a daylight bomber, and it disliked dirty weather more than most combat planes because it was so heavy for its wing and so hard to handle, even under the best conditions.

It was, of course, a "maximum effort" mission. Normally, a Marauder group put 36 planes in the air. This time every B-26 on the base was scheduled—54.

When we got out to the aircraft hardstand, our ground crew wasn't there at all. The air crew (I was an observer)—pilot, copilot, navigator, bombardier, engineer-gunner, radio-gunner, and tail gunner—stood around in the drizzle in a numb, frustrated way. As I joined them, the pilot, an ordinarily cheerful captain named Hixon, swore prodigiously.

"Well, look her over as fast as you can. It's all we can do."

Hixon stood a moment as though dazed; his nerves, already under the strain of the impending night takeoff and the possibility of low-altitude flying, had to take on the added strain of the non-appearance of his ground crew. He climbed in and took his seat.

At this point another outlandish thing became apparent. The plane's "putt-putt," an auxiliary gasoline motor which was used to start the big four-bladed electric propellers turning, was not in the plane. Its proper place was in the waist compartment, but on this fabulous morning it squatted outside on the wet tarmac of the hardstand like a cold brass toad. It was still connected; its long leaders coiled up into the fuselage like a black snake.

When Hixon shouted: "Start the putt-putt!" over the interphone about 40 seconds later, the engineer dropped out of the plane, started the putt-putt where it squatted, and climbed back in.

The props revved up like charms. The lack of a preflight had apparently done no harm. It was time for "Taxi Out."

We moved out of the hardstand and started slowly down the perimeter track. Looking out of the navigator's bubble, I was barely able to make out a Jeep that whirled up to a wild stop. Figures jumped out, gesticulating. I could see by their mouths that they were yelling blue murder, but the roar of the engines made it impossible to hear what they were saying.

Both pilots had seen them, but once a bombardment mission has started to move, screaming and pointing men are not reason enough to halt a taxiing plane and throw the whole takeoff out of gear.

Over the interphone, to nobody in particular, Hixon said: "What the hell was eating them?"

After we had been airborne an hour: "Tail gunner to Pilot, Tail Gunner to Pilot, we got a tail!"

"What?"

"Yes, sir! I just now noticed it. It's whippin' around out there behind us and it's snappin' and jerkin' and givin' off red, green, and blue sparks!"

"Hendershot, are you flak-happy?"

"No, sir."

The engineer, standing beside me, suddenly bent double with laughter. "I know what it is. It's the putt-putt. I forgot to tell Ames to disconnect it."

Pilot: "Christ in the foothills, that means we taxied out with it, too! Right past Operations and General Anderson!"

Engineer: "That must be what those men were pointing at."

Pilot: A Groan.

Tail Gunner: "It just fell off, sir."

We were still over England, climbing, forming our boxes, and heading for our rallying point on the coast.

The big three-box formations started across the Channel at 3,000 feet. The plane shook to a series or rat-tat-tat-tats that sounded like a steam riveter at work in the plane; our gunners were clearing their .50-caliber machine guns and test-firing them. We kept going into and out of clouds, losing, resighting, and losing again the wing of the Marauder which, ahead and to our left, was our visual contact for keeping our place in the formation.

Above the clouds, the sky was purple and the stars and moon was brilliant. The undercast looked in the moonlight like a field of incredibly piled-up snowbanks. Some of the cloud-snowbanks towered so high that we had to fly through them.

The interior of the clouds was solid white. Each time we plunged from transparent purple light into opaque white, I recalled, with unpleasant vividness, things I'd heard about vertigo: "In a cloud, you won't know, you can't know, which way is up." "You can be in a bank and think you're straight and level." "You have to trust your instruments, you have to trust them absolutely." "If you lose your nerve in a cloud, you've had it!"

We lost the formation twice. Interphone conversations ceased as we strained our eyes for the wing of our "contact" sister. It wasn't cloud vertigo the crew feared, for our pilots were very sharp. It was collision.

By a combination of luck and skill of our pilots, we regained our proper position just before our box started its long slant down for the kill.

We put on our helmets and struggled into our heavy flak suits, which cuirassed us front and back. It was then, through a hole in the undercast, that I saw, in the dawn's early light, a sight I will never forget—hundreds on hundreds of ships heading toward France in a leagues-long semicircle spread out on the gray, white-capped waters. From our height they were toy ships with toy wakes showing the unanimous direction of this segment of the invasion armada.

We left the ships behind. It was 0612. The navigator tapped me on the shoulder and pointed down through his blister. "Navy offshore batteries!" he roared in my ear. Looking down, remembering our soldiers crouched in the approaching landing craft, it was good to see the flashes of the big Navy guns.

The hole below us was gone; we were over the cloud-snowfield again. We put our nose down as the box began to lose altitude. We were in the white for what seemed hours. When we came into the clear, the undercast was an overcast. The altimeter read 6300 feet and the French Channel coast was below.

Looking out of the radio operator's window I saw red streaks slanting up between us and the plane on our left. The streaks looked like red, reversed rain. I watched them without any reaction, because, combat missions being the exception and not the rule in my military routine, I didn't know what they were. I had been watching for the black puffs of typical flak.

The streaks had stopped by the time we heard:

"Bombardier to Pilot, opening bomb bay!"

"Roger."

A terrific clatter was audible to all of us over the sound of the engines and the grating of the opening bay. The navigator, radio man, and I looked at each other blankly.

"What in the name of God was that?" Hixon asked over the interphone.

"Damned if I know, sir," said the engineer.

"Didn't you check the bomb bay?"

"I flashed a light in there and saw that the bombs were in. There wasn't time."

"Bombardier to Pilot, straight and level!"

The climactic moment came at exactly 0620.

"Bombs away!"

The yell of "yay-y-y-y!" that filled our earphones sounded as though it came from one throat. Although no flak was visible, our box went into violent evasive action, as briefed, then turned off across the peninsula.

Bombardier: "A superior, I think!" "Check off one Kraut strongpoint!"

It was nearly daylight.

Tail Gunner: "Ten million planes at four o'clock!"

Pilot: "That'll be the heavies."

Over water again, heading north, we saw heavy flak to our left over Guernsey Island much too far away to threaten us. As we flew over England, singing and laughing, we sounded like a B-26 full of happy magpies. Early morning sunlight flooded in through the plexiglass nose.

The interrogation room buzzed with relief, high spirits, and the general excitement of The Day.

The "Bridge Busters" had not lost a ship or a man, although Box One, whose target was an ammunition dump, had to go in at 1200 feet. All three boxes reported "Superior" results, but six of Box One's planes were hit by machine-gun tracer bullets, the red rain I had watched with the fearlessness of ignorance. One Box One crew swore that a Kraut heaved a rock at them, they were so low.

Hixon was sarcastically congratulated because of our "tail." It had been marvelled at during the taxiing and takeoff by the entire groundling population of the base—over 2000 officers and enlisted men. The screaming, gesticulating men we had seen as we started to taxi turned out to have been our ground crew. They had been awakened late.

And gradually the explanation came out on the clatter we heard when our bomb bay opened. Inside the bay, resting on the doors, had been 15 Army cots, dozens of new, shiny kitchen pots and pans, and seven cases of K-rations. Our crew chief had drawn these things for his barracks and mess hall and had laid them on the bomb bay doors, after the bombs were in, to prevent them from a "moonlight requisition." He had intended to remove them while preflighting the plane, then take them to their destination after takeoff. When the bomb bay swung open, the whole conglomeration fell out into German-occupied France.

It was the considered opinion of everybody that a case of K-Rations was at least as lethal as a 250-pound bomb.

Probably the most amazing thing about the entire 9th Air Force Marauder armada's participation was that there were no midair collisions! Although all the groups had been practicing predawn takeoffs and join-ups all during the month of May on days when no mission was scheduled for the morning, it was still a risky business trying to join up with a set of navigation lights as opposed to a clearly defined aircraft shape.

D-Day morning proved to be blacker than any of the practice session mornings, and the intermittent rainfall even further distorted the navigation light flashes that the pilots were homing in on.

Once joined up, it became a little easier to maintain visual contact, but flying in and out of cloud layers on the way to the targets only amplified the risk of disorientation.

It required 100 percent concentration on the part of the "old hand" pilots, and the rookies must have had to put forth 110 percent to bring the whole thing off as successfully as it turned out.

After D-Day the usual targets were still bombed, but added to the list were road junctions, troop and armor concentrations, strongpoints in German defenses, supply and ammunition dumps, etc. (Figs. 6-46 through 6-49). Direct support of the Allied ground forces was the mission, and it was fulfilled. In the long daylight hours of "Double British Summer Time," two and sometimes three missions per day became standard operating procedure for the B-26 groups when the weather permitted. Crews eager to get their missions in and go home were many times disappointed at being recalled from a mission because George Patton's armored columns had overrun a target before the bomber formation could get there.

John Meehan, now of Ft. Lauderdale, Florida, was a radio-gunner in the 599th Squadron of the famous 397th Bomb Group, the "Bridge Busters." John joined the group when it was being formed in April 1943, and was assigned to Captain Powers' crew.

Shortly after the group became operational in April 1944, the Squadron Commander, L/C E. H. Berkenkamp, now of Tacoma, Washington, pirated John from Powers to be the radio operator on his lead crew. Meehan naturally took a dim view of this and let his feelings be known to the Colonel. After all, he'd trained with the Powers crew, gone all through OTU with them, shared the fun of cross-country trips to Oklahoma City, Reading, Pennsylvania, and other favorite destinations while they were stationed at Hunter Field, Savannah, Georgia, and had flown the south Atlantic route with them to England. Berkenkamp understood, so didn't belabor the point with Meehan at the time.

Fig. 6-46. *Lead and low flight of the first 344th BG box on the 7 June mission. Target was gun positions at Barfleur, France, just inland on the Cherbourg Peninsulas and south of the landing beaches. No pre-dawn takeoff involved, just the routine mid-morning mission. Bomb load was eight 500-pound fragmentation bombs.*

212

Fig. 6-47. *On the return flight to England from the 344th's 7 June Barfleur mission, landing craft of the invasion forces heading for Normandy could be seen in the Channel below.*

Sometime later, after Powers' crew had racked up between 25 and 30 missions, they were shot down over France and Berkenkamp couldn't resist telling Meehan that if he'd stayed with Powers, he'd now be a POW.

This fact gave little solace to John, as no report was forthcoming that his former crew buddies were actually POWs. Likewise, no confirmation came through that they had been killed, so they were officially listed as "Missing in Action."

Unbeknownst to the group, the entire crew had evaded capture after bailing out and had made contact with the French underground. Amazing as it may seem, they didn't become separated, and at one time were hidden out in the attic above a bakery in a French village. Many anxious moments were sweated out listening to Germans coming into the bakery to buy bread during their stay there. Eventually the underground spirited them out of France.

Soon after D-Day the entire crew came back to the 397th for a visit before being sent back to the States and Meehan got back at Berkenkamp by saying: "See, Colonel, if I'd been with them, I'd be going home now!"

John went on to fly 65 missions with "Fearless Fosdick" Berkenkamp, and now they kid one another about the deal at their annual unit reunions. Powers made a career of the Air Force, retiring as a Colonel; he now lives in San Antonio.

Back around mid-May some of the new F models had begun to filter into the 9th AF's inventory. It took a little getting used to flying on the wing of an F leading a formation. The new angle of the wing made it appear that she was flying straight and level even though she was slowly climbing.

Fig. 6-48. *Marauder of the 323rd BG coming off the target on a post D-Day mission against a German airfield installation in France. (photo courtesy Glenn L. Martin Co.)*

Since no engineering drawings or data are now available, the exact nature of the proposed E model changes that didn't carry over into the production F model could not be determined—namely, the revised gun arrangement, new escape hatches, and the reloadable twin-tube bazooka for rocket bombs. The first two would have been well-accepted by the combat groups, although it is difficult to imagine how the defensive firepower could have been improved except

Fig. 6-49. *Nose art on 497th Sqdn. Commander D.D. Bentley's ship in the 344th BG. The dual-meaning name worked and it was never "got" by flak or fighters during Bentley's tenure as 497th CO. As a Lt. Col. he was transferred to the 322nd BG as Deputy Commander in August 1944.*

by covering the small "dead zone" cone below the tail. Of course, new escape hatches would have been welcomed with open arms because the Marauder was not the easiest airplane from which to bail out.

The bazooka tubes, on the other hand, would have been given a very jaundiced reception, as they only smacked of a return to low-level operations. Maraudermen would probably have said: "Let the Pacific B-25s with their 75mm nose cannons get the glory if they want it. We don't need bazookas!" Likewise, Peyton Magruder must have held his head in his hands and moaned: "Oh, no! They'll never learn!" when some AAF armament whiz kid suggested this installation. It's just as well they weren't incorporated, as the 75s in the Mitchells didn't prove to be all that successful anyway.

As our ground forces began to move out of the Normandy area, the 9th Air Force left England and moved to France in various stages. In August all but two of the 20 fighter groups had moved to fighter strips on the continent. The remaining two moved over in mid-September. Sometimes the runways they used were nothing but perforated steel matting laid down, but they were operational in record time (Figs. 6-50 through 6-53).

When the first fighter groups moved over in late June and early July, the ground troops were still fighting to drive the Germans out of the hedgerows. Close air support was "close" in more ways than one. In many cases the strips were so close to enemy lines that instead of taking off in a southerly direction,

Fig. 6-50. *Yankee ingenuity welds the old to the new to direct air traffic at a 9th AF P-51 Mustang fighter strip in Normandy. (USAAF photo courtesy Major Richard C. Harris, USAF Ret.)*

Fig. 6-51. *Typical temporary mess facilities in the early days in France. Chow line of the 497th Sqdn., 344th BG, November 1944. Airman facing camera with mess gear in hand is Sgt. Wojack, who painted most of the beautiful girls on the 497th ships.*

Fig. 6-52. *Typical of bomb-gutted Luftwaffe hangars on air bases the 9th occupied are these on Station A-59, Cormeilles-en-Vexin, near Pontoise, France—home of the 344th BG.*

Fig. 6-53. *French agri-business as usual at A-59—a peasant lad doing his fall plowing on the air base area. At first, security on the air bases was even more relaxed than in England.*

the fighters were forced to start off towards the north and circle to gain altitude before crossing the enemy-held positions just to the south of the strip!

The Marauders and Havocs of the 9th followed the fighters over to France a month or so later and got a little taste of what their predecessors in Alaska, the Pacific, and the Mediterranean had been putting up with all along. All the airfields they occupied had formerly been Luftwaffe bases, so what facilities the 9th hadn't destroyed in the months previous with their bombing, the Germans had demolished before abandoning them. Squad tents became the standard housing shelter, and, in many cases, mess halls were out in the open until temporary structures could be erected many weeks later.

The runways were pretty much intact, but hangars had been destroyed, as well as all other support buildings, barracks, administration buildings, water supply (the Germans had even placed explosives in the water supply or contaminated it so it couldn't be used), etc.

Maraudermen could tell from the ruins on the various bases that the Luftwaffe had fared pretty well during their occupation of France. Even the washrooms and shower facilities in the hangars for the use of mechanics had been finished off in ceramic tile.

The dates on which the various bomb groups became operational in France and the airfield locations they occupied are shown below:

22 August 1944:	387th BG at A-15, Cherbourg/Maupertis
25 August 1944:	394th BG at A-13, Tour-en-Bessin
26 August 1944:	323rd BG at A-20, Lessy
28 August 1944:	397th BG at A-26, Gorges
19 September 1944:	391st BG at A-73, Roye/Amy
29 September 1944:	322nd BG at A-61, Beauvais/Tille
30 September 1944:	344th BG at A-59, Cormeilles-en-Vexin
2 October 1944:	386th BG at A-60, Beaumont-sur-Oise

Just to countersink the Marauder's battle-proven integrity, we find the B-26 *Truman's Folly* appearing on the scene again in France (Fig. 6-54). A. Jackson Lawrence III, now of Ocean Springs, Mississippi, relates he flew quite a lot of his missions in her with the 453rd Squadron of the 323rd Bomb Group. When the outfit moved to France, the ship was still going strong and Jackson says she ended her career with an amazing total of 186 missions without an abort! It makes one wonder if the stats on this remarkable ship ever got back to "Hard-nosed Harry."

As the Allied ground troops moved across France to the east and up into Belgium in the west, some Marauder groups moved closer to the action at the front (Fig. 6-55). The four groups that made these interim moves are shown below:

323rd BG:	To A-40, Chartres, 21 September 1944
	To A-69, Laon/Athis, 13 October 1944

<pre>
387th BG: To A-39, Chateaudun, 18 September 1944
             To A-71, Clastre, 30 October 1944
394th BG: To A-50, Bricy, 28 September 1944
             To A-74, Cambrai/Niergnies, 8 October 1944
397th BG: To A-41, Dreux, 11 September 1944
             To A-72, Peronne, 6 October 1944
</pre>

Moving a fighter group was one thing, but to move a medium bombardment group took on the aspect of an operation of gargantuan proportions. Yet the 394th Bomb Group moved *twice* within 10 days!

Col. Arthur M. Brewer, ANG Ret., now of Cape Coral, Florida, didn't join the 344th Bomb Group until September 1944, so didn't have the need for his Mae West on cross-channel missions for very long. However, in the seven months from then until the war ended in May 1945, he managed to fly 45 missions with the 495th Squadron and was on hand when Lt. Col. Lucius D. Clay, Jr., became Squadron Commander.

Brewer got a taste of all Air Force worlds in the intervening years until his retirement in 1967 as a Base Commander in the Michigan ANG. When WWII ended, he transferred to the ATC and flew C-47s all around Europe until April 1946. In May he tried a heavy bombardment aircraft by flying a B-17 from England to Morrison Field, Florida, after only four hours checkout time. He then joined the Air Force Reserve flying P-51s at Selfridge Field, Michigan, and in June 1948 transferred to the Michigan Air National Guard. As the roles

Fig. 6-54. *Lt. Lawrence standing by* Truman's Folly *on steel matting at Station A-40, Chartres, France in late 1944. (photo courtesy A. Jackson Lawrence, III)*

Fig. 6-55. *Line crew finishes up last-minute cleaning of plexiglass surfaces on this 322nd BG Marauder as one of the combat gunners, in parachute harness, patiently waits on the left. Station A-61, Beauvaix/Tille, France. (photo courtesy W. J. Johnston)*

and missions of his unit changed over the years, he alternately flew the A-26, P-51, F-84, RF-84, and F-89, including a two-year stint of active duty at Luke Field, Arizona, instructing jet pilots in various F-84 models.

During his "French Connection" with the 495th, he flew the *Barracuda*, and the accompanying photographs (Figs. 6-56 through 6-59) from his collection show a few familiar combat scenes.

Emmett J. Lancaster, now of Tempe, Arizona, the artist who did the cover and two other paintings in this book, had flown overseas as a copilot with the 497th Squadron of the 344th Bomb Group in January 1944. When the group moved to France, he was a qualified unlimited first pilot with over 50 missions flown.

While musing over the fortunes of war in his semi-underground hut in the Squadron area at A-59 one evening—and probably recalling his D-Day experience—he penned this little gem, which told it like it was:

Poet and Pilot Overture

To fly on wings of war in alien skies,
To know exalted life and sudden death;
Then lay your spirit on the line and by
The churning in your gut to realize,
That fear and courage draw a common breath.

Fig. 6-56. *The* Barracuda *with Lt. Brewer and Lt. Friar in front at Station A-59, France. She's a C-45 model. (photo courtesy Col. Arthur M. Brewer, ANG Ret.)*

Fig. 6-57. *Brewer in* Barracuda*'s cockpit among aircraft of the 495th Squadron in dispersal area on Station A-59, France. Group headquarters in on high ground at upper left. Note new configuration of radio operator's window. (photo courtesy Col. Arthur M. Brewer, ANG Ret.)*

Fig. 6-58. *Lt. Brewer easing up into formation on bombing mission. Note backpack parachute, headset helmet, and anti-glare goggles. (photo courtesy Col. Arthur M. Brewer, ANG Ret.)*

Fig. 6-59. *View of Numbers Three and Four as Brewer eases into Number Six position of 495th Squadron flight. Radio compass at left and electric gunsight view plate at left. (photo courtesy Col. Arthur M. Brewer, ANG Ret.)*

With the approach of winter, the weather conditions worsened, and the use of a new bombing technique was employed more often than ever before. Earlier on, a select number of Marauders and crews were cut from the pack and the First Pathfinder Squadron—Provisional was formed. These Marauders were equipped with the first crude equipment for bombing through the overcast, which carried the code name "OBOE." Crews that flew the PF ships were specially trained in the use of this equipment, and a Pathfinder ship would lead a group on a mission if the target was obscured by weather.

An instant dislike for Pathfinder missions developed among Marauder crews for two reasons—weather and flak. Formation flying through intermittent layers of cloud above a solid undercast was a bit hairy at best, and the OBOE ship needed a long, drawn-out bomb run in order to zero in on the target. A run of from three to five minutes was not uncommon, and staying straight and level for that length of time was a gilt-edged invitation to the German AA gunners.

Frank Brown, LTC USAFR Ret., now of Stillwater, Minnesota, piloted a Pathfinder aircraft and now bemoans the fact that WWII Pathfinders have become as extinct in memory and utilization as bombardiers. In fact, he says hardly anyone in today's aviation circles seems to know just what a Pathfinder was! Even many WWII Air Force contemporaries had never heard of them.

Frank and the author reminisced about those days in the ETO at a chance meeting in January 1986, when both were lounging outside their travel trailers at the Laughlin AFB, Texas, Famcamp. It's a rare occasion when two former B-26 pilots meet these days (other than at unit reunions), but when one of them is a Pathfinder, it's a memorable event, indeed.

When told of the dislike the bomb groups had for Pathfinder missions, Frank replied: "Hell's fire! We didn't especially relish tooling around in the soup risking collision with you clowns on the way to the target, either! As for the long bomb runs, it was necessary to stay straight and level because the OBOE beam was only 30 feet wide!"

On one of the few decent weather days in early December when a Pathfinder mission was not required, the author was flying copilot in the Number Five ship in the low flight of the second box, checking out a recently arrived replacement crew on their first mission. The target was a German airfield near Cologne, and, being in the last ship in the formation to take off, the author was able to take the photographs shown in Figs. 6-60 through 6-67.

Brig. Gen. Paul Hughes, USAF Ret., now of Stuart, Florida, was also a Pathfinder pilot who joined the squadron in September 1944. He led a total of 55 missions as a first lieutenant, leaving the outfit in March 1945. Since his tour of duty only covered something under 180 days, the reader can deduce the amount of extended periods of bad weather the 9th Air Force was faced with during the fall and winter of 1944-45. Hughes supplied the author with some added details and personal observations during an interview in February 1987.

Pathfinder pilots had of necessity to be thick-skinned and determined individuals. Not only was every mission they flew a "bad weather" type, but

Fig. 6-60. *Unshaven author standing outside his semi-underground hut on Station A-59 just before going to briefing for the Cologne mission. Note winter flying gear and .45 pistol belt. Propeller blade is from an FW-190 wreck on the base.*

Fig. 6-61. *344th BG aircraft marshalling for takeoff on Cologne mission. Group headquarters was located in chateau on the hill at upper right.*

Fig. 6-62. *Mission lead aircraft from 495th Squadron ready to start takeoff roll on Cologne mission.*

Fig. 6-63. *First box joined up over A-59 on first orbit. After second orbit, the second box will be in position.*

Fig. 6-64. *On the way to the target, last element of low flight of first box is lagging behind. In cockpit of author's ship, note radio compass on windshield center post and view plate of electric gunsight at left. Old-style ring gunsight is still in place on nose, although somewhat askew by now.*

Fig. 6-65. *First box starting bomb run on Cologne mission. Crack in windshield of author's airplane is result of flak fragment hitting it just moments before.*

Fig. 6-66. *497th Sqdn. airmen eating chow after the mission. Coffee was made in the bomb bay tank to left of water trailer.*

Fig. 6-67. *Aftermath of the Cologne mission. 1/Lt. A. E. Eberhardt, Eureka, California, standing beside remains of his C-45 model. Al had been on leave in Paris and another crew flew his ship that day.*

they had to bear up under the critical eyes of group commanders and their deputies, some of whom had been leading missions since mid-1943. These colonels and lieutenant colonels took a dim view of entrusting their groups to young first lieutenants or captains with less combat experience than they had.

The only noticeable exterior difference between a Pathfinder ship and other Marauders was a plexiglass tube, two feet long and four inches in diameter, that protruded from the belly just forward of the waist windows. This housed the OBOE antennae, and PF crews understood that there was at least $5000 worth of gold used in the mechanism. The balance of the beam receiving equipment—installed, serviced, and maintained by the RAF (since it was a British invention)—was located in the radio compartment.

The Pathfinder Squadron consisted of 18 OBOE-equipped Marauders and each was crewed in a "lead ship" manner, which included a navigator and a bombardier. The Pathfinder ship flew the Number Three position in the four-ship lead flight of the group. At the IP the Pathfinder took over the lead, the Number Four man in the lead flight assumed the Number Three position, and the group leader slid into the Number Four spot under the Pathfinder.

Precision flying was the prime requisite of a Pathfinder, as the time of arrival at the IP had to be within plus or minus one minute of the scheduled time in order to receive the OBOE signal. This signal came through the Pathfinder pilot's headset in the form of a Morse code E (dot) if he was to the left of course and a T (dash) if he was to the right. When he was on course, it blended into a steady hum. Supplementing the audio signal was a small four-light panel located on the pilot's instrument panel and a duplicate panel in the bombardier's compartment. The first bulb would light up when the IP was reached; the second indicated time to open bomb bay doors; the third indicated one minute to drop time, and when the fourth one lit up, it was time to drop. Considering that the audio signal and the signal activating the light panel both came from the OBOE ground stations, this was quite an advanced system for the time.

The accuracy of the system was an amazing circle of error of only 300 feet, and on certain critical targets (close to the bomb line,etc.), the dictate was either drop on the Pathfinder or don't drop at all. On others, the group leader had the option of dropping visually if the conditions warranted. In the latter case the group leader would reassume the lead, and the Pathfinder ship would slide into the Number Four slot of the lead flight.

The Pathfinder navigator made extensive use of the "Gee Box" (the forerunner of SHORAN) since the PF missions were always associated with bad weather. In rare instances, when the Pathfinder ship couldn't make it to the base of the group it was to lead because of the weather, a rendezvous enroute to the target would be accomplished. This called for even more precision.

Between missions, the Pathfinder crews flew extensive practice missions to sharpen their technique and this OJT instrument flying paid off in ultimate target destruction. The bomb group personnel used to gripe about flying in bad weather occasionally, but with the Pathfinder crews it was a way of life.

While the Pathfinder Squadron had its own organization, it was always based as a tenant on the fields occupied by other bomb groups, beginning with the 322nd in Braintree, England, and after the move to France at Beauvaix-Tille with the 322nd, then A-72 at Peronne with the 397th, and finally at Y-55 in Venlo, Holland, with the 394th and 397th.

Immediately after V-E Day the Squadron was disbanded, the crews and aircraft returned to their Bomb Group of record, and the outfit that had provided the 9th Air Force with about 50 percent of its capability to strike targets during the critical winter weather of 1944-45 was gone—almost without a trace!

1945

With the German army in full rout by mid-February, a new tactic was employed—or rather, part of an old tactic was rejuvenated. A group would bomb its primary target in formation and on the way back to base would break up into three-ship elements to drop down on the deck and strafe targets of opportunity. Anything that was German was fair game, whether it was moving or stationary. Some of the crews relished this legalized buzzing, but most realized that on the deck the B-26 was still vulnerable to everything from cannon to small arms fire.

Although they wouldn't have been operational a full year until 6 March 1945, the 344th Bomb Group flew its 200th mission on 13 February 1945—the first medium bombardment group in the ETO to complete 200 missions within a year's time. Considering that at least half of the days in this 344-day time span were those on which bad weather forced all groups to stand down, it was quite an accomplishment (Figs. 6-68 through 6-70).

The new year brought more base changes and all but one group moved up into Belgium and Holland:

322nd BG:	To A-89,	LeCulot, Belgium, 31 March
323rd BG:	To A-83,	Denain/Prouvy, France, 9 February
344th BG:	To A-78,	Florennes/Juzaine, Belgium, 5 April
386th BG:	To A-92	St. Trond, Belgium, 9 April
387th BG:	To ?	Beck, Holland, 29 April
391st BG:	To Y-29,	Asche, Belgium, 16 April
394th BG:	To Y-55,	Venlo, Holland, 2 May
397th BG:	To Y-55,	Venlo, Holland, 25 April

Here's a bit of interesting trivia: Not only was the 344th Bomb Group the first to hit the beachhead targets on D-Day and the first group to complete 200 missions within a year's time, but it held the record for drawing base locations with the longest names. In England it had been at Stansted-Mountfichet; in France it was at Cormeilles-en-Vexin, and finally in Belgium, it was at Florennes/Juzaine. Even after hostilities had ceased and the 344th moved into Germany for the occupation, they were based at Schleissheim, so the tradition carried on right up to the end.

Fig. 6-68. *A flight of the 497th Sqdn. buzzing the squadron area during low-level strafing practice. Station A-59, February 1945.*

Fig. 6-69. *An unidentified Marauder strafing a target of opportunity in the wooded area to the left in Belguim or Western Germany, February 1945. (photo source unknown)*

230

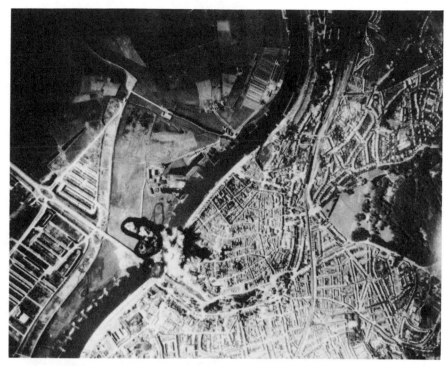

Fig. 6-70. *344th Bomb Group strike photo of hits on bridge across river at Arnhem, Germany. February 1945. (photo courtesy Joe Chiozza)*

Fig. 6-71. *The remains of 42-95864 after crashing on takeoff at Station A-59, France, 29 January 1945. (photo courtesy R. E. Wilson)*

Pulitzer Prize-winning novelist MacKinlay Kantor (*Andersonville*, 1956) was a war correspondent during WWII and flew combat missions with the RAF early in the war. Subsequently he was assigned to cover the 305th Bomb Group (H), which was then commanded by Curtis E. LeMay. An intimate friendship with LeMay resulted, and in 1965 Doubleday published Kantor's book *Mission with LeMay*. Other books followed—*Storyteller* (1967), *The Day I Met a Lion* (1968), and *Missouri Bittersweet* (1969). His articles also appeared regularly in *Esquire* magazine in the postwar years.

Kantor flew combat missions with both the 8th and 9th Air Forces and recounted many of his experiences in the *The Day I Met a Lion*. He also flew a string of missions with the 92nd Bomb Wing during the early stages of the Korean War and served as technical consultant to the Chief of Staff, USAF, during 1951-53. He was even set to fly some missions with an AC-47 gunship outfit during the Vietnam war, but an attack of the Asian flu intervened.

He wrote an epic poem on airpower in the fall of 1945, entitled "The Things Thou Hast Seen," but it remained unpublished until it appeared in the Summer 1969 issue of *Aerospace Historian* magazine. One stanza of the poem refers to an incident that occurred while he was flying with the 495th Squadron of the 344th Bomb Group (M) in France during early 1945:

> "I am the '26 that plowed to its burning against
> The road embankment between Cormeilles and
> Genicourt. Remember, Pearson? Remember,
> Minnahan? Remember, Major Clay?

While Pearson, Minnahan, and Clay (Lucius D., Jr.) were pilots in the 495th Squadron of the 344th Bomb Group, the '26 that Kantor refers to as crashing and burning was from the 497th Squadron. The incident stands out in the author's mind, as he attended the funeral of the crewmembers at a military cemetery just outside Paris.

Snow blanketed the countryside when on 29 January 1945 Serial Number 42-95864 took off from Station A-59, France, on what was to be her last mission. She was flown by a young, recently arrived replacement pilot with very little experience in the B-26, and this may have contributed to what followed. A snowstorm was in progress at the time, and visibility was so poor that the far end of the runway could not be seen from the takeoff position. Weather over the target for the mission was clear, however, so the word from the mission planners was "Go!"

Number 864 lost the right engine just after takeoff and the pilot turned onto the downwind leg, hoping to get back to the runway for an emergency landing. He never made it. Becoming disoriented in the snowstorm, he couldn't find the field, and realizing he couldn't waste precious time trying to find it, he chose to crash-land on a frozen lake. It would have been successful but for the fact that after touching down, there was no way to slow the ship down. She slid into and up over a road embankment at the lake's edge. The resulting jolt and bounce up onto the embankment broke the fuselage in half and the ship burst into flames, the conflagration preventing the crew from escaping. They all perished.

In contrast with such tragedies as 864, there was the occasional jubilation when combat tours were completed and orders were received for that long-awaited rotation to the ZI (Zone of the Interior—the code name for the United States). Figure 6-72 shows a group of officers of the 344th Bomb Group elatedly displaying their orders outside the 497th Squadron Operations tent.

It became a tradition among 497th Squadron members to have their picture taken in *Johnny Come Lately* if their first name was John. This was usually done sometime before their return to the ZI.

The ship was so named because the pilot, J. J. Nemeth, the copilot, J. S. Hollinger, and one of the gunners were all named John. Nemeth's crew had completed their combat tour before the 344th left England and had been rotated home, so *Johnny Come Lately* became one of the many ships in the squadron in the same category that were subsequently flown by a variety of crews. The author remembers it as a "sweet-flying" ship and, since he'd flown quite a few missions in her after the original crew left, it seemed all the more appropriate to have this John's picture taken in her cockpit (Fig. 6-73).

Brig. Gen. Paul Hughes is currently trying to contact former Pathfinder crewmembers in the hopes of forming an association and having a reunion. One of his first contacts was E.B. (Ned) Grubb, now of Ft. Myers, Florida, who was a Pathfinder pilot and recalls those days here:

Fig. 6-72. *Orders for home! L to R: Author, Pilot J. R. Balach, Pilot F. J. Healy, and Bombardier J. W. Curley. 13 February 1945, Station A-59, France.*

233

Fig. 6-73. *Last photo of author taken at A-59 before his return to the ZI. Battle-scarred* Johnny Come Lately *had 124 missions in at the time of this shot. Red-tipped bombs indicate post-D-Day runs. St. Valentine's Day, 14 February 1945.*

"The 1st Pathfinder Squadron (M) Provisional was conceived by General Samuel E. Anderson, Commander of the 9th Bomber Command, 9th Air Force. As early as January 1944, the Command had been working on a method to continue bombing attacks during periods of bad weather—a constant threat during the winter months in England and on the continent. This technique was put into actual service after long months of practice, trial missions, and intense study.

"When I arrived in England in September 1944, I had never heard of the 1st Pathfinder Squadron. It was highly classified. I was assigned to the 452nd Squadron, 322nd Bomb Group in Braintree, where I flew only a few missions as I was recovering from a long bout with lockjaw. However, after crossing the Channel into France, the 322nd shared an airfield at Beauvais with the 1st Pathfinder Squadron. The field had been badly damaged by the 9th, and among the groups striking this target was the 322nd. It was here—after blowing a left tire on takeoff for a mission, and luckily sparing the aircraft from serious damage—that I was reassigned to Pathfinder. During the next six months we moved from base to base, lived mostly in tents through the winter, and finally finished out the war in Venlo, Holland (Figs. 6-74, 6-75).

"Since the Pathfinder Squadron was provisional—this meant that it did not have its own Table of Organization—all crews were selected from various groups of the 9th Bomber Command. This also meant, among other things, that all promotions ceased while serving in the Squadron, as the groups from which

234

Fig. 6-74. *Bombardier Joe Chiozza's 494th Squadron Marauder in flight over Station A-59, February 1945. D-Day invasion stripes had all but worn off by then. Note former German flak tower under trailing edge of right wing. Joe's crew came in for a lot of razzing because of their ship's squadron ID letters—K9★P. Remarks such as "Here comes old Dog Pee's bombardier" made Joe cringe. (photo courtesy Joe Chiozza)*

we came were reluctant to promote those of us who were actually on TDY (temporary duty).

"The main and only reason for the existence of our Pathfinder Squadron was to lead groups of the 9th Bomber Command to their targets during periods of bad weather. This resulted in increased harassment to the enemy, who were being severely bombed by the RAF during night raids by individual aircraft and by the 8th and 9th Air Forces during daylight hours. The enemy now had to worry about bombing attacks during rotten weather—a time that up to now was a period of relative relaxation, when they could attend to the maintenance of flak guns, aircraft, etc., and possibly get some rest.

"Many of the Pathfinder pilots had been B-26 Marauder flight instructors, as I had been, and most had considerable B-26 flying time. I had already experienced blown tires, engine failures, and a belly landing before arriving overseas and had accumulated over 750 hours flying time in the Marauder. This experience helped tremendously when it came time to lead formations as smoothly as possible—and the previous instrument flying time proved invaluable. One of the plusses of being a Pathfinder pilot was the freedom we were given

Fig. 6-75. *The Wermacht may have been about ready to throw in the towel in March of 1945, but the Luftwaffe experts with the 88mm flak guns were still knocking down an occasional Marauder. This is the ship of Assistant Operations Officer of the 497th Sqdn., 344th BG, Major Chapman, just after receiving a direct hit. (USAAF photo)*

by General Anderson to fly when we wanted to, despite the weather, to and from the various bases in Europe.

"A Pathfinder crew usually had a day something like this: The weather would deteriorate—snow, low clouds, fog, etc., over the target area. The OD would awaken the crew very early—two or three AM—and we would grab a cup of coffee and head for briefing at Operations. Since each of our aircraft was scheduled to fly with a different group, we naturally had briefings for our individual targets. We would then board our planes, take off at night, and fly to the Group's base. We would then attend their briefing and coordinate the mission with the Group Commander.

"Then it was time to take off, often at or before dawn, climb through the overcast—if there was one locally—form up on top, and proceed to the target. Pathfinder planes usually carried four 500-pound bombs, which were used strictly as a reference for the Group to drop on. When our bombs fell away, the Group also dropped. Our bombardier would calibrate the proper release point depending upon the trajectory of the bombs the Group was carrying. As soon as the Group bombardier saw our bombs drop free, he toggled out his bombs and the rest of the formation followed suit.

"We often dropped from on top of an overcast, but often the entire formation would be in overcast or light snow or between layers. At times like these it was to the great credit of the Group that they were able to maintain formation under very severe conditions.

"Add to this the always-present flak—radar-controlled towards the end of the war—which, in spite of all the chaff we tossed out into the slipstream from every bomber in the formation, was always a menace. More often than not most of us returned to base with a variety of holes in our aircraft, much to the dismay of the ground crews who always did a magnificent job repairing the damage.

"After the drop, the Pathfinder had the option of returning to base alone or staying with the formation for protection if the penetration was fairly deep into enemy territory, or if German fighters were in the area. If the weather cleared over the target, usually the Group Commander assumed control and bombed visually.

"The equipment we carried in Pathfinder aircraft was mostly of British design and was highly classified. Any time our Marauders were parked, there was always a military guard posted. And, of course, there were self-destruct devices attached to the equipment so that it could be destroyed if the aircraft was shot down over enemy territory.

"The crew, including the pilot, had no precise knowledge of what made the equipment work. We knew how to interpret the signals we received in our radio headsets (a separate set of signals in either ear) and how to fly the slightly curved beam that was sent out from ground stations, first in England and then in France. This beam bisected the target and was about 30 feet wide—less than half the wingspan of a B-26! Pathfinder crews called the system "Cat and Mouse"—the Cat was the aircraft and the Mouse the elusive beam.

"The IP or Initial Point was located 25 or 30 miles from the target in order to allow time for the Pathfinder pilot to 'bracket' the beam and nail it down for an accurate run. This resulted in a much longer-than-usual straight flight path to the target, which was most unpopular with the Groups as it provided a better-than-usual opportunity for the enemy gunners to set up their flak patterns.

"At times, if the flak was extremely heavy, the Group Commander would perform evasive action along the flight path until we fired a flare, which meant we were approaching the target, and he would then pull his formation behind us for the drop. As we proceeded along the beam, various radio signals told us where we were with respect to the drop point.

"When the release signal was heard, the Pathfinder bombardier would toggle our four bombs and the Group would immediately follow suit. The Group bombs would strike the target, and this technique was surprisingly accurate when all the equipment was working. Although we rarely saw the target or the bombs strike, later reconnaissance photos proved that the 1st Pathfinder Squadron was indeed effective during periods of bad weather."

Ned Grubb's remark "when all the equipment was working" brings up a salient point regarding the OBOE system. The least malfunction in any portion of the equipment was cause for the mission to be abandoned. The author recalls flying many PF missions on which no bombs were dropped after starting the bomb run. Although credit for such a mission was given, it was very discouraging to have sweated out all the weather and flak to no avail. Marauder crews would vent their wrath in verbal abuse directed at the Pathfinders and their "Mickey Mouse" equipment.

Of course, the Pathfinders didn't rate this kind of belittlement, because they too were just as disappointed when a malfunction occurred. What the Marauder crews didn't realize at the time was that this "secret" equipment was still in its operational infancy and that reliability bugs still had to be worked out. As sensitive and precise as the system was, it's a wonder *more* glitzes didn't occur.

Because of the classified nature of the Pathfinder operation, there was never any publicity about the outfit, so, hopefully, these accounts will inform those interested of the important part a small group of brave, talented, and dedicated men played in the air war over Europe.

A typical Pathfinder mission was flown on 18 March 1945 by the 394th Bomb Group out of Station A-74, Cambrai, France, to a target at Worms, Germany. First Lieutenant James V. Fontana, now of Meriden, Connecticut, was the pilot of the 586th Squadron's C-41, Serial Number 43-34213, a G model, that day. He relates that the bomb load for the mission was four 1000-pounders, and the mission was three hours and 40 minutes long (Fig. 6-76).

Bombing altitude was 13,000 feet, and flak at the target was heavy and accurate. Although his ship was riddled with holes from flak bursts so close they could see the flame in the center, the group received an "excellent" on the bombing results. To top it off, they were also hit by German Me-262 jets but returned safely to base (Figs. 6-77).

The next day, 43-34213 was flown by another pilot and was shot down over the target at Dulmen, Germany, killing the pilot, copilot, and bombardier.

Fig. 6-76. *Ships of the 394th BG lined up for takeoff on the PFF mission described. A few F or G models are evident in the lineup by their upward-canted engine nacelles. (photo courtesy LTC James V. Fontana, USAFR Ret.)*

238

Fig. 6-77. *Lt. Fontana's ship at point of bomb release on the PFF mission described. Note 10/10 cloud cover below. Pathfinder lead ship flight is out of camera range off to the right. The second element of the flight under 4T★C's tail is flying an extremely loose formation and the Number Five ship was slow in toggling his bombs. The target must have been unusually large in area for the Group to have received an "excellent" with such a wide separation of flights. (photo courtesy LTC James V. Fontana, USAFR Ret.)*

Tragically, the copilot was Lt. Turner, who had come all the way from Barksdale with Fontana's crew.

Robert A. Grubb, now of Selinsgrove, Pennsylvania, and an M.D. in the Doctor's Convalescent Center there, was a pilot in the 397th Bomb Group from 1944 right up until occupation duty in Germany was discontinued. Figure 6-78 shows the typical casual attire of 9th Air Force Maraudermen flying combat missions. In this case, with milder weather beginning, flight jackets and coverall flight suits constituted the flight uniform of the day. From their nonchalant pose one would not guess they went up to face flak bursts every day (Fig. 6-79).

As the war in Europe drew to a close, the 386th Bomb Group converted to the new Douglas A-26 Invader in March, and the 391st followed suit in April. The handwriting was on the wall, and the rumor going around was that after the job was done in Europe, all medium outfits would be transferred to the Pacific to help finish off the Japs—but equipped with the A-26. What was to become of the Marauders, no one seemed to know—and at that stage of the game, there wasn't even much speculation about it.

Fig. 6-78. *1/Lt Robert A. Grubb, far right, and his crew in front of their Marauder on the steel matting at Venlo, Holland, in April 1945. (photo courtesy Dr. Robert A. Grubb)*

Fig. 6-79. *Marauder of the 397th's 597th Squadron dropping two 2000-pound "blockbusters" on a mission over Germany, 16 April 1945. This was the largest size bomb the B-26 bomb bay would accommodate. (photo courtesy Dr. Robert A. Grubb)*

240

Fig. 6-80. *1/Lt James Fontana leaning out of the pilot's escape hatch of one of the 394th BG's ships at Kitzingen, Germany in the summer of 1945. The 394th's white diagonal stripe group identification shows up well on the ships in the background. (photo courtesy LTC James V. Fontana, USAFR Ret.)*

Soon after V-E Day some groups were demobilized, but others moved to Germany to serve with the occupation forces. The 344th, as an example, moved to Schleissheim, and the 394th moved to Kitzingen (Fig. 6-80).

At this late point the author would be remiss if mention was not made of the other ETO Marauder Groups' rudder insignia. The 322nd, being the first to enter combat, carried the distinction of no rudder insignia; the 323rd's was a white horizontal stripe at the tip; the 344th's was a white triangle at the tip; the 386th's was a yellow horizontal stripe at the tip; the 387th's was a band of diagonal yellow and black stripes along a horizontal band at the tip; the 391st's was a yellow triangle at the tip; and the 397th's was a yellow diagonal stripe running the same direction as that of the 394th's.

The dates of the first and last operational missions and the total number of missions each Marauder Group in the ETO completed are shown below:

322nd BG:	14 May 1943—24 April 1945	428
323rd BG:	16 July 1943—25 April 1945	318
344th BG:	6 March 1944—25 April 1945	266
386th BG:	30 June 1943—3 May 1945	409
387th BG:	30 June 1943—19 April 1945	393
391st BG:	15 February 1944—3 May 1945	294
394th BG:	23 March 1944—20 April 1945	271
397th BG:	20 April 1944—20 April 1945	239

The Marauder had proven the skeptics wrong and had come through the war with an enviable combat record not matched by any other bomber! In the ETO, the loss to enemy action had dropped to an amazing less than one-half of one percent!

Peyton M. Magruder could well afford to be proud of his brainchild!

CONCLUSION:
R.I.P.

In the late fall of 1945 all of some 500 or more B-26s in the ETO were ferried to a huge disposal site near Landsburg, Germany. Here they were stripped of engines, radio equipment, and any other items the Air Force deemed salvageable. Having determined that the use of explosives would be the most economical method to reduce these aircraft to scrap, the salvage workers tied TNT packs to the wing roots to blow them off and then to the fuselage to break it into bits. Bulldozers pushed the remains into huge scrap piles to be later melted down. Ironically, the metal thus reclaimed went into a program to give German industry associated with aluminum products a rebirth.

Three Associated Wire Service photos appeared in newspapers all around the country late in 1945 depicting the Landsburg lachrymose liquidation of the Marauder. One shot was an aerial view of the disposal site, showing hundreds of Marauders and Havocs parked in neat rows awaiting destruction.

The second photo showed firefighters putting out a fire (which frequently occurred during the process) that resulted from the explosive charge that had broken the back and blown the wings off *Heaven Can Wait,* a 344th BG veteran of 99 missions. Viewing this scene, one could not help but wonder just how many flak bursts this tired old ship had endured, only to suffer the indignity of being deliberately destroyed by the very Air Force that had conceived her.

The last shot showed the results of progressive TNT charges reducing two Marauder fuselages to bits. The rudder of one, bearing the diagonal striping of the 387th Bomb Group, still towered intact above the debris as if in final protest to this disgraceful destruction.

Efforts to obtain copies of these photographs were to no avail, as AP could find no record of them in their archives. Maybe it's just as well that they don't appear here. Most Maraudermen would probably prefer to remember their ship as she was when she was in peak fighting trim. (The three photos can be seen in Roger Freeman's 1978 book *B-26 Marauder at War*, Charles Scribner's, if you can find a copy.)

I had the dubious privilege of seeing my airplane destroyed at Landsburg—not personally, but through the medium of a newsreel. It was early December when my wife and I went to the movies one Sunday night in our home town of Sterling, Illinois. During the newsreel showing, the camera first showed an aerial view of the Landsburg disposal site as the commentator explained what was to take place. Then a ground camera panned along down a long line of Marauders, hesitating at one for a few moments to show two airmen removing some radio equipment from a cockpit.

Already shaken by the sight, I sat bolt upright in my seat and yelled: "My God! That's my plane!" It wasn't until after they'd shown the demolition boys tie TNT packs to the wing roots and blow them off that my wife could get me calmed down enough to keep half the theater audience from staring at us.

Having no stomach for the rest of the show after that shocking viewing, I went to the theater manager, whose sons were personal friends, and asked him to clip one frame from the newsreel film as a final remembrance of the airplane that brought me home safely from over 50 missions. Mr. C. J. Kontos, having lost his second son in the Phillipines, was kind enough to accommodate my request. That clip from the newsreel film is shown in Fig. 7-1.

About the same time as the newsreel showing, a similar operation was in full swing at a huge disposal site at Walnut Ridge, Arkansas. Somewhere around 1000 or more Marauders from all over the continental United States were ferried there for disposal.

This location had formerly been the Walnut Ridge Army Air Field, a USAAF Basic Flying Training School during the war, and which had been traded to the Navy for a base in New England at the end of the Aviation Cadet program in early 1945. The Navy used it as a training base until after V-J Day, and then turned it back to the AAF for use as a disposal site.

Not only were there B-26s at this site for disposal but many other types as well, among them PT-19s, PT-22s, PT-23s, BT-13s, P-47s, P-61s, C-45s, C-46s, C-47s, C-54s, B-17s, B-24s, B-25s, B-32s, and A-20s.

Aviation buffs have been used to seeing photos of the huge disposal and storage sites at Kingman, Arizona, and Davis-Monthan Air Force Base near Tucson, as well as the naval disposal site at Goodyear, Arizona, near Phoenix, but the little-known Walnut Ridge operation was the largest of all. Over 11,000 airplanes stood wingtip-to-wingtip and nose-to-tail on the site. The operation began in the fall of 1945, and by spring of 1946 the entire field was filled with the largest group of aircraft in one location in history (Fig. 7-2).

Fig. 7-1. *Members of the 497th Sqdn. Communications Section removing radio equipment from* Terre Haute Tornado, *Serial Number 42-95906, just prior to her demolition in the fall of 1945, Landsburg, Germany.*

In the beginning, the Reconstruction Finance Corporation handled the disposal task; later on it was taken over by the General Services Administration. The entire operation took until October of 1947 to complete.

The aircraft were first offered for sale and many were bought by France, China, and South American countries for military or airline use. After all sales possibilities had been exhausted, the remaining aircraft were stripped of engines, propellers, radio equipment, etc., and chopped into sections by a huge guillotine-type blade 15 feet long and two inches thick. Then bulldozers pushed the sections into the maws of two huge furnaces that had been built below grade near the site (Fig. 7-3). After meltdown, the aluminum ingot end product was shipped off to be made into pots and pans. Little did Maraudermen realize that they would one day be eating their omelets from a pan that once may have been a part of the airplane in which they sweated out mission after mission, fighters and flak, weather, and the Pathfinder's long bomb runs.

In a typical military dictum, all multi-engined aircraft being ferried to the site were required to stop in St. Louis for refueling, regardless of where their flight had originated. As a consequence, they all arrived at Walnut Ridge with practically a full fuel load on board. Since 100 octane aviation fuel was at a

Fig. 7-2. *Aerial view of a small corner of the aircraft disposal site at Walnut Ridge. This area includes some of the B-26, B-25, and A-20 aircraft on the site. Since only a few of the 1000-plus B-26s show up here, some idea of the immensity of the operation can be visualized. In actuality, this represents only a little over one percent of the total area involved! (photo courtesy Rudy Vetter)*

premium right after the war, many bidders actually bought aircraft solely for the gas in the tanks. They'd drain out the gas and leave the airframe for the scrappers. During the scrapping operation the Texas Railway Company, the outfit that performed the scrapping meltdown, salvaged over a million and a half gallons of aviation fuel from the ships.

Fig. 7-3. *A bulldozer preparing to push aluminum aircraft parts into a melt-down furnace at Walnut Ridge. The guillotine blade already had done its work. (photo courtesy Rudy Vetter)*

Retired Air Force Brigadier General Paul J. Hughes, the former Pathfinder pilot who had finally been promoted to Captain, flew two B-26s from Laughlin Army Air Field Transition Training School to Walnut Ridge in the late fall of 1945. In the Laughlin Operations prior to one of these ferry flights, he overheard one of the other pilots filing a flight plan for Walnut Ridge remark that he'd always wanted to land a '26 gear-up, but the emergency situation had never presented itself. Hughes probably thought to himself: "If you'd been flying this beast where I was, you'd have had plenty of opportunity to fulfill your dream," but said nothing and continued filling out his own flight plan.

What later transpired is best told in the General's own words: "My departure from Laughlin was delayed because of a mechanical problem, and when I finally arrived at Walnut Ridge several hours later, the tower advised me that I should be aware of a disabled aircraft on the grass adjacent to the active runway. In response to my question, the tower said the B-26 had landed gear-up several hours earlier due to a mechanical problem! That's why we won the war I guess!"

Whether it was a bona-fide emergency or whether the pilot fulfilled his desire and faked an emergency to land one gear-up is not known, but it all turned out well in the end. They were just going to be scrapped anyway (Fig. 7-4).

Fig. 7-4. *The last ship left on the flight line at Lauglin AAF, Del Rio, Texas, in the late fall of 1945. This last ship to be ferried to Walnut Ridge for disposal from Lauglin was a "straight" model, Serial Number 40-1500. (USAAF photo courtesy Richard F. Love)*

In relating this story, the General wished me well in endeavoring "to do justice to a remarkable airplane that the bureaucrats buried without the military honors it so richly deserved."

Eight pre-production B-32 Dominators came to Walnut Ridge directly from the Consolidated Aircraft factory, and there were no doubt other types that had just come from factories as well (Fig. 7-5). The personal B-24s of Admiral Halsey and General MacArthur were in the lot, but no entrepreneur saw fit to purchase them as a memorial or put them to commercial use as a tourist attraction—or a hot dog stand. However, Slick Airways, the first air freight line to go into operation after the war, bought 12 C-46s from the site, and the B-25 used by Bill Odom on his famous round-the-world flight sponsored by the Reynolds Ball Point Pen Company came from this lot.

Marauder aficionados were convinced that the disposal operations at Landsburg and Walnut Ridge were a travesty of justice and that the dependable Pratt and Whitney engines on the B-26 could have been later replaced by jet engine pods to convert the ship into a 500-mile-an-hour jet bomber still way ahead of its time in design. Many would have bet their bankroll that Peyton Magruder could have pulled it off. After all, the 3M combination of World War II—Martin, Magruder, Marauder—was a winner!

Leaving the distastefulness of the scrapping of the Marauder but continuing the requiem, it is interesting to note that the Marauder flew in all theaters of operation except the CBI during World War II. Retired General Gunter Rall, a former Luftwaffe Chief of Staff, even claims he saw some in the Russian inventory that had been flown into Russia through Iran. General Rall and Brig. Gen. Chuck Yeager were at the Air University, Maxwell AFB, in the fall of 1985

Fig. 7-5. *View of the silver preproduction B-32s parked just off the ramp to the left, with the Walnut Ridge Operations building in the foreground. Ten other Dominators, which had seen service in the CBI, can also be seen. On the ramp are three different models of the P-47, a P-39, and two P-40s. At the upper right is the beginning of the vast storage area. Fall 1945. (photo courtesy Rudy Vetter)*

to lecture a class of professional military students on their WWII experiences. I was doing the research for this book in the Library archives and met General Rall when he came up to search the records in hopes of finding the name of the American pilot who shot him down late in WWII. In a short conversation, he told me he had indeed seen Russian B-26s when he was flying combat on the Russian front on his way to becoming the third ranking ace in the world with 275 aerial victories.

Not disputing the General's words, but wanting to verify this heretofore unknown fact, I searched the Maxwell archives, but there were no procurement or destination records in the files. Later contact was made with Ray Wagner, curator of the San Diego Air Museum and perhaps the foremost authority on B-26 history in the U.S., who determined that the General must have mistaken an A-20 for a B-26. The Russians did have some A-20s, but Mr. Wagner informed me that when the Soviet lend-lease delegation, headed by General Michail Gromov (the same Gromov who flew over the pole to the U.S. in 1937) came to the U.S. in September 1941 to select the types of aircraft they wanted, they tested the B-26 at Bolling Field, Washington, D.C., but judged it unsuitable for their particular medium bomber requirements and chose the B-25 instead.

Even so, maybe Uncle Joe Stalin and FDR had hatched another one of their secret deals, and some '26s might have slipped into Russia on the QT.

One conclusive thought is appropriate at this point: Although General James H. Doolittle will be remembered by future generations for leading the first

American air raid on Japan in the B-25 Mitchell, he, probably more than any other general officer in the USAAF, had the most influence on the success of the Marauder through his analysis of the problems, recommendations for their solution, initiating the remedial action, and changing the bombardment tactics to a true "medium concept" while commanding the units in Africa.

Of course, it must be pointed out that General Samuel E. Anderson was the driving force behind the success of the 9th Air Force Marauders performing at medium altitudes after the Ijmuiden disaster, so he must be given credit along with Doolittle.

While these statements are basically true, it is typical of how the ball bounces—whether it be in the military, government, or big business. The brass gets the credit but the spadework is done by their subordinates. Not to take anything away from Doolittle—because it was his rank and reputation that could get things moving, obtain results, and get the ears of people in a position to save the Marauder—but it was in reality through the ability and dedication of one man that the Marauder survived those early days—Vincent W. "Squeek" Burnett!

Now, to end this sad chapter on a light note . . .

Maraudermen had always been proud of the fact that they had mastered a "hot" airplane and were prone to brag about it when in the company of contemporaries flying "that other medium," lights, heavies, or transports. Just to illustrate how all things change—and sometimes sooner than we'd like to admit—the story was often told during WWII of two macho "hot pilot" B-26 types cycling across the tarmac to the club at their base in England one late summer afternoon in 1944.

They looked up in admiration as a lone B-26 zoomed across the field in a low pass at tower level, pulled up in a steep bank, and made a tight circle to approach for a landing. The wheels came down as the ship rolled out onto the final, followed by the flaps as its wings leveled for the touchdown, and it greased in for a perfect landing and turned off at the first intersection.

One pilot turned to the other and proudly exclaimed: "Now, that's a man's airplane!" The second one replied: "You can say that again! Let's wheel over to the ramp and see who this 'hot rock' replacement is who makes a fighter approach."

Imagine their chagrin when out from the nosewheel well dropped a diminutive damsel of the WAAF (Women's Auxiliary Air Force), who had ferried the ship from the Martin factory in Baltimore across the North Atlantic to England.

"Is nothing sacred anymore?" they muttered, as they stood on their pedals and pumped away to the club to satiate their deflated egos and wounded pride with shots of scotch washed down with mild and bitter.

Epilogue: She Flies Again!

Of all the 5000-plus Marauders built, there are only four in existence today, and only one of these is in flying condition.

The story of *Flak Bait*, whose nose section is on display at the Smithsonian, has already been told in Chapter 1, but the history of the second B-26, on display at the U.S. Air Force Museum at Wright-Patterson AFB, Ohio, is indeed unique.

Martin B-26G-10, Serial Number 43-34581, was accepted by the U.S. Air Force at the Martin Baltimore factory on 11 September 1944 and officially delivered to the Air Force at Baltimore on the 14th. On the 15th she was flown to Hunter Field, Savannah, Georgia, where she underwent the usual modifications for combat duty, and on the 25th she arrived at Morrison Field, Palm Beach, Florida, to begin her flight overseas.

Flying the South Atlantic route, she left Morrison Field on 26 September and was delivered to the Free French Air Force in Italy sometime during October 1944. The only thing we don't know for sure is whether this "man's" airplane was flown across by a male ferry pilot or by one of those cute little WAAFS.

From the time of her delivery to the FFAF, she flew on bombing missions in the Mediterranean Theater of Operations, including Italy, Sardinia, Cassino, the beaches of Provence, and targets from the Rhone to the Rhine until the end of the war in May 1945.

Along with other FFAF Marauders, she was then declared surplus and placed in storage at the French Air Base at Mont de Marsan. She would have eventually been scrapped, along with all the others, but for a strange quirk of fate.

In 1951 Air France was looking for an aircraft whose shell and engines could be dismantled and rebuilt by inexperienced personnel without any serious consequences. The airline needed such an aircraft to permit practical instruction for its mechanic training program at their Vilgenis installation in the Seine and Oise district.

Seeking aid from the French Air Force in locating such an aircraft, Air France personnel were told to take their pick of the discards at Mont de Marsan. They selected the B-26 and in so doing unknowingly paid a tribute to Peyton M. Magruder and the Glenn L. Martin Company, the designer and builder of the Marauder. Its advanced design embodied certain construction techniques and methods that were similar to those of transport planes of that period, and its near-perfect hydraulic system was still considered a valuable training aid even as late as 1965.

Old 43-34581 was disassembled and transported by truck to Vilgenis, where she was reassembled and placed on a concrete slab among the trees and offered to the curiosity of young mechanics, who for 14 years subjected her to fictitious repairs. Her engines were rendered inoperative only to be put again in functioning order, and all her parts, one by one, were given to the attention of future airline mechanics (Fig. E-1).

Fig. E-1. *The Air Force Museum Marauder when she was being used as a training facility for Air France Mechanics. Vilgenis, France, 1965. (U.S. Air Force Museum photo courtesy Hugh V. Morgan)*

Without a doubt, she would still be on the test stand for the generations of mechanics (of which the oldest were working on Caravelle and Boeing jets), were it not for the chance visit to the Air France college for mechanics of an American officer stationed in the area in early 1963.

Knowing that the U.S. Air Force Museum had been searching for a B-26 since 1954, this officer notified the Air Attache at the U.S. Embassy in Paris of his discovery. The Embassy contacted Col. William F. Curry, Director of the Air Force Museum, who promptly sent technical adviser Mark C. Sloan to France to check out the find. On many previous occasions the museum had followed up on leads, only to find that the aircraft was a Douglas A-26 and not a Martin B-26. This time they struck pay dirt.

Confronted by such interest, Air France made a gift of the B-26 to the U.S. Air Force, which, in exchange, gave the airline a DC-3. After the official presentation ceremony in 1965, Air France mechanics began removing the engines, flaps, and tail assembly and were soon joined by a U.S. Air Force team from the Chatearoux Air Base maintenance shop, who dismantled the wings, tail section, and fuselage in four days of dusk-to-dawn toil.

The ship was then transported to Chatearoux on flatbed trailers, where it was crated and loaded aboard a C-124 Globemaster transport for its last flight to the Air Force Museum.

At Wright-Patterson, countless hours were spent by the restoration team in reassembly and outfitting her in the WWII colors and identification of the 556th Squadron of the 387th Bomb Group (M) (Fig. E-2).

The story of *Carolyn,* the C model that has been restored to flying condition in the combat configuration and markings of the 386th Bomb Group (M) of the 9th Air Force by the Confederate Air Force—headquartered in Harlingen, Texas, at the site of the WWII AF gunnery school—is probably the most amazing of all.

Fig. E-2. *The U.S. Air Force Museum B-26 Marauder on one of the display ramps. The museum employed a bit of aviation license by giving her the serial number, squadron ID, group tail marking, and name of a famous ship in the 387th Bomb Group, a B-50 model; the airframe is actually a G-10. (photo courtesy U.S. Air Force Museum)*

It is one of dedication, determination, ingenuity, and improvisation. CAF "Colonel" Jerry Harville, B-26 Squadron Project Officer, supplied the following details of the metamorphosis miracle performed on the Marauder. But first, a word about the Confederate Air Force.

The CAF is a group of inspired individuals dedicated to the preservation of WWII aircraft for posterity. While many museums around the country have the same purpose, the CAF is unique in that all their aircraft are in flying condition and regularly perform in airshows and flight demonstrations all over the continental U.S.! While the CAF Headquarters, museum, and main restoration and maintenance facilities are located at Harlingen, many of the CAF aircraft are stabled at various satellite bases around the country. Included in their inventory are aircraft from all three U.S. military services, plus those representing the German and Japanese air forces.

All funds for the restoration, maintenance, and operation of CAF aircraft come from donations by members. One of the distinctions of being a member is the bestowing of the honorary rank of "Colonel" in the Confederate Air Force. There is no rank discrimination in the CAF—regardless of a member's background, station in life, or the size or scope of his contribution, everyone is a "Colonel."

The saga of the CAF Marauder actually began at Omaha, Nebraska, when B-26C-20-MO, Serial Number 41-35071, rolled off the Martin assembly line there in late 1941. She was accepted by the Army Air Force in April 1942 and during WWII was based at various training fields in Florida, North Dakota, and Texas. She was declared surplus in June 1945 and went off the inventory, when she was purchased by a private concern at the disposal site in Walnut Ridge, Arkansas.

In 1949 Lee Cameron, a United Air Lines pilot, flew her in the Bendix Trophy Race, but didn't finish due to a mechanical failure. Shortly thereafter she was purchased by Tennessee Gas Corporation (now Tenneco) and converted to an executive transport. They squared off the wingtips, cut large windows in the sides, installed a drop-down passenger door, added a dorsal fin forward of the rudder, a long, tapered cone aft of the rudder, and replaced the plexiglass nose with a radar dome. The CB-16 engines turned three-bladed Hamilton standard propellers.

Tennessee Gas eventually sold the bomber when more economical and higher performance executive aircraft became available from the various aircraft manufacturers, and it was owned by at least two other companies, was at one time registered in Mexico, and eventually wound up in the hands of the Greeley State Bank of Greeley, Colorado, where it had been offered as collateral for a loan, and the bank ended up with it.

The CAF heard of it and, in November 1967, acquired it from the bank and flew it to Harlingen. It was in very bad mechanical condition, and since there were no funds available at the time to work on it, it sat for a year practically forgotten.

254

Disaster struck during an engine run-up in 1968. The downlock pin on the right main gear became disengaged and the airplane fell on its side. Besides ruining the engine, propeller, and engine mounts on the right side, other major damage included bent wing spars and crushed ribs on the underside of the fuselage, leaving the ship in a basket case condition. Considering how many WWII Marauders had made crash landings with less damage than this after receiving battle damage, it is almost unbelievable that so much damage could occur just from the gear collapsing while at rest—but it did.

Former Maraudermen in the CAF organization began to wonder if the old "Widow-Maker" jinx of 1942-43 was coming back to haunt them.

For the next seven years this cripple sat on the CAF back lot awaiting funds to repair it. Even though sufficient funds were still not available to authorize extensive work on it, the determined Colonels pulled it into a hangar in October 1975 and started to work on it. Complicating the process was the absence of technical manuals and related structural information. All the B-26 engineering and production data had been destroyed in a fire at Martin's Baltimore plant years before, so some manuals were purchased and others were donated by persons interested in the project.

The realization that no Marauder structural parts were available anywhere in the world came after a fruitless search for wing spars. Now the restorers knew that any parts required would have to be handmade by either themselves or by a metalworking shop. Material for the wing spars was purchased and, using the original ones for patterns, a machine shop was told to make new ones—minus the bend that had resulted from the collapse (Figs. E-3, E-4).

Fig. E-3. *The CAF restoration began by removing the civilian tail cone in the Harlingen CAF hangar. Note the different age groups of the talented and dedicated men in this photo. (photo courtesy Col. Jerry Harville, CAF)*

Fig. E-4. *The tail cone has now been replaced by the beginnings of the tail turret, a picture window in the aft fuselage has been sealed off, and the waist window is being reworked. (photo courtesy Col. Jerry Harville, CAF).*

If money had been readily available, the restoration could have been completed in two years, but in reality the whole process took nine long years! A B-26 restoration squadron was formed within CAF, and donated funds began to trickle in. The B-26 became known as "the airplane that nobody loves," and the restoration crews were now indeed convinced that history was being repeated, that this Marauder was "jinxed."

Each dollar that came in had to be judiciously allocated and spent, and the priorities were constantly changed according to funds available. First priority still remained to repair the collapse damage. The ribs were handmade by first fashioning wooden ones, then using them as patterns to fabricate metal items. The tail cone, dorsal fin, and radar dome were removed, and the tail turret and top turret added. The side windows were removed and the openings sealed, the engine and propeller replaced, and every foot of electrical wiring was replaced, along with much of the hydraulic system. A new plexiglass nose was fashioned using photographs taken of the B-26 in the Air Force Museum. Rounded wingtips were added, and, slowly but surely, the Marauder was returned to a combat-configured airplane.

The new engines were zero-timed by JRG Enterprises in Minneapolis, and eventually the day of first flight arrived. 11 September 1984 was an equally auspicious occasion in the eyes of the CAF as was that November day 44 years earlier when Martin officials watched the first flight of the B-26. By a somewhat ironic twist of fate, FAA certification was done by Inspector Owen Magruder. Although no relation to Peyton M. Magruder, the designer of the B-26, "Colonel" Harville figured it was poetic justice that the last remaining B-26 in flying condition should receive her certification from a Magruder (Figs. E-5 through E-8).

The CAF Marauder was named *Carolyn* in honor of a generous contributor to the restoration fund and flew for almost a year with the three-bladed props. A search for original Curtis electric four-bladed fans proved fruitless, but wanting the B-26 to be as correct in every detail as possible, the CAF team had special four-bladed Hamilton Standard propellers made by San Antonio Propellers.

Harville estimates the restoration cost a minimum of $350,000, and men of lesser caliber might have resorted to hari-kari when in October 1985 the nose gear malfunctioned on landing and collapsed. The plexiglass nose was smashed, the props bent out of shape, and the engines ruined!

To illustrate the dauntless spirit of the CAF, quoted herewith are Harville's comments on the catastrophe and the aftermath:

"The B-26 Squadron was sick to its collective stomach. We all threw up, washed our faces, and started to work again. New nosewheel doors had to be made from scratch, the gear repaired, the glass nose redone, new props found, and the engines overhauled.

"Work began in earnest. One year later the airplane was ready to fly again. The only things necessary were the willingness to work and $120,000 to pay for it. The bottom line to this story is that we have mortgaged the lives of our great grandchildren, but we have the most beautiful airplane in the world!"

Topping the CAF Marauder saga would be difficult, but David Tallichet, president of Specialty Restaurants Corp., of Anaheim, California, is responsible

Fig. E-5. *Running up the engines prior to the first flight in 1984. Note that engine cowlings are still in the civilian configuration and the props are still the three-bladed Hamilton Standards. (photo courtesy Col. Jerry Harville, CAF)*

Fig. E-6. *She flies again! The momentous first flight resulting in the Magruder FAA certification. Turrets and package guns are now in place. (photo courtesy Col. Jerry Harville, CAF)*

Fig. E-7. Carolyn *in all her restored splendor on the Harlingen ramp in October 1985. Engine nacelles are now in the correct configuration. (photo courtesy Col. Jerry Harville, CAF)*

258

Fig. E-8. *Shades of the ETO! With a few trees in the background, this takeoff at Harlingen could have appeared to have taken place at either Great Dunmow, Essex, England, or Beaumont-sur-Oise, France! Wheels are just coming up as the CAF Marauder takes to the air just prior to the ill-fated nose gear collapsing incident. (photo courtesy Col. Jerry Harville, CAF)*

for a B-26 restoration story equally as amazing. A wholly-owned subsidiary of his corporation, Military Aircraft Restoration Corp., is restoring a Marauder to flying condition in its hangars at the Chino (California) Airport.

David flew B-17s in the 8th Air Force during WWII and has been involved in military aircraft restoration ever since. Also being restored at the Chino facility are a P-38 and various Air Force and Navy fighters of WWII vintage. He maintains a low profile, and his hobby has gained little notoriety in the outside world. In fact, the B-26 restoration has been rather secretive—I only learned of it through informants who had seen the aircraft at Chino during the past two years. Eventually, in January 1988, I made a visit to Chino and confirmed the restoration as a fact.

Mrs. Tallichet facetiously claims that Specialty Restaurants exists for the express purpose of supporting the Military Aircraft Restoration subsidiary, and why not? To give the reader an insight into SRC, the famous ''Castaways'' restaurants around the country are a part of the chain, as are the unique 391st Bomb Group Restaurant in Palm Beach, Florida, and the 91st Bomb Group Restaurant in Memphis, Tennessee. These latter facilities are replicas of the operations buildings and briefing rooms of WWII USAAF bomber bases in England, and are crammed with memorabilia of the period.

Tallichet heard of a crash-landed P-39 near Watson Lake, Canada, in 1964 and flew up to investigate. The P-39 turned out to be non-existent in the area described, but a local told him that there were still three B-26s out on the tundra that had never been recovered. Tallichet immediately flew out there and confirmed that the three aircraft were still there. Ecstatic over his find, he immediately began negotiations with the U.S. Air Force, the Canadian government, and the U.S. Air Force Museum for recovery rights to the aircraft. Permission was finally granted, and Tallichet contracted for their removal from Canada in the fall of 1971 by Al Reddick, of Reno, Nevada—another well-known aircraft restoration entrepreneur.

What was unknown at the time, and remained unknown until January 1988, was that these aircraft were the same three that Howard F. Smiley tells of crash landing in Chapter 4 of this book. Unknown to Smiley was the fact that the Air Force had cannibalized the "Million Dollar Valley" B-26s only to the extent of removing the engines, propellers, armament, and instruments, so Tallichet was able to bring out the remaining hulks in their entirety.

The intensive cannibalizing began in Chino when Tallichet's restoration crews began restoring one of the three to flying condition. By some strange quirk of fate, Serial Number 40-1464 (Smiley's airplane) was chosen as the one to restore. Fate had entered the scenario because, although the nose and nose gear of 1464 were demolished, the main gear was intact. The Air Force had removed the

Fig. E-9. *Howard F. Smiley in the cockpit of his Million Dollar Valley airplane at Chino (California) Airport, March 1988. (photo courtesy Howard F. Smiley)*

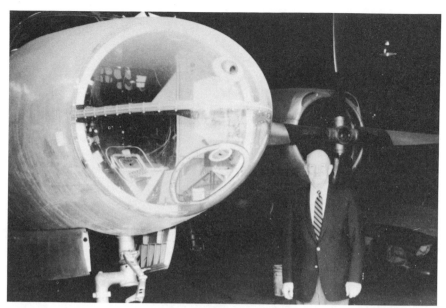

Fig. E-10. *Howard F. Smiley proudly stands beside his restored B-26, Serial Number 40-1464, at Chino, 46 years after crash landing it in Canada. Howard informed Tallichet and crew that it was SOP to "X" the props to prevent prop-tip damage in case of a strut failure or tire deflation when the aircraft was parked. So they immediately "X'ed" them after this photo was taken. (photo courtesy Howard F. Smiley)*

main gear from the other two planes but had left the nose gear intact. The long, tedious process of rebuilding began.

When I visited Chino in January 1988, I found 40-1464 standing regally in the hangar, looking as if she were ready to be rolled out. This could have been Boise, Idaho, some 46 years earlier. Crawling up into the cockpit, I discovered that most of the instrumentation had not yet been installed. Tallichet estimated this would take about a year—what with other aircraft restoration priorities sometimes interfering with the B-26 project. Otherwise, she was ready to fly; the engines had been zero-timed and all was in readiness.

She already had the distinction of being the oldest B-26 in existence—the 103rd B-26 built—the old, straight model with the short wings, short rudder, and underpowered engines!

The amazing coincidence of the story of 40-1464 came to light during my interview with Tallichet in his Anaheim office on 11 February 1988. Upon learning that 40-1464 had been Smiley's aircraft, Tallichet immediately picked up the phone and called Howard in Sioux City, Iowa. You can imagine Smiley's surprise when all was revealed to him, and the climax of the whole thing is graphically portrayed by the accompanying photographs taken when Smiley visited Chino in March (Figs. E-9 and E-10).

Hopefully, when 40-1464 finally takes to the air again, Smiley will be on board!

Bibliography

Air Force Magazine, December 1943, April 1944, July 1950.

Stars and Stripes Weekly Newspaper, August 1944.

A History of the Martin B-26 Marauder, Glenn L. Martin Co., 1944.

Partial Battle Record of the B-26 Marauder, Glenn L. Martin Co., 1944.

The Martin Star Monthly Magazine, Feb., Mar., Apr. 1942; Aug. and Nov. 1943; Jan. and Feb. 1946.

The Martin B-26B & C Marauder, Ray Wagner, Profile Publications No. 112.

Walnut Ridge Times Dispatch, 1985 Anniversary Issue.

B-26 Marauder at War, Roger A. Freeman, Charles Scribner's Sons, New York, 1978.

B-26 Marauder in Action, Steve Birdsall, Squadron/Signal, 1981.

Index

264

Edited by Steven H. Mesner